THE
BREATHING
PLANET

NEW SCIENTIST GUIDES
Series Editor: Michael Kenward

The Understanding of Animals
Edited by *Georgina Ferry*

Observing the Universe
Edited by *Nigel Henbest*

Grow Your Own Energy
Edited by *Mike Cross*

Building the Universe
Edited by *Christine Sutton*

The Making of the Earth
Edited by *Richard Fifield*

The Breathing Planet
Edited by *John Gribbin*

A new**scientist** GUIDE

THE
BREATHING
PLANET

Edited by
JOHN GRIBBIN

Basil Blackwell & New Scientist

First published in book form in 1986 by
Basil Blackwell Limited
108 Cowley Road, Oxford OX4 1JF, UK

Basil Blackwell Inc.
432 Park Avenue South, Suite 1505,
New York, NY 10016, USA

British Library Cataloguing in Publication Data
The Breathing planet.——(A New Scientist guide)
  1. Climatic changes
  I. Gribbin, John   II. Series
  551.6   QC981.8.C5
  ISBN 0-631-14288-6
  ISBN 0-631-14289-4 Pbk

Library of Congress Cataloging in Publication Data
The Breathing planet.

  (New scientist guides)
  Reprints of articles originally published in New Scientist.
  Includes index.
    1. Weather——Addresses, essays, lectures.
  2. Climatic changes——Addresses, essays, lectures.
  3. Atmospheric chemistry——Environmental aspects——
  Addresses, essays, lectures.   4. Man——Influence on
  nature——Addresses, essays, lectures.   I. Gribbin, John R. 1946-
  II. New scientist.   III. Series: New scientist guide.
  QC981.4.B74   1986   551.5   85-26878
    ISBN 0-631-14288-6
    ISBN 0-631-14289-4 (pbk.)

Typeset by Katerprint Co Ltd, Oxford
Printed and bound in Great Britain by
T. J. Press, Padstow

Contents

Contents

Contributors

MICHAEL ALLABY is a freelance writer who specialises in environmental topics.

LORD ASHBY, FRS, was formerly Eric Ashby before being granted a peerage in 1973. Among his many contributions to science and society in Britain, he chaired the Royal Commission on Environmental Pollution.

DR KEN BAILEY worked in the Department of Geology at the University of Reading at the time he wrote about volcanic activity for *New Scientist*.

DR LLOYD BERKNER worked with Lauriston Marshall at the Southwest Center for Advanced Studies in Dallas, Texas.

WILLIAM BURROUGHS is a freelance writer, based in England, who has a special interest in climate and weather. He was a researcher in atmospheric studies at the UK National Physical Laboratory, Teddington.

NIGEL CALDER used to be a staff writer with *New Scientist*, and edited the magazine from 1962 to 1966. His interest in climatic change developed through a BBC TV special and associated book, both called *The Weather Machine*, which he wrote.

CATHERINE CAUFIELD writes for *New Scientist* on environmental topics. She is the author of *Tropical Moist Forests: The Resource, the People, the Threat*, May 1982, Earthscan.

DR TONY COX worked with Alan Eggleton at Harwell.

ANDREW CRANE is a Research Officer at the CEGB's Central Electricity Research Laboratories at Leatherhead, Surrey. He is the co-author, with Dr Liss, of the book *Man-Made*

Carbon Dioxide and Climatic Change: A Review of Scientific Problems (Geo Books, Norwich, 1983).

MICHAEL CROSS is a staff writer for *New Scientist*, and was the first journalist to visit and report from the drought-stricken region of Ethiopia in 1984.

TAM DALYELL is a British Member of Parliament who writes a weekly column for *New Scientist*.

DR DICK DERWENT worked with Alan Eggleton at Harwell.

DR MARCEL VAN DIJK is with the Bureau of Meteorology in Melbourne.

DR ALAN EGGLETON wrote from the Environmental and Medical Sciences Division of the Atomic Energy Research Establishment, Harwell.

DR SIDNEY EPTON was working with Shell at the Thornton Research Centre at the time of his collaboration with Jim Lovelock on the Gaia hypothesis.

DR PETER FRANCIS is a lecturer in the Department of Earth Sciences at the Open University. His books include *Volcanoes*, published by Pelican.

DR JOHN GRIBBIN has been Physics Consultant to *New Scientist* since 1978. His books include a standard text *Climatic Change*, which he edited for Cambridge University Press, and, at a "popular" level, *Future Weather*, a Pelican paperback.

DR ANN HENDERSON-SELLERS has worked at several British universities and in the United States. She is the author of a major book, *The Origin and Evolution of Planetary Atmospheres*, published by Adam Hilger.

PROFESSOR SHERWOOD IDSO is a research physicist with the US Department of Agriculture's Water Conservation Laboratory in Phoenix, Arizona. His booklet *Carbon Dioxide: Friend or Foe?*, available from IBR Press, Tempe, Arizona, provides the most coherently argued case for the, at present minority, view among scientists that there is no need for alarm at the build-up of carbon dioxide in the atmosphere.

DR ARTHUR JONES wrote for *New Scientist* from Cleveland, Ohio.

CHRISTOPHER JOYCE is the Washington Correspondent of *New Scientist.*

DR MICHAEL KELLY works at the Climatic Research Unit at the University of East Anglia, where he is a Senior Research Associate. His research interests focus on anthropogenic influences on climate, from the likely repercussions of large-scale river diversions to the carbon dioxide "greenhouse effect" and the threat of a "nuclear winter".

MICHAEL KENWARD is the editor of *New Scientist.*

DR LEO KRISTJANSSON wrote for *New Scientist* from the Science Institute of the University of Iceland.

PROFESSOR HUBERT LAMB spent many years with the UK Meteorological Office, before leaving to establish the Climatic Research Unit at the University of East Anglia. He was the Unit's first Director, and although now officially retired he is still actively involved in climate studies and retains his association with the Unit. His many books include *Climate History and the Modern World* (Methuen).

PETER LISS is a Reader in the School of Environmental Sciences, University of East Anglia, and was formerly a Scientific Adviser to the CEGB.

PROFESSOR JAMES LOVELOCK, FRS, is one of a rare and vanishing breed of scientists. He works independently of any established institution such as a university or large industrial laboratory, in a private laboratory attached to his home, formerly in Wiltshire and now on the edge of Dartmoor. From that small laboratory, he has designed instruments used by the Viking landers to sniff the atmosphere of Mars, and on the walls hang certificates from NASA marking his major contributions to their space programme, while in the UK his achievements have been marked by his election as a Fellow of the Royal Society. In spite of battling against serious illness, he recently added a new string to his bow with a successful work of fiction, written with Michael Allaby, about the human colonisation of Mars.

DEBORA MACKENZIE is a member of *New Scientist's* team of consultants.

PROFESSOR LAURISTON MARSHALL's ideas about the evolution of the Earth's atmosphere developed while he was working at the Southwest Center for Advanced Studies in Dallas, Texas.

DR DAVID MERCER works in the Department of Geography at Monash University, Melbourne.

FRED PEARCE is News Editor of the *New Scientist*.

DR JIM PETERSON works in the Department of Geography at Monash University, Melbourne.

PROFESSOR SHERRY ROWLAND was the scientist who, with Dr Mario Molina, "blew the whistle" on the possibility that propellant gases from aerosol sprays might damage the ozone layer of the atmosphere. He works in the chemistry department of the University of California, Irvine, and has served as a member of the US National Academy of Sciences Ad Hoc Panel on the Stratospheric Effects of Chlorofluoromethanes.

BRYAN SAGE is a writer who specialises in environmental issues.

DR GERALD WICK worked at the Scripps Institution of Oceanography at La Jolla, in California, at the time he wrote about oceans and climate for *New Scientist*. He had previously been the magazine's Physical Sciences Editor, and is now a Buddhist monk living in Los Angeles.

DR DEREK WINSTANLEY is a British scientist who was the first to suggest, in the early 1970s, that droughts in the region of Africa south of the Sahara marked a global weather shift and were likely to persist. Since then, he has visited the region as a volunteer worker and obtained more evidence to support this argument. He is now working with the US Department of Energy, on a study of acid rain, on secondment from a post with the National Center for Atmospheric Research, in Boulder, Colorado.

Foreword

In November 1956 a small and enthusiastic team of journalists and scientists launched *New Scientist*. Ever since then, with a few interruptions, *New Scientist* has provided a weekly dose of news from the world of science and technology.

Over the years, the magazine has reported research as it happened. Sometimes the findings that we described turned out to be less enduring than their discoverers first thought. Sometimes they went on to win Nobel prizes for the scientists involved. Theories that first provoked severe scepticism became established wisdom. Established wisdom was cast aside.

These guides bring together that "history in the making". In these pages you will find more than a scientific account of a particular subject. You will find the personalities and the problems; the excitement of discovery and the disappointment of wrong turnings and the frustration of delays. I hope, too, that you will find something of the excitement that scientists feel as they push back the frontiers of knowledge.

Science writing does not stand still any more than does science. So the past quarter of a century has seen changes in the way in which *New Scientist* has presented its message. You will find those changes reflected here. Thus this guide is more than a collection of articles carefully plucked from the many millions of words that have appeared over the years. It is a record of science in action.

Michael Kenward
Editor, New Scientist

Preface

"Some are weather-wise, some are otherwise." So wrote Benjamin Franklin, in *Poor Richard's Almanack*, in February 1735. The need to be weather-wise has never been greater than it is in the last quarter of the twentieth century, when rapidly growing populations in the developing world provide the possibility for famine on a previously unprecedented scale if the weather does not perform as anticipated (or hoped) and the crops fail. The fact that modern technology and more efficient farming practices have helped to keep the potential productive capacity of the world's farmlands increasing even more rapidly than the increase in population is no consolation to starving people in the Sahel, or Ethiopia. "Politics", in the broadest sense of the word, is doubly responsible for their plight, first because political boundaries prevent the nomadic migrations that were until recently a natural response to a shift in the rains, and secondly because it is thanks to political decision making that poor countries choose, or need, to grow cash crops with which to earn precious foreign exchange (all too often to spend on armaments) instead of food to eat. But whatever the root causes of the problem, the fact remains that hundreds of millions of people today live on a knife edge, fed barely adequately in the good seasons and sure to starve if and when the crops fail.

So the need to understand weather and climate is greater today than it has ever been. The problems of changes in the climatic patterns of the globe are most immediate and pressing in those dry regions where a little rainfall has to be made to go a long way. But the implications of changes in climate are no less important in the affluent states of the rich north, where a severe spell of cold weather can reduce industrial production by 25 per cent, destroy crops and boost demand for energy dramatically. It is only in the 1970s and 1980s that it has become clear just how much the climate of the world, and of particular regions, can and does change naturally from decade to decade and from century to century. The implications for policy making are profound. Should water authorities in Europe, say, plan for a rainfall pattern like that of the 1960s in the 1990s? Or might the 1890s provide a better guide to what to expect? Unfortunately, just when the science of climatology is on the brink of being able to provide useful forecasts of such natural changes in our environment, a spanner has been thrown into the climatic works – by our own activities.

The polluting activities of humankind, blithely destroying the bulk of the world's forest, boosting the amount of carbon dioxide in the atmosphere, creating acid rain and (perhaps) changing the composition of the ozone layer above our heads, all go to complicate the business of forecasting future weather. Jim Lovelock and his colleagues have introduced into scientific debate the concept of all life on Earth as components of one organism, Gaia, roughly in the way all the cells in your body make up one organism, yourself. The natural changes Gaia can take in her stride, even if they make us (or some of us) uncomfortable from time to time. But the impact of human activities on the atmosphere of our planet may be sufficient to destroy the natural balance, posing a real threat to Gaia. Is the atmosphere of the Earth a fragile bubble that mankind is about to burst? Or is it a rugged system that can cope with our worst excesses? Either way, the one sure thing is that changes are coming, in our lifetime. This collection of articles from the pages of *New Scientist* may help you to know what to expect, and how to cope with those changes. The best advice comes, once again, from Ben Franklin: "We must indeed all hang together, or, most assuredly, we shall all hang separately."

John Gribbin

PART ONE

Gaia

Life on Earth exists in an almost symbiotic relationship with the atmosphere of our planet. Indeed, life "on Earth", meaning the land surface of our planet as opposed to the oceans that cover so much of our globe, has only been in existence since the time that earlier living organisms, themselves restricted to the oceans, converted a large proportion of the original atmosphere of our planet into oxygen. The oxygen itself gave life a leg up the evolutionary ladder by providing a sufficiently reactive "fuel" to power mobile, energy-burning organisms – animals. And it also provided a protective shield beneath which some of those new animals could crawl out of the oceans and onto the land, following the spread of plants onto the dry surface of the Earth. That protective layer lies between about 15 and 50 km above our head; its major constituent is ozone, a form of oxygen in which each molecule is made of three atoms instead of the two that are present in every molecule of oxygen in the air that we breathe. Ozone has the important property, for us and for all life on Earth, of absorbing ultra-violet radiation from the Sun. Before the ozone layer was in place, this sterilising radiation scoured the surface of the Earth and made life out of the water impossible. Today, as for the past few hundred million years, it provides a natural sunshield, maintained by the life processes of photosynthesising plants.

The balance between life and the oceans and atmosphere of our planet is maintained so accurately to suit life as we know it that Jim Lovelock and his colleagues were moved to suggest, in the mid-1970s, that the whole region of life on Earth, the ecosphere, forms one giant living organism, in a way analogous to the way the many cells in your body cooperate to produce one living organism, you. Lovelock gave this hypothetical super-organism the name "Gaia", after the Greek Earth goddess. The keynote article in which the concept of Gaia was first announced to the world deserves pride of place as the first article in this book. It is followed, in this introductory section, by a series of articles in chronological order, which show how our ideas about the origin and evolution of the atmosphere have developed over the past twenty years. And as a cautionary footnote I include at the end of the section a brief report from the Monitor section of *New Scientist*, as the Science News section used to be called, which stresses a point that needs always to be borne in mind – that all of our ideas about the details of geophysical history remain to some extent cloudy and uncertain.

1

The quest for Gaia

JAMES LOVELOCK AND SIDNEY EPTON

Consider the following propositions:

(1) Life exists only because material conditions on Earth happen to be just right for its existence.
(2) Life defines the material conditions needed for its survival and makes sure that they stay there.

The first of these is the conventional wisdom. It implies that life has stood poised like a needle on its point for over 3500 My. If the temperature or humidity or salinity or acidity or any one of a number of other variables had strayed outside a narrow range of values for any length of time, life would have been annihilated.

Proposition (2) is an unconventional view. It implies that living matter is not passive in the face of threats to its existence. It has found means, as it were, of driving the point of the needle into the table, of forcing conditions to stay within the permissible range. This article supports and develops this view.

The Sun, being a typical star of the main sequence, has evolved according to a standard and well established pattern. A consequence of this is that during the Earth's existence the Sun's output of energy has increased substantially. The Earth now receives between 1.4 and 3.3 times more energy than it did just after its formation 4000 My ago. The Earth's surface temperature at the time when life began has been calculated. These calculations take into account the solar input, the radiative properties of the surface and the composition of the atmosphere. At that time, the atmosphere probably contained ammonia and other complex molecules which acted like the glass in a greenhouse, that is, by reducing the radiation of heat and long-wave infra-red radiation from Earth. The calculations show that the surface temperature could indeed have been within the range we now know to be needed to start life off.

Once life began, it fed on the atmospheric blanket. Unless some means had existed for restoring to it heat-retaining gases such as ammonia, or of altering the Earth's surface to make it more heat retentive, the planet would surely have become uniformly ice-bound and lifeless. The rate of increase of solar energy would have been too small to compensate. Yet the fossil record and the continuity of life gives no support to this conclusion. At the time of supposed emergence from glaciation, that is, when the radiation from the more active Sun had made up for the radiation loss due to loss of the heat-retaining gases, and when only the feeble beginnings of a new life should have been possible, complex multi-celled organisms had already evolved. Life must have found a way of keeping the temperature of the Earth's surface within the critical range of 15–30 °C for hundreds of millions of years in spite of drastic changes of atmospheric composition and a large increase in the mean Solar flux. The calculations were wrong because they left out the effect of the defence mechanism that life uses to protect itself.

Extinction through glaciation was not the only danger. Over-production of ammonia and other heat-retaining gases could have resulted in the opposite effect, known as the "runaway greenhouse", that is to a rapidly increasing surface temperature that would have scorched the Earth and left it permanently lifeless, as is the planet Venus now. The evidence that this did not happen is plain – we would not have written these words nor would you be reading them.

Has life been able to control other conditions of existence besides the surface temperature of the Earth? A most significant fact about the Earth is the composition of its atmosphere. Almost everything about its composition seems to violate the laws of chemistry. If chemical thermodynamics alone mattered, almost all the oxygen and most of the nitrogen in the atmosphere ought to have ended up in the sea combined as nitrate ions. The air we breathe cannot be a very fortunate once-off emanation from the rocks; it can only be an artefact maintained in a steady state far from chemical equilibrium by biological processes.

The significance of this was first realised some years ago when one of us, in association with Dian Hitchcock, took up the problem of deciding whether it would be possible to detect life on Mars by the use only of spectroscopic observations on its atmosphere. Our suggestion was to look for any combination of constituents that was far from chemical equilibrium; if such was found life might exist there. (So far no such combination has been detected on either Mars or Venus.)

Gaia

It appeared to us that the Earth's biosphere was able to control at least the temperature of the Earth's surface and the composition of the atmosphere. *Prima facie*, the atmosphere looked like a contrivance put together cooperatively by the totality of living systems to carry out certain necessary control functions. This led us to the formulation of the proposition that living matter, the air, the oceans, the land surface were parts of a giant system which was able to control temperature, the composition of the air and sea, the pH of the soil and so on so as to be optimum for survival of the biosphere. The system seemed to exhibit the behaviour of a single organism, even a living creature. One having such formidable powers deserved a name to match it; William Golding, the novelist, suggested Gaia – the name given by the ancient Greeks to their Earth goddess.

The past three years have been spent in exploring and elaborating the Gaia hypothesis (in collaboration with Lynn Margulis) and checking its implications against fact. It has proved to be fruitful. It has led us along many paths and by-paths, and valuable insights have been gained especially about the consequences of Man's interaction with the biosphere. The following is a selection of some of the interesting things we have found on the way.

Atmospheric constituents

If Gaia is a living entity we have the right to ask questions such as "what purpose does constituent X serve in the atmosphere?" As an example, the biosphere produces about 1000 million tons of ammonia a year. Why?

As already pointed out, in early times, when the Sun was cooler than it is now, ammonia served to keep the Earth warm. At the present time, the need for ammonia is different and just as important, because we believe that ammonia keeps the soil near to pH 8 which is an optimum value for living processes. It is needed because a consequence of having nitrogen- and sulphur-containing substances in the air in the presence of a vast excess of oxygen is their tendency to combine to produce strongly acid materials – thunderstorms produce tons of nitric acid and if there were no regulator such as ammonia the soil would become sour and hostile to most organisms.

Another of our beliefs is that one of the purposes of the small but definite amount of methane in the atmosphere is to regulate the oxygen content. Methane is a product of anaerobic fermentation in soil and sea. Some of the methane rises into the stratosphere where it oxidises to carbon dioxide and water, so becoming the principal source of water vapour in the upper air. The water rises further into the ionosphere and is photolysed to oxygen and hydrogen. Oxygen descends and hydrogen escapes into space. In effect, methane production is a way of transporting hydrogen from the Earth's surface to the stratosphere in sufficient quantity to maintain oxygen concentration in the lower atmosphere.

We have also found interesting and unexpected trace gases in the atmosphere, such as dimethyl sulphide, methyl iodide and carbon tetrachloride. There is no doubt that the first two are biological emissions and they may well serve to transport the essential elements, sulphur and iodine, from the sea to the land. Carbon tetrachloride does not seem to have a biological source but its uniform distribution in the atmosphere, showing no difference between the northern and southern hemispheres, and other evidence suggest that it is not a man-made pollutant either. Its origins are an intriguing puzzle as is the question of its function, if any.

For more than 3500 My in the face of a big increase of Solar output, the mean temperature of the Earth's surface must have remained within the range of 15–30 °C. How did Gaia do this? She must have used several ways to keep surface temperatures so constant. Before there was a significant amount of oxygen in the air, the emission and absorption of ammonia by simple organisms may have been the control process, so making use of its heat-absorbing and heat-retaining properties. Variations of the concentration of ammonia in the air would therefore be a means of temperature control.

There must have been other ways as well, for the failure of only one year's crop of ammonia would have led to a self-accelerating temperature decline and extinction of life. One can envisage advantage being taken of the ability of certain algae to change colour from light to dark, thereby influencing the emissivity and the albedo of the surface. Later, when photosynthesising and respiring organisms existed and oxygen became a major constituent of the air, the control of the concentration of carbon dioxide, which is also a heat-absorbing and heat-retaining gas, may have been used to play a role in stabilising temperature.

Gaia and Man

Gaia is still a hypothesis. The facts and speculations in this article and others that we have assembled corroborate but do not prove her existence but, like all useful theories, right or wrong, Gaia suggests new questions which may throw light on old ones. Let us ask another. What bearing has she on pollution, population and Man's role in the living world?

Gaia has survived the most appalling of all atmospheric pollutants, namely oxygen, which was put into the atmosphere in substantial quantity about 2000 My ago when the photosynthesisers had completed their task of oxidising the surface and the atmosphere. Whole ranges of species must have been killed off or driven into dark, oxygen-free prisons from which they have never been released; the appearance of the whole planetary surface and its chemistry were completely changed. To appreciate the impact of oxygen, think of what would happen to us if a marine organism began to photosynthesise chlorine and was successful enough to replace oxygen in the air with chlorine. This is science fiction, but oxygen was as poisonous to the primitive ferments as chlorine would be to us today.

Man's present activity as a polluter is trivial by comparison and he cannot thereby seriously change the present state of Gaia let alone hazard her existence. But there is an aspect of Man's activities more disturbing than pollution. If one showed a control engineer the graph of the Earth's mean temperature against time over the past million years, he would no doubt remark that it represented the behaviour of a system in which serious instabilities could develop but that had never gone out of control. One of the laws of system control is that if a system is to maintain stability it must possess an adequate variety of response, that is, have at least as many ways of countering outside disturbances as there are outside disturbances to act on it. What is to be feared is that Man-the-farmer and Man-the-engineer are reducing the total variety of response open to Gaia.

The growing human population of the Earth is leading us to use drastic measures to supply this population with resources, of which food has prime importance. Natural distributions of plants and animals are being changed, ecological systems destroyed and whole species altered or deleted. But any species or group of species in an ecological association may contribute just that response to an external threat that is needed to maintain the stability of Gaia. We therefore disturb and eliminate at our peril; long before the world population has grown so large that we consume the entire output from photosynthesisers, instabilities generated by lack of variety of response could intervene to put this level out of reach.

Puzzling climate

Are there any signs that we might have triggered something off already? There is at least one such possibility – the present puzzling climate. Unprecedented temperature decreases have occurred in northern regions, such as Iceland, along with many other unfamiliar manifestations, such as modified wind systems and rainfall distributions.

Many explanations of these climate trends have been put forward. Some mechanism that either reduces the amount of the Sun's radiation reaching the Earth or increases the amount radiated is required. Ecologists, not unexpectedly, place the blame on the products of man's activities. Increasing dustiness of the atmosphere, nuclear explosions, supersonic aircraft have all been proposed and considered, but within our admittedly limited theoretical understanding of what goes on, none has stood up well to criticism.

Another possibility that we are exploring is that one of the trace gas emissions such as that of nitrous oxide serves as a biological climate regulator. Nitrous oxide is produced naturally by soil micro-organisms at a rate of hundreds of millions of tons annually. The output varies, however, as a result of agriculture, particularly from the use of nitrogenous fertilisers. We do not know how nitrous oxide could modify the climate, but the evidence suggests that it has been increasing in concentration and it is known to penetrate the stratosphere where its decomposition products could affect the ozone layer.

This climatic trend may be "just another fluctuation" of the kind that has occurred before and will cure itself. This tends to be the meteorologists' view but the uncomfortable thought remains that none of the earlier occurrences has been explained. Perhaps some unidentified activity of Man has been the common factor and nowadays there are a good deal more people about, active in many more ways. The consequences this time could well be much more serious and prolonged. We await developments somewhat uneasily.

Finally, a brief prospective look at the relation between man and Gaia, which also sums up the implications of this article. Socially organised Man has the ability possessed by no other species to collect, store and process information and then to use it to manipulate the environment in a purposeful and anticipatory fashion. When our forebears became farmers they set themselves on a path, which we are still beating out, that must have had an impact on the rest of Gaia almost as revolutionary as that of the evolution of photosynthetic organisms millenia before. The area of the outside world that we, as a species, are capable of regulating to our short-term advantage has gradually expanded from the immediate locality of a settlement to vast geographical regions. This path could take us finally to the point at which the area of manipulation becomes the whole world. What happens then?

Nineteenth-century technocracy would say that we would then have won the final victory in the battle against Nature. The Earth would be our spaceship, we the passengers and crew, the rest of Nature, living and dead, our life-support system. But the price of victory might well be that we should have immobilised Gaia's control systems which she had established to keep the conditions on our planet at the level necessary for her and therefore our survival. The responsibility for the task of maintaining system stability would pass to us alone and it would be dauntingly difficult. As well as carrying technical burdens, we should also have to make agonising social and moral decisions, such as how many passengers the spaceship could afford to carry and whom to throw overboard to make room.

A need to survive

The easier path is to rid ourselves of nineteenth-century techno-cratic thinking, to reject the idea that human existence is necessarily a battle against nature. Let us make peace with Gaia on her terms and return to peaceful co-existence with our fellow creatures. Thirty thousand years ago some of our ancestors did something like this. They abandoned primitive hunting and took up what has been called the transhumane way of life. Men lived and migrated with the animal herds, defended them against other predators and systematically culled them for food. This ensured them a more plentiful and regular supply of animal products than the random hunting mode that it superseded. But out first priority as a species is to choose from the numerous technically feasible means of limiting our own population those that are socially acceptable in social and moral terms.

Now for one more speculation. We are sure that Man needs Gaia but could Gaia do without Man? In Man, Gaia has the equivalent of a central nervous system and an awareness of herself and the rest of the Universe. Through Man, she has a rudimentary capacity, capable of development, to anticipate and guard against threats to her existence. For example, Man can command just about enough capacity to ward off a collision with a planetoid the size of Icarus. Can it then be that in the course of Man's evolution within Gaia we have been acquiring the knowledge and skills necessary to ensure her survival?

6 February, 1975

2

Oxygen and evolution

LLOYD V. BERKNER AND LAURISTON C. MARSHALL

When the close connection is traced between the build-up of oxygen in the Earth's atmosphere on the one hand, and the environment and physiology of living organisms on the other, a model emerges that accounts for periods of explosive evolution. It may also explain subsequent catastrophes, such as the one that overtook the great reptiles

---

The possibility of direct exploration of the planets with space vehicles has directed attention to the constitutions of planetary atmospheres. Moreover it is only since the International Geophysical Year that we have had a reasonably detailed picture of the structure of the Earth's atmosphere. The facts at hand suggest that analysis of data obtainable on the Earth, combined with new data from the planets, may be exceedingly useful in developing a broad theoretical basis for the rise and stability of planetary atmospheres, and related development of life.

Our present study concerns the history of the Earth's atmosphere – not so much what it is now, but how it got here, why it is, and what may have been the intermediate steps. As will be seen, these questions have significant bearing on the initiation and evolution of life on Earth.

One of the most interesting facts about the Earth's atmosphere is the relatively large content of oxygen – about 21 per cent – a condition unique among the planets of our Sun. It presents an interesting paradox. Life could not have been generated in the beginning with the present quantity of oxygen in the atmosphere – yet we cannot live and breathe without it. Most modern forms of life, even many plants, are highly dependent upon oxygen, and in most cases a rather precise amount of it, for their existence. This means that oxygen in the atmosphere must have been relatively stable in its concentration for a considerable time. Yet the very origin of life on Earth would have been frustrated if oxygen had been abundant at that time. The amino acids and other vital but vulnerable materials needed for incorporation in the incipient organisms would have been promptly oxidised.

Until recently, scholars have not been able to agree fully on how a stable atmosphere came into being with the present amount of oxygen. On the one hand there is a very useful principle propounded about 150 years ago by Hutton which has found wide acceptance – it is called *uniformitarianism*. This explains geological and evolutionary variety by the slow changes we observe under the conditions encountered today. On this view, all developments have occurred at almost imperceptible rates compared with human events and concepts of time without the need to postulate at any time significant changes in the environment. But, as we shall see, a modern interpretation of the geological record can show sudden bursts of evolutionary activity that are hard to explain unless we allow for decisive changes in the environment.

Thus, we observe that multi-cellular forms of life in the sea came into being only at the opening of the Palaeozoic – that is to say, 600 My ago. Plant life on dry land has existed only about 420 My (preceded for a few million years by some fossil spores) and animal life on land perhaps about as long. The only evidence of any life before the Palaeozoic consists of certain bacteria, and other very primitive organisms. Yet such algal material is found by Hoering and by Abelson to be trapped in the oldest rocks in curious formations known as bioherms, some dating back nearly three billion years. The Gunflint shales of the Great Lakes, laid down nearly two billion years ago, teem with the fossils of single-celled organisms, and the deposition of certain ores may have required bacterial action in their chemical deposition. But there is no evidence that life existing in the waters progressed during these billions of years, to even a modest degree of sophistication, until about 600 My ago.

The Earth was probably formed from small objects – planetesimals or meteorites – which did not bring with them any primordial atmosphere. The birth of its atmosphere was a secondary phenomenon, arising after the Earth's formation from the escape of gases from its rocks, usually by localised heating, melting and volcanic action. As the primaeval atmosphere appeared, it would be dominated by hydrogen, water vapour and carbon dioxide, and subsequently modified by gradual escape of the lighter gases (hydrogen and helium) and by the absorption and precipitation of carbon dioxide in carbonates as the oceans became widespread.

At present there are about 500 volcanoes classified as active around the world; about 400 are situated in the Pacific ring. Wilson estimates that slightly less than a cubic mile a year of solids is added to the continents at the current rate of activity. Multiply this number by the lifespan of the Earth and one has a figure of about three billion cubic miles, which is very close to the present estimates of the total volume of all the continents.

Accompanying this solid effluent, the volume of volcano gases is considerable. The largest single constituent is water vapour, which can be as high as 97 per cent by volume. This is mixed with varying amounts of nitrogen, carbon dioxide, hydrogen, sulphur dioxide and chlorine, plus much smaller quantities of hydrogen sulphide, carbon monoxide, methane, ammonia and others. All these volcanic vapours and gases have been bound in the rocks, to be released, sometimes explosively in the throat of the volcanoes.

The water vapour and gases released over three or four billion years are thought to be more than sufficient to account for the volume of the oceans, and for the nitrogen and other constituents of the present atmosphere, excepting only oxygen. But this exception is particularly important. There is no free oxygen produced by volcanic activity. Volanic temperatures and the presence of iron, sulphur and other materials in chemically reduced states lead to violent chemical reactions that ensure that all oxygen comes out in combined form.

Thus oxygen was virtually absent from the primitive atmosphere. This view is confirmed in other ways. Ancient sediments formed by erosion billions of years ago are known to be only partially oxidised, suggesting an atmosphere low in oxygen. More recently, Holland has concluded that the early atmosphere must have been chemically reducing in character (that is, dominated by hydrogen). The origin of life itself appears to forbid the existence of much oxygen at the beginning, as we observed earlier in posing a paradox.

Since the evidence suggests an absence of oxygen in the primitive atmosphere, the immediate question is how to account for a build-up of oxygen and a resolution of the paradox. The free oxygen must be derived chiefly from the break-up of water molecules into hydrogen and oxygen. It can occur via one of two routes: by direct photo-dissociation of water vapour exposed to ultra-violet light (primarily in the waveband 1500 to 2100 Å), and by the indirect process that occurs during photosynthesis in green plants. On a primitive planet without life, only the first alternative is available. How much oxygen will this photo-dissociation yield?

We have made a study of the ultra-violet content of the radiation from the Sun. Observations of rockets and satellites have shown the amounts of ultra-violet light from the Sun that are reaching the atmosphere at the effective wavelengths. It comes from the visible photosphere of the Sun, and has been shown by Wilson, in his study of stars similar to the Sun, to be sensibly constant over geological time.

Of the products of photo-dissociation, the hydrogen is light enough to escape rather quickly from the atmosphere (the exact rate is still under debate). Nor would the nascent oxygen, formed by photo-dissociation, stay around long in the primitive atmosphere, where it was produced at the surface. It would react very quickly with partially oxidised rocks and materials. In the atmosphere, some of the oxygen forms ozone – reactive molecules containing three atoms of oxygen. Ozone itself reacts at a high rate with surface rocks. Thus, in a primitive atmosphere, oxygen is used up at a definable rate in surface oxidation, and possibly also by reconstitution of water vapour at certain levels in the atmosphere.

Simple calculation demonstrates that ultra-violet energy could release oxygen by photo-dissociation of water vapour which is more than 100 times that necessary to account for the oxidation of all the sedimentary rocks in the continents and on the floor of the oceans over geological time. But when we ask whether photo-dissociation can account for the present high level of oxygen in the atmosphere itself, the answer is no – not by a factor of more than a thousand.

Dr Harold Urey has pointed out that the mechanism becomes self-regulatory because the water vapour is shaded from the solar ultra-violet by absorption by the very oxygen that is so produced. We call this limiting process the "Urey effect". The detailed calculations allow but a slight build-up of oxygen in the atmosphere.

Water vapour is mainly limited to the lower atmosphere, since it is readily precipitated as rain from the colder regions above. As the water vapour is broken down by ultra-violet light to provide a supply of free oxygen to the atmosphere, this same oxygen is distributed above the principal water vapour levels. It turns out that this oxygen absorbs the very wavelengths that are needed for the continued breakdown of the water vapour. When oxygen reaches a certain very small concentration it simply cuts off its own further production.

The ultimate concentration of oxygen in the primitive atmosphere is determined by the rate of loss which, at equilibrium, must be balanced by the supply. This balance can be calculated and identified. We find that the concentration of oxygen in the primitive atmosphere did not exceed about 0.1 per cent of the present oxygen concentration. We suspect that the same processes control the present oxygen content of the atmosphere of Mars as seen by *Mariner IV*.

In our present atmosphere we are shielded from lethal ultraviolet by very small amounts of ozone, principally at a height of about 30 miles. The total quantity of ozone amounts only to about 50 to 70 billionths of the atmosphere below 30 miles, yet it is sufficient to protect life from lethal sunburn.

But in the primitive atmosphere, when oxygen was less than one-thousandth of its present levels, ozone was produced very close to the surface. The protective ozone layer was very thin – not enough to protect incipient life at the surface from the lethal ultraviolet glare of the Sun at the surface. Our calculations show that the combined effect of absorption of ultra-violet by the oxygen and ozone in the primitive atmosphere, plus a layer of water, provides conditions favourable to the synthesis of living molecules and promotion of the simplest forms of life processes in water at depths of about 30 to 40 feet – but not on, or even near the surface. Carl Sagan has independently reached a substantially similar conclusion.

Thus we can imagine organic compounds synthesised through the energy of ultra-violet light at the surface and gently convected downward away from ultra-violet damage into regions where more complex organisms could be synthesised in the presence of visible non-lethal radiation. This primitive ecology calls for shallow pools with a depth of 30 feet or more, sufficient to shadow the deadly ultra-violet, but not so deep as to cut off too much of the visible light. The model also calls for convection currents in the water, too slight to sweep the primitive organisms up from the bottom, yet sufficient to carry organic nutrients downward from the surface. At this early stage, life in the oceans seems very improbable – the waves and currents of the oceans would circulate the early organisms to the surface or disperse them downward into darkness. Therefore, they could exist only in lakes and protected shallow seas as bottom-dwelling organisms at a depth of 30 or 40 feet.

We have noticed a very curious coincidence. In the primitive atmosphere the greatest protection occurs around 2600 Å. The location of this wavelength zone of maximum protection is a fact of our Solar System, depending only on the distribution with wavelength of ultra-violet radiation from the Sun, and the absorption characteristics of ozone and water. Now this is the very region where present-day nucleic acids (2630 Å) and proteins (2750 Å) are most sensitive to damage. This might suggest a selective advantage to nucleic acids and proteins synthesised with such absorption characteristics. We have not calculated how much another Sun with quite a different radiation pattern might shift this protective zone, nor do we know whether other nucleic acids or proteins with different absorption characteristics can exist, but this point ought to be kept in mind in projecting life to other solar systems.

We are still faced with the problem of accounting for the further build-up of oxygen to present levels capable of supporting higher life-forms, and of protecting them from fatal radiation in the oceans and on the land. The rise of oxygen can only have occurred through a process of photosynthesis whereby oxygen is released from water during the reduction of carbon dioxide into carbohydrate. The crucial point is that photosynthesis employes visible light, whose intensity is not curtailed by the presence of oxygen or ozone in the atmosphere. The Urey effect does not limit its production.

The first cell life possibly incorporating photosynthesis appears to have been identified at about 2.7 By ago. The subsequent oxygen balance would be determined by:

+ *generating mechanisms*
(1) photo-dissociation (Urey effect limits);
(2) photosynthesis (Urey effect does not limit);
− *removal mechanisms*
(1) oxidation of surface materials;
(2) biological processes, including decay and respiration;
(3) dissolving of oxygen in water;
(4) some re-association of hydrogen and oxygen in the atmosphere.

At first, the effect of photosynthesis would not seriously disturb the primitive balance at 0.1 per cent of present atmospheric level.

Eventually, however, as the areas covered by photosynthetic release of oxygen enlarged, atmospheric accumulation of significant amounts of oxygen would begin. For this to happen, oxygen must be supplied faster than it is dissociated and lost through its active forms, permitting us to estimate that the pools must have covered an equivalent of somewhat more than one per cent of present land areas in order to provide enough photosynthetic activity and consequent oxygen production to overpower the Urey effect.

From this, one can form a graphic picture of how continental areas must have looked. The lands were barren, with no vegetation, but possessing bodies of water in which the photosynthetic activity took place at their shallow bottoms. Anyone who has flown over Northern Canada and Labrador, can readily visualise how much of the Earth's surface must have appeared.

The mechanisms available so far have provided the early organisms with only limited amounts of energy. As oxygen began to increase slowly, to a point about ten times the amount that existed at the early stages, or one per cent of the present oxygen level, the possibility of energy supply to organisms through *respiration* begins to appear. This mechanism provides 30 to 50 times the energy per molecule made available to organisms through more elementary chemical processes of fermentation. In many primitive organisms, the changeover from fermentation to respiration occurs when oxygen reaches about one per cent of its present concentration in the atmosphere. Pasteur pointed out this effect nearly a century ago during his study of the spoilage of wines, so it is known as the "Pasteur effect".

Respiration creates altogether new evolutionary opportunities – for a circulatory system to convey the oxygen, a digestive system to employ it, a nervous system to control the process – in short, for complex multi-celled organisms with advanced mechanisms of energy capture, control and utilisation. Respiration has always been recognised as a major evolutionary development. What has been overlooked is that the physical opportunity for respiration is the key that unlocks the whole catalogue of advanced biological function and development. Only as oxygen concentrations permit respiration is there created an evolutionary demand for complex biological function to maximise its energy capture, with the consequent employment of that energy for the advantage of the organisms.

The increase in oxygen in the atmosphere to about one per cent of its present level is automatically accompanied by a calculable increase in the total ozone content. When we consider the absorption of ultra-violet in oxygen, ozone and water we find that the lethal rays of ultra-violet are cut off at depths of only a foot or so of water.

The level of oxygen in the atmosphere at one per cent of the present amount is referred to as the *first critical level*. Life is still confined to the water but now can survive at very shallow depths. The spread of life to the oceans is permitted since lethality is now limited only to the very surface of the waters and more advanced organisms can now evolve that have some control over their situation in that environment. Indeed, as one reads Hardy's charming account of the unexplained diurnal depth control of pelagic organisms, found so generally in the seas, it is suggestive of a protective response inherited from these very times.

11 November, 1965

3

The evolution of the Earth's atmosphere

ANN HENDERSON-SELLERS

Interest in the evolution of the Earth's atmosphere is at a peak as a result of predictions that Man's activities may be becoming a significant force in modifying the "natural" state of affairs. An international conference on planetary atmospheres is being held this week in Nice; here, one of the participants at that conference sets the scene by discussing how the Earth got the atmosphere it has today

The fascinating topic of the evolutionary processes that produced the atmosphere we have around the Earth today is no longer a specialist preserve of the planetary scientists, but has become a puzzle of broader, and more practical, importance. The study of climatic change, both natural and man-made, is now at the forefront of the Earth sciences as many experts wonder whether conditions as pleasant for life as those of the past few decades are likely to persist. And a full understanding, and prediction, of climate depends on a full understanding of the atmosphere, where it came from, and how it got into its present state.

The interdependent cycles affecting life in the atmosphere and oceans (and in the longer term, influences from continental changes) combine in our planetary ecosystem, which seems to have serenely withstood 4.5 By of traumatic upheavals. These include an increase in Solar luminosity, volcanic activity, the formation of oceans, mountain building and continental drift, and the origin of life on the planet. It is difficult to obtain evidence relating to the prevailing climatic conditions over timescales comparable with the age of the Solar System itself; but something can be said about the value of the average global surface temperature and its changes over most of this time.

The present-day temperature is 288 K (15 °C), and is clearly compatible with a hospitable environment for life as we know it. Geological evidence suggests that this global mean surface temperature has not varied outside the range 280–300 K throughout the Earth's history. Liquid water first appeared on our planet around 3.8 By ago, so this particular ecological niche seems to have been relatively stable for a very long time. Researchers' attempts to model mathematically the dynamic interactions between the Earth and its atmosphere have, one has to admit, been grossly inadequate. Nevertheless, two views seem to be emerging: one, that our present position on Earth is a happy, but statistically unlikely, chance situation; the second, a considerably less anthropocentric view, is that the planetary environmental evolution is inherently stable.

Experts now generally agree that the Earth and other planets near the Sun (the terrestrial planets – Mercury, Venus and Mars) lost any primordial atmosphere through Solar heating early in their lives. The present atmospheres are thought to be a result of loss of gas from the mantle, including both volcanic outgassing and the vaporisation produced by the impact of meteorites. But

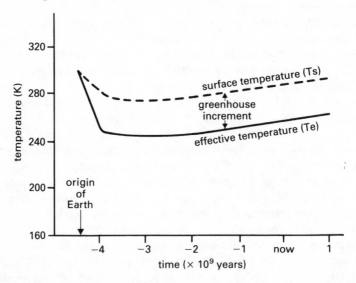

Figure 3.1   *Stable evolutionary track of the Earth's surface temperature. The "greenhouse effect" increases rapidly during the early stages of the evolution. T_s remains above 273 K throughout*

the experts are not agreed on just what kind of atmosphere this outgassing produced in the first place.

The same degassing processes today would liberate mainly water vapour and carbon dioxide, so the simplest guess is that the Earth's atmosphere started out from a mixture of these two gases. But instead the usual argument is that the atmosphere produced initially was rich in gases like methane and ammonia – reducing gases similar to those dominating the atmosphere of Jupiter and the other giant planets today. This conventional view seems to be inherited from the early theories of the origin of life, which were based on the build-up of complex organic molecules from a reducing atmosphere and water, stimulated by sunlight and lightning discharges. Now, though, experiments have shown that complex amino acids can build up in an atmosphere dominated by carbon dioxide, and there is an extreme view (put forward by Sir Fred Hoyle and Chandra Wickramasinghe) that life might originate in interstellar space, not even requiring a planetary base (*New Scientist*, vol. 76, p. 402). In addition, both Venus and Mars are now known to have carbon dioxide atmospheres. The simplest explanation is that all three planets started out in the same way, with predominately carbon dioxide atmospheres produced by degassing. So how did the three planets – especially the Earth – get to their present-day states?

The most important parameter, by a long way, is the mean global surface temperature at the time when an atmosphere began to form. This determines where the water goes to, and that in turn determines the evolution of the planetary system from then on. Without an atmosphere, the temperature is simply the effective temperature, T_e, which results from the balance between incoming Solar radiation and the rate at which heat is lost to space by the planet. The values appropriate for rocky planets in the orbits of Earth, Venus and Mars are given in Table 3.1 – these are the surface temperatures the three planets must have had 4.5 By ago.

Crucially, the temperature on Venus then was high enough for water to be kept in its vapour state; from the very beginning, the water vapour in the atmosphere of Venus must have trapped infra-red radiation, eventually producing a runaway greenhouse effect

Table 3.1

	Venus	*Earth*	*Mars*
T_e(4.5 By ago)	360 K	300 K	245 K

which has made Venus a hot desert today. At the other extreme, on Mars, the water couldn't even melt, let alone evaporate, so the atmosphere remained thin, with water trapped in frozen reservoirs below the surface. On Earth, however, things were – and remain – more interesting.

The intermediate position of our planet resulted in temperatures that ensured condensation of water vapour released into the atmosphere, forming large ocean areas, permitting carbon dioxide solution and leading to the formation of sedimentary rocks as rain carried eroded material into the seas. With carbon dioxide removed from the atmosphere (see Table 3.2) the path of future surface temperature evolution was determined.

Once the atmosphere is established, the planet becomes more reflective to Solar radiation, and also a better radiator of heat; the effective temperature drops, but later must increase again as the Sun's luminosity rises. Now, however, the average global surface temperature, T_s, depends not only upon T_e but also upon the greenhouse effect – the extent to which the atmosphere acts as a blanket, trapping heat that would otherwise be radiated into space. This depends on the kind of gases in the atmosphere, and how much there is of each (Figure 3.1).

Water is critically important for many biological, chemical and physical processes. It also controls temperature on Earth both by the greenhouse effect and by the extent to which snow and ice cover, or clouds, change the reflectivity of the Earth (its albedo). These feedback processes have ensured temperatures on Earth close to 290 K, permitting liquid water to dominate the planet's surface and providing a hospitable home for life.

Table 3.2   *Inventory of carbon near the Earth's surface (normalised)*

Reservoir	Proportion of total carbon
Biosphere marine	1
non-marine	1
Atmosphere (in CO_2)	70
Ocean (in dissolved CO_2	4000
Fossil fuels	800
Shales	800 000
Carbonate rocks	2 000 000

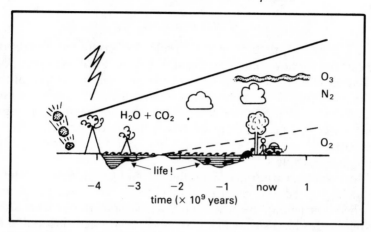

Figure 3.2 *Schematic diagram of the history of the Earth's atmosphere. The influence of the biosphere has been considerable*

Once life came on to the scene it too played a part in determining the chemical composition of the atmosphere. Figure 3.2 shows, in a highly schematic form, atmospheric and biospheric evolution over the history of the Earth. Although complex life-forms developed only recently, biological processes have combined with physical and chemical mechanisms overall to change the input of 80 per cent water vapour, 20 per cent carbon dioxide and traces of nitrogen and sulphur compounds into the present atmosphere dominated by nitrogen and free oxygen.

Primitive life originated, according to the most widely accepted theories, in the sub-surface layers of the early oceans, where it was protected from ultra-violet radiation. To the first organisms, oxygen was a dangerous poison, a waste product produced from their life process and dissolved in the ocean waters, slowly diffusing into the atmosphere above. The released oxygen was bound up by chemical reactions into the surface rocks, including the iron oxide "redbeds" formed about 2.6 By ago. But once enough oxygen was around, it changed the rules for living organisms in two ways. First, it provided a new source of energy for life-forms that learned the trick of respiration; secondly, by building up in the atmosphere and then forming an ozone layer that absorbed incoming Solar ultra-violet radiation, it made it possible for life to emerge from the protecting layers of the ocean.

Enter mankind

Now life could spread on a grand scale, with a dramatic effect on the carbon dioxide content of the atmosphere. Sedimentary deposits buried plants and animals, their remains rich in carbon, in the rocks, resulting in the semi-permanent removal of vast quantities of carbon from the atmosphere. Only semi-permanent, though, since now life, in the form of Mankind, is deeply involved in extracting some of that carbon-rich material, in the form of fossil fuels, and burning it.

More subtle variations of biological and atmospheric systems could have produced short-term changes in surface temperature, as when flourishing "tropical" jungles have spread over wide areas of the Earth's land surface and changed the surface albedo and its infrared absorption. One suggestion (J. Lovelock and S. Epton, *New Scientist*, vol. 65, p. 304) proposes that the atmosphere should be seen as part of the biosphere, producing a complete self-regulating ecosystem which is named after the Mycenaean Earth

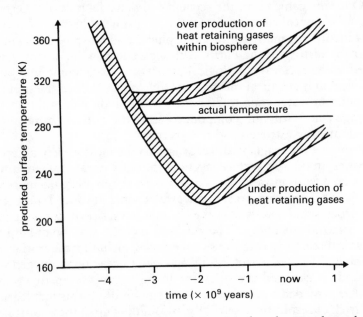

Figure 3.3   *The temperature histories for the Earth under the control of the biosphere. The "Gaia hypothesis" allows temperature control and may have produced the stable temperature curve*

goddess, Gaia. On this picture, temperatures are confined to a stable narrow band suitable for life by the processes of life itself (Figure 3.3).

Climate predictions

The two main schools of thought in climate studies give very different points of view. One sees the evolution of the atmosphere as like a wandering walk along a valley floor, with occasional slight excursions up the side of the valley, but soon returning to the most stable conditions at the bottom. The other sees a continuing "ridge walk" balancing in a narrow region of stability with doom of one kind or another but a step away on either side. The role of cyclic changes such as the Milankovitch mechanism which modulates climate at various cycles with periods in the range 10–100 000 years (see *New Scientist*, vol. 75, p. 530) must also be taken into account, together with evidence that these fluctuations can only modulate glacial epochs when the continents are in the right place – near the poles – for a glacial epoch to occur in the first place (Figure 3.4). So continental drift affects the changing atmosphere!

Other processes, involving more rapid feedback, are still poorly understood. Will increase in carbon dioxide from burning fossil

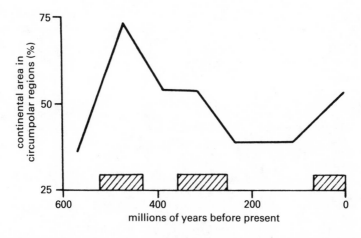

Figure 3.4 *Areas of continental mass close to one or both poles seem to correlate well with (shaded) periods of glacial activity*

fuels produce a runaway greenhouse effect? Or will a slight temperature increase encourage more clouds to form, increasing the
albedo, reflecting Solar heat away and cancelling out the greenhouse effect? Predictions of future climatic variations depend first
on understanding past evolution of the planetary atmosphere. We
are still far from that ideal, but perhaps the current conference in
Nice will take us a step further along the road.

26 October, 1978

4

Volcanic activity: the continual degassing of the Earth

KEN BAILEY

The creation of the Earth's atmosphere was not a "once and for all" event in the remote geological past, but continues even today

---

One of the most promising guides to the history of the Earth lies in the evolution of the gases now residing in its outer zones – the atmosphere, the hydrosphere, and the rocky shell of the lithosphere. Most of these gases have accumulated through time, and, if properly understood, they must give us some constraints on theories of the planet's evolution. Among the processes by which gases may be expelled from the interior, the favourite has always been the upward movement of molten rock (magma), producing volcanic activity at the Earth's surface.

Traditional images of volcanoes depict a majestic cone emitting a plume of vapour, the identifying symbol of a volcano. Yet most general discussions of the development of the Earth's lithosphere, hydrosphere, atmosphere and biosphere give scant attention to volcanic variability, treating the activity as if it were uniform, and the vapour plume as inconsequential. Active volcanoes are, however, highly variable in their distribution, rates of production, modes of eruption, and in the compositions of their solid products, lavas and ashes. There should be no reason to suppose, therefore, that volcanic gases always contain the same types of substances. Nor is there any good reason to suppose that they are inconsequential in amount. The vapour plume signature on pictures of volcanoes should alert us to the fact that periods of lava and ash eruptions represent only a small fraction of the lifespan of most volcanoes, but that during this time, even while "dormant", they are still fuming.

The role of gases in volcanic geology has been neglected largely because of their evanescent character. The record that gases leave in the rocks, which is all that remains when activity has ceased, is incomplete and difficult to decipher.

The variability in amount and function of volcanic gases can be seen in the different eruptive styles of different magmas. Some lavas well up through the volcanic vent, or even along a surface fissure, and flow easily over long distances (such as at Mauna Loa, on Hawaii). Others erupt with violent explosions, building up cones largely by showers of fragments deposited around the vent. This form of eruption characterises the volcanoes around the rim of the Pacific, the classic steep-sided cone being typified in the beautiful symmetrical form of Mount Fuji in Japan.

Explosive, gas-rich, fragmental eruptions are characteristic of the alkali-rich volcanoes that typify volcanic activity in the stable interiors of the Earth's plates, especially within continental plates. It is to be expected that the composition of the gases might vary just as strongly as the compositions of the solid products in these different kinds of volcanoes, but the effects of this have received little consideration.

Our ignorance about the chemical compositions of volcanic gases is due to the difficulty of getting hold of samples. Even when it is possible to collect a sample free from contamination by air or atmospheric water, the composition of the erupted gas will vary with temperature of emission, and there may be significant losses of some of the volatile species by sublimation and precipitation on the cooler rocks around the point of escape. Volcanic sublimates are characteristically rich in halogens and sulphur, so the collected gas will be depleted in these constituents. The total amounts of these sublimates are difficult to estimate because of their dispersal in the porous structure of a volcano, and because many of them are relatively soluble in surface and ground waters. As the temperature of the collected gas decreases, so the likelihood of its contamination by atmosphere and ground water increases. Consequently, the hottest gas is the best sample, and this is preferably collected as it escapes from molten lava, at temperatures between 900 and 1200 °C.

Suitable sites where the gas collection tube can be placed close to strongly degassing molten lava are not often available, and nearly always present arduous and hazardous conditions for the collector. An additional cause for concern is that major emissions of gas from volcanoes are violent, most commonly explosive, and collection during such eruptions is impossible. Some analyses of erupting gas columns have been made using remote-control instruments, but these have been limited to one or a few molecular species and give no indication of the total gas composition. It may be that the violent mode of eruption involves gases significantly different in composition from those that are collectable.

Even when a good gas collection has been made, the gas geochemist is left with the realisation that his sample represents only one moment in the geological life of a volcano. Furthermore, his volcano is but part of the variable world-wide volcanic pattern available only at this instant in the immensely longer life of the planet. If we are concerned with the development of the Earth's atmosphere, then we should also have regard to variations in gas output through time. Variations in the total amounts of volcanic action, and in relative proportions of different types of volcanoes, during the past 4500 million years complicate the evolutionary pattern.

Because of the sampling problems, there are only a few analyses of high-temperature gases, the best known being from the tholeiitic basalt volcano, Kilauea, on the big island of Hawaii. Most generalisations about the evolution of the Earth's gases have turned to the Hawaiian analyses as representing the volcanic contribution: the comparison is then made between the volcanic gas and the proportions of volatiles now residing in the atmosphere, hydrosphere and lithosphere (see Table 4.1). Even this simple comparison reveals important differences that demand explanation. One explanation is that the samples of gases from

Table 4.1 *Comparison of volcanic gases with "excess" volatiles in atmosphere, hydrosophere and sedimentary rocks. Values in weight per cent*

	Average Hawaiian gases	"Excess" volatiles
H_2O	64.3	92.8
CO_2	23.8	5.1
Cl	0.16	1.67
N	1.60	0.23
S	9.97	0.12
H	0.05	0.06
Others	0.07	0.02

Hawaii are unrepresentative of juvenile gas emission. It is clear, for instance, that andesite volcanism, such as that around the Pacific border, is richer in water, and this type of volcanism is now seen by some people as one of the main contributors to the surface waters of our planet. The dominance of water on the Earth's surface lends plausibility to the popular assumption that water is the dominant product in volcanic gases generally, but alkali-rich volcanism runs counter to this assumption. Magmas rich in alkalis are characteristically erupted in the interior regions of the Earth's lithospheric plates, especially where these are rifted, with the East African Rift presenting the most comprehensive display in recent geological history. In the southern part of the zone which is now active, there are some of the best examples of carbonate magmatism, with observed eruptions of carbonate ashes and lavas from Oldonyo Lengai, in northern Tanzania. The carbonate lavas (which are simply another erupted form of carbon dioxide) are essentially anhydrous. They are also rich in fluorine. Associated with the carbonate magmatism are silicate lavas with very low contents of silicon dioxide (such as nephelinites), and analysed gases from the active nephelinite volcano, Nyiragongo, in Zaire, are also rich in carbon dioxide. Recent experimental studies confirm that the melting of peridotite (the average composition of the Earth's upper mantle) in the presence of carbon dioxide yields nephelinitic liquids. Clearly, this type of magmatism requires the participation of carbon dioxide rather than water. It is not generally appreciated, however, that the more silica-rich magmatism in the Kenya section of the East African Rift is also rich in halogens and highly deficient in water. Although it is not retained in solution in the silicic melts, carbon dioxide is much in evidence in these volcanic fields. All along the Rift Valley carbon dioxide escapes from the ground, sometimes at such high pressures and of such purity as to be commercially exploitable.

The East African Rift is probably the most spectacular example of alkali-rich magmatism in recent times, and this type of magmatism is generally rich in carbon dioxide. This confirms the view that has been growing in the past few years that variations in volcanism are closely linked to the amount and composition of the associated gases, which may even have a controlling influence on the generation and character of the magma itself. A new picture thus emerges of the East African Rift as a great gash in the continental lithosphere from which large quantities of carbon dioxide have been issuing since Miocene times, for the past 23 My.

The earliest phases of activity were probably dominated by carbo-nite/nephelinite eruptions. Similar alkaline volcanoes erupted in other rifts, and pushed up parts of the plate interiors, but during the same period volcanic zones along the plate margins were erupting different sorts of magma with different associated gas compositions (in which water may have been the chief constit-uent). Enough has been said to show, however, that the once generally accepted simplified volcanic gas budget, dominated by water, is in need of re-appraisal before indulging in speculation about atmospheric processes.

If we assume that volcanic volatiles are a characteristic and intrinsic part of the magmatism, the variations in composition from place to place provide a special insight into heterogeneity in the Earth's mantle. During high-pressure melting within the Earth most free, volatile species would be soluble in the melt formed first: any volatile-bearing minerals will be generally among the least refractory and also consumed in the early melt. The rising magma would then not normally lose its dissolved volatiles unless

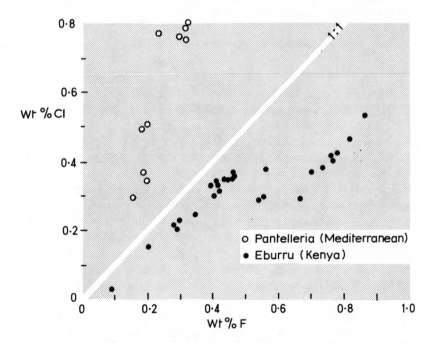

Figure 4.1   *Fluorine and chlorine distributions in glassy lavas of the same type from Eburru and Pantelleria*

it precipitated volatile-bearing solids, or reached oversaturation in gas. These two conditions will be recognisable in the finally solidified rock by the presence of large volatile-bearing crystals (phenocrysts) and trapped gas cavities (vesicles). Many erupted magmas do not contain volatile-bearing phenocrysts, and often show little signs of vesiculation, so that the volatiles trapped in the rock may be regarded as intrinsic. In different lavas, these intrinsic volatiles vary significantly in amounts, and especially in proportions, indicating that the source materials were compositionally variable.

As an example, we may consider the distributions of fluorine and chlorine in glassy lavas. These two elements are highly soluble in silicate melts and are difficult to extract, even during fusion under vacuum, so it is fair to assume that we are seeing them in intrinsic proportions. Figure 4.1 shows the variations in two sets of glassy lavas from Pantelleria, in the Mediterranean, and Eburru, in Kenya. In their major element chemistry the two sets of lavas are indistinguishable, so the differences in the halogens must reflect the source chemistry in the mantle below these two volcanoes. A similar pattern is emerging distinguishing oceanic from continental volcanoes of the same type.

Evolutionary degassing

Whenever the calculated inventory of volatiles in the outer parts of the Earth has been compared with the time-integrated present-day volcanic gas output (even with the uncertainties already noted) it has indicated an approximate balance for the major gaseous species, requiring continuous volcanic emission throughout the Earth's history. An even simpler check is to calculate the carbon dioxide equivalent of all the carbon now residing in hydrocarbons and carbonates in sedimentary rocks. This would provide an atmosphere with a partial pressure of carbon dioxide of about 14 bars! If such an atmosphere had existed in the past it should have left clear evidence in the geologic record, but none has yet been reported. Since carbon dioxide is a common volcanic gas it is reasonable to suppose that it has been gradually added to the atmosphere, from which it has been continually removed by solution, rock weathering and biological activity, to become fixed in sedimentary rocks. This hypothesis of evolutionary degassing has always had its advocates, and it is receiving new support in studies of rare gases from volcanic sources. The concentrations, and ratios, of different gases show strong departures from atmospheric values, indicating continuing release of rare gases, now reaching the surface for the first time ("juvenile" gases). Probably the most straightforward evidence of juvenile emission is in the isotopes of helium, because they readily escape from the Earth's gravity field, and their residence time in the atmosphere is geologically short-lived. The isotope ratio, ^{3}He/^{4}He, is much greater in deep ocean waters, volcanic gases, lavas and deep rocks than in the atmosphere, indicating continuing juvenile emission. What is more, this ratio varies considerably between different regions, consistent with the evidence of mantle heterogeneity already noted for the more abundant reactive gases. Juvenile helium in the volcanism around the Pacific margin also re-enlivens the debate about the source of the water that seems to characterise this type of magmatism. Most current hypotheses postulate the main contribution of volcanic water coming from wet ocean-floor rocks that have been overridden by the continental plates, so the water is regarded as re-cycled atmospheric/oceanic water, but the helium suggests that a juvenile origin of water – from within the Earth – is required.

Sometimes, it has been suggested that essentially all the gases being erupted today are re-cycled, having their sources in old surface rocks that have been subducted into the mantle, or buried in the deep crust, during earlier episodes of mountain building. In other words, there is no genuine juvenile gas coming from the deep interior. The concentrations and *ratios* of gases from most volcanoes, however, are quite incompatible with re-cycled atmosphere, atmospheric waters, or crustal rocks, so there is *no* observational basis for the suggestion that some combination of these could be a regenerative source for volcanic gases.

It is possible to piece together from the interiors of the continental plates a geological story going back to the oldest known rocks (about 3.8 thousand million years). The older rocks now exposed at the surface were, at the time of their formation, deeply buried to depths between 20 and 60 km below the Earth's surface. Typically these rocks are of the type known as granulites, which are poor in volatiles and elements of large ionic size ("incompatible" elements): they are generally thought to have crystallised under anhydrous conditions and to represent a volatile-depleted residue from the depths of the continental crust. It must be presumed that during the process of granulite formation the immediately underlying mantle will also have been severely depleted in volatiles and incompatible elements. Yet many parts of the ancient continental

shields (particularly where there has been rifting) have been penetrated by subsequent episodes of alkaline magmatism, rich in
volatiles and incompatible elements. This magmatism has been
repeated at intervals in some parts of the continents through to the
present time, showing that the deeper parts of the Earth still hold
reserves of volatiles that may be released episodically. The continents have been sites of chemical heterogeneity in the outer part of
the Earth since they first started to form.

Seen against the background of the potential variability of
volcanic gas output throughout the past 4500 My, the modern,
Man-produced gas pollutants, such as carbon dioxide, must be
seen geologically as a new outburst. But as yet there is nothing to
say that fluctuations in volcanic gas output have not produced
comparable, or even greater, perturbations in atmospheric composition, possibly over even longer periods in the past. Geological
evidence indicates that the relatively small mass of the atmosphere
is balanced by changing rates of weathering and deposition in the
lithosphere/hydrosphere/biosphere in the long term, and probably
in the short term as well. Essentially, our oceanic buffer system
seems to have coped with the presumed variations in the volcanic
contributions to the atmosphere. Any threat from atmospheric
pollution would be greater if we render the oceans sterile by a
pollution "catastrophe", but even then some calculations indicate
that the atmosphere would not go out of control. This is not to
invite complacency, only to suggest that we must make greater
efforts to study the geologic record before we panic about producing a "runaway greenhouse". The overriding reason for husband-
ing the diminishing store of fossil hydrocarbons is that these
chemicals are *too precious to burn*. Our descendants, while still
enjoying an equable climate, may well look upon this as the
"profligate age", when we burned their inheritance in full knowledge of what we were doing.

1 February, 1979

5

Carbon dioxide, ammonia – and life

JOHN GRIBBIN

Astronomers and geophysicists now seem to be reaching agreement on their interpretation of the early atmosphere of our planet, and hence the conditions in which life on Earth began

Pick up an encyclopaedia and look up the section on the Earth's atmosphere. It will probably tell you that the primeval atmosphere of our planet was dominated by methane, and that this hydrogen-rich gas was necessary for the formation of the first complex organic molecules, the precursors of life. But an increasing number of geophysicists, biologists and climatologists would take issue with the encyclopaedias on both these claims. These scientists would base their objections on modern evidence provided by other planets, by the effects of volcanic eruptions and other strands from a broad spectrum of scientific research.

The gases released by volcanoes today are dominated by water vapour and carbon dioxide, and there seems no reason to expect the volatile products of volcanic activity to have been substantially different in the Earth's youth. Both Venus and Mars have atmospheres of carbon dioxide, presumably produced by the outgassing of volatile materials from within the planets. And although the Earth's atmosphere today contains very little carbon dioxide, the absence of this gas can be explained by a combination of the effects of water (dissolving carbon dioxide and laying it down as carbonates in sedimentary rocks) and life (taking up carbon dioxide and releasing oxygen through photosynthesis) acting upon a primeval atmosphere of carbon dioxide. But where did the life come from that played such a key role in producing the atmosphere we breathe today?

It used to be widely thought, and widely taught, that the original "primitive" atmosphere of the early Earth was a "reducing" atmosphere, that is with no oxygen but rich in hydrocarbons such as methane and ammonia, which can combine with oxygen. This would be similar to the atmospheres of the giant planets, such as Jupiter and Saturn, today. The reasoning behind this assumption developed primarily from the belief that such an atmosphere would be ideal, and might be essential, for the development of the complex but non-living molecules that preceded life. This idea, and by implication the idea that the Earth's first atmosphere was a reducing one, received a great boost in 1953, when Harold Urey and Stanley L. Miller at the University of Chicago carried out a simple experiment. They set up a closed system in which water vapour, ammonia, carbon dioxide, methane and hydrogen circulated past an electric discharge. Chemical reactions stimulated by the input of energy produced a brown sludge at the bottom of the reaction vessel. The sludge contained amino acids: complex molecules regarded by many scientists as the building blocks of life, which are used in the construction of the body's proteins, for example.

Similar results can be obtained using ultra-violet light as the energy source, and ultra-violet (from the Sun) and electric discharges (lightning) must both have been around to energise chemical reactions in the terrestrial "primeval soup". This picture captured the popular imagination, and the story of life emerging in the seas or pools of a planet swathed in an atmosphere of methane and ammonia soon became part of the scientific folklore that "every schoolchild knows".

It is rather less well known, however, that some of the earliest experiments of the kind that Miller and Urey pioneered, were carried out using carbon dioxide, water vapour and only traces of ammonia, and that these experiments too produced an organic broth containing amino acids. In the early 1950s, it seems, the received wisdom was that the young Earth's atmosphere was rich in ammonia and methane, so these equally interesting results languished in obscurity for a couple of decades. When astronomers and geophysicists started to come round to the view that

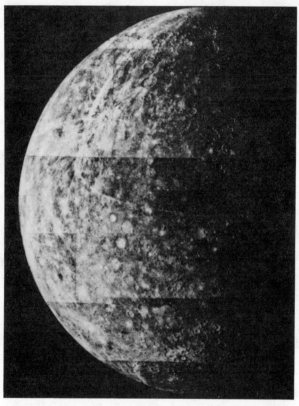

(a)

Figure 5.1 *The four terrestrial planets exhibit a wide range of atmospheres. Mercury* (a) *has none while Venus* (b) *is swathed in dense clouds mainly of carbon dioxide. Mars* (d) *has a thin atmosphere which also is largely carbon dioxide. It now seems that the Earth* (c) *at least began with a carbon dioxide atmosphere like its neighbours (Credit* (c) *MBB (Messerschmitt–Bölkow–CMBH),* (d) *NASA, California)*

(b)

the Earth's primitive atmosphere may, after all, have been dominated by water vapour and carbon dioxide, they were confronted
by the enshrined "fact" of scientific life that the Miller–Urey
experiments "proved" both that life originated in an ammonia-
rich atmosphere and that the Earth therefore started out with a
reducing atmosphere.

But now, this particular card-house seems to have been demo-
lished, and a new scientific edifice is arising in its place. In order to
convince people that the Earth started out with a reduced, not a
reducing, atmosphere – that is one with oxygen already locked up

in gases such as carbon dioxide, and which cannot take up more oxygen – astronomers, geophysicists and, more recently, climatologists have had to explain how life could arise on a wet planet with a carbon dioxide atmosphere laced with traces of ammonia. By such devious routes is scientific progress made.

Keeping the Earth warm

The primary feature the physical scientists have to explain, apart from the existence of an atmosphere around the Earth, is the remarkable constancy of the surface temperature of the Earth, shown by a variety of pieces of geological evidence, over the past 4000 My. The astronomers assert confidently that during the course of the Earth's evolution the Sun's heat output has

(c)

(d)

increased, so with the present-day atmosphere and the same reflective properties (albedo) the seas would have been frozen earlier
than about 2300 My ago. Over the whole span of geological time,
the Sun's luminosity has increased by about 40 per cent, if the
astronomical models of how stars work are as good as they seem
to be.

Ten years ago, Carl Sagan and George Mullen, of Cornell
University, presented in *Science* the results of some calculations
and these signalled the start of a new round in the debate. Sagan
and Mullen assumed that the Solar luminosity had increased by
"only" 30 per cent since the Earth formed and, keeping other
factors constant, they ran their computer model of the variations

in the Earth's surface temperature backwards in time from present-day conditions. The observed mean surface temperature of the Earth today is about 286 K (13 °C), and as the Sagan–Mullen model runs backwards through time the seas freeze 2.3 aeons ago (1 aeon is 10^9 years): beyond 4 aeons ago, near the beginning of the geological record, the computed temperature is a chilly 263 K (− 10 °C). But pillow lavas, ripple marks in rocks and other items of evidence point to the presence of an abundance of liquid water 3.2 aeons ago, and the earliest known microfossils, from about the same epoch, include blue-green algae, which are hardly characteristic of a frozen planet.

So how did the Earth keep warm that long ago? Assuming the Solar variations were as calculated, the only options open are to vary the albedo of the planet or to change its atmospheric composition to include gases with a stronger greenhouse effect. Sagan and Mullen argued that the albedo must have remained essentially the same over the Earth's history, and that therefore all the required increase in temperature must come from the greenhouse effect. "Major variations in the carbon dioxide abundance" they said "will have only minor greenhouse effects because the strongest [absorption] bands are nearly saturated."

They concluded that, as recently as two aeons ago, the Earth's atmosphere contained "some constituent or constituents not now present with significant absorption in the middle infra-red" part of the spectrum. The best candidate, they decided, was ammonia, which could produce appreciable infra-red absorption in the wavelength band from 8 to 13 μm at a concentration of only 10^{-5} parts by volume. (The present concentration of ammonia in the atmosphere is estimated, rather uncertainly, as about one thousandth of that figure, or less.) Noting that ammonia is "a very useful precursor" for pre-biological chemistry, Sagan and Mullen concluded that, all round, an early atmosphere laced with ammonia must have been a good thing for life on Earth, first providing the raw material, then ensuring a warm home on which life could develop.

However, even this half-way house between the "every school-child knows" picture of an early reducing atmosphere and the contrasting image of an atmosphere dominated by carbon dioxide has now been superseded. The albedo of the Earth really may have been significantly different long ago, while life might have managed to get a good grip on the planet without any more ammonia than we find in the atmosphere today.

Doubts about the assumption of more or less constant reflective properties for the Earth over its long history were raised by Ann Henderson-Sellers and Jack Meadows, of the University of Leicester, in a "letter" to *Nature* in 1977 (vol. 270, p. 589). Their argument came in two parts. First, if the atmosphere of the Earth had accumulated by outgassing over a significant period of time, then the albedo would have changed gradually from the value for a rocky, airless planet to the value for a planet surrounded by atmosphere. This covers a range from about 0.07 for the airless state (that is, only seven per cent of incoming Solar radiation reflected) up to 0.33 today. So a slow process of degassing could compensate for some of the variation in Solar luminosity, allowing more heat to reach the surface of a planet with a thinner atmosphere so keeping the surface temperature above the freezing point of water.

But the available evidence suggests that the degassing was probably faster earlier in the Earth's history than it is today, for the young planet was vigorously geologically active. The rapid build-up of an atmosphere that would tend to act as a reflective barrier to sunlight means that some other process must have been at work to explain the evidence of liquid water two or three aeons ago. Rather than invoke a greenhouse effect due to ammonia, Henderson-Sellers and Meadows considered changes in the Earth's rotation, as it has slowed down over the aeons due to the Moon's tidal influence.

The Moon, scientists generally believe, either formed at the same time as the Earth or was captured at least four aeons ago; a more recent capture should have produced geological upheavals that would be clear today in the record of the Earth's rocks. For all that time tidal forces have been at work slowing the rotation of the Earth and increasing the length of day, from an original value of only a little more than 2 hours to the present 24 hours. In the process, the distance of the Moon from the Earth has increased, and the strength of the tidal influence has diminished. So the most pronounced changes in length of day occurred early in the history of the Earth–Moon system, over the crucial first two aeons.

If a planet with very little atmosphere spins rapidly, then it has problems re-radiating the energy it receives: only the night side of a planet does much re-radiating, and on a rapidly rotating planet night does not last long enough for much energy to be lost before the surface is whisked round again into the glare of the Sun to absorb more heat. According to Meadows, the young Earth, with an atmosphere a bit less than that of Mars today, would have had an albedo of about 10 per cent (that is, 90 per cent of incoming radiation is absorbed) and the surface temperature would have been above the freezing point of water, even if the planet were not spinning rapidly. With the two effects of spin and albedo, working together, the calculations of Henderson-Sellers show that the early Earth (between about 2000 My ago and something over 3000 My ago) may even have been warmer than the present-day Earth, without a greenhouse effect any more pronounced than the atmosphere produces today.

Indeed, some calculations suggest that adding compounds such as methane and ammonia to the primitive atmosphere of the Earth would be too much of a good thing. Michael Hart, of the NASA–Goddard Space Flight Center in Maryland, has attempted to model on a computer the evolving temperature of the Earth while supposing the composition of the atmosphere varied as new material was outgassed and as life began to play a part. He has allowed for changes in the Sun's luminosity, and the greenhouse effect, but not for all the changes in the model of Henderson-Sellers and Meadows, and he included 1.1 per cent methane in an initial atmosphere made up of 84.4 per cent water, 14.3 per cent carbon dioxide, 0.2 per cent nitrogen and traces of ammonia and argon (*Icarus*, vol. 33, p. 23).

Gloomy prognostications

The atmosphere that develops from this mixture ends up very like the present-day atmosphere of the Earth after 4.5 aeons, but along the way it passes through two crises. After only 800 My, the surface temperature reaches a peak of 317 K (26 °C), with a pressure of 1.4 atm – conditions very close to initiating a runaway greenhouse effect of the kind that makes Venus a searing desert today. And after 2.8 aeons the surface temperature falls to such an extent that the model "Earth" comes within one degree of freezing into a permanently ice-shrouded state and becoming a frigid desert like Mars. Interpreting these results in *New Scientist* (vol. 78, p. 671) Keith Hindley commented that the implication is that the habitable zone around the Sun is "much smaller than previously thought . . . as narrow as only 10 million kilometres, greatly reducing the estimate of [the number of] planets in the Galaxy suitable for the evolution of advanced life-forms".

Such a gloomy prognostication depends in no small measure on

the assumption that reducing gases are present initially to provide
the seeds of life and to give a large boost to the early greenhouse
effect. Using an improved version of the alternative scenario she
had developed with Meadows, Henderson-Sellers "predicted" a
much smaller range of variations over the past four aeons in a
temperature that remained close to 280 K (7 °C) rising slightly to
present-day levels (*New Scientist*, vol. 80, p. 287).

The way the Earth's temperature seems actually to have avoided
the extremes of heat and cold suggests to some people that life
itself plays a part in the feedback processes regulating the temperature; indeed "independent scientist" Jim Lovelock and Lynn Margulis, from Boston University, developed the idea of "Gaia", the
Earth's biosphere as a living entity regulating conditions on Earth
to suit herself (*New Scientist*, vol. 65, p. 304). But it appeared that
seekers after life in the Universe, at least of Earth-type life, were
caught in a bind. You could make a nice, warm planet for life to
live on if you left almost all of the reducing gases out of the
atmosphere, but if you tried to make a planet like the Earth with a
decent lacing of ammonia to start the ball of life rolling, you ran
the risk of a rapidly developing "runaway" greenhouse effect,
producing conditions decidedly unsuitable for life as we know it.

Could the Earth really be a freak? Or was there a way out of the
bind? Henderson-Sellers, by then working at the University of
Liverpool, and A. W. Schwartz, of the University of Nijmegen, in
the Netherlands, came up with at least a clue to the answer in
1980. Writing in *Nature* (vol. 270, p. 589), they suggested one
way in which ammonia might be produced locally in the quantities
needed for life to begin, without ever reaching a global concentration sufficient to cause problems with a greenhouse effect. Their
idea hinged on the observation that titanium dioxide is an effective
catalyst for the photochemical reactions that convert nitrogen to
ammonia, and that some deserts are so rich in titanium that they
"produce" up to 20 kg of ammonia from each hectare in a year.
Apart from the novel suggestion that life on the early Earth may
thus have owed its existence to the presence of deserts as much as
to the availability of liquid water, this model has built into it some
interesting feedback loops. The deserts also produce some ammonia, so a slight warming from a greenhouse effect might have
encouraged the spread of the dry deserts and allowed more ammonia to be produced, thus improving the chance of life getting a
grip. Then, once life existed ammonia would be quickly locked up

in amino acids and DNA, reducing the threat of a runaway greenhouse effect.

In 1981, the results of more calculations and experiments were published, suggesting that even the production of ammonia from desert sands might not be necessary for the origin of life. A team from the University of Hawaii and the NASA Ames Research Center, headed by Clair Folsome, described how experiments using spark discharges through a nitrogen "atmosphere" onto aqueous suspensions of calcium carbonate produced small but significant yields of complex molecules such as hydrazine and carbohydrazide (*Nature*, vol. 294, p. 64). Such reactions could, they said, "have supplied a pathway for chemical evolution and the origin of life on a primitive Earth" without the need for methane or ammonia, and that "more productive processes may yet be found".

But a little ammonia must be a good thing if amino acids are to be built up in any chemical system. Climatologists Tom Wigley and Peter Brimblecombe, of the University of East Anglia, point out that although it is possible to make organic molecules in the absence of ammonia, amino acids are unstable and break down if there is no ammonia around at all. (They are referring to "free" amino acids; the ones locked up in the body are in a rather different environment.) In the sort of watery environment where life presumably first arose, amino acids are stabilised if the concentration of the ammonium ion is sufficiently high, and this depends on how much ammonia there is in the air above the water. The team at the University of East Anglia has calculated just how much ammonia is needed to do the job. They find that a minimum partial pressure of ammonia of 10^{-8} atm ensures that amino acids could be stable in the acidic ocean waters of the early Earth. The measured partial pressure of ammonia in the air over the oceans today is two to six times this figure, so everything looks good so far.   *13 May, 1982* © *John Gribbin; all rights reserved*

Rewrite those textbooks

If life started out in smaller pools in a freshwater environment, the partial pressure of carbon dioxide in the atmosphere is also an important factor, determining the activity of carbonate ions in the establishment of the crucial equilibrium in the solution (*Nature*, vol. 291, p. 213). Wigley and Brimblecombe, less sanguine than

Sagan and Mullen, believe that an early carbon dioxide atmosphere could have contributed significantly to warming the Earth through the greenhouse effect, but they find that even in freshwater pools, allowing for the presence of a carbon dioxide atmosphere, ammonia concentrations in the atmosphere comparable to those found today are sufficient to ensure sufficient activity of ammonium ions for amino acids to be stable. This is a key new insight into the processes by which precursors of life may have formed on Earth. Using the data from Henderson-Sellers and Schwartz's study of the effect due to titanium oxide, they calculate that the partial pressure of ammonia in the carbon dioxide atmosphere of the early Earth was between 1.3×10^{-8} and 1.3×10^{-6} atm, ample to do the job and much less than the limit of 10^{-5} atm at which a significant greenhouse effect sets in. Their most important conclusion is that "a strongly reducing atmosphere does not seem to be necessary for the origin of life", with the unstated corollary that life can develop on planets that do not run the risk of being made uninhabitable through a runaway, ammonia-based greenhouse effect.

All things considered, the news is rather good for people who hope and believe that life as we know it exists somewhere else in the Universe, and for proponents of the "principle of terrestrial mediocrity", which says that the Earth is such a very ordinary place that there must be many more places rather like it out there. All we have to do now is rewrite all those textbooks and ensure that "every schoolchild knows" what the best theory of the evolution of the Earth's atmosphere and the origins of life is today: that life developed in the pools on the surface of a planet with a carbon dioxide atmosphere bearing only a trace of ammonia, perhaps itself the product of chemical reactions in the desert sands.

13 May, 1982

COULD CLOUDS HAVE KEPT THE EARLY EARTH WARM?

Why was the Earth *not* frozen long ago when the Sun was cooler? Since the Solar System formed, some 4500 My ago, the Sun has warmed by about 25 per cent, while the temperature of the Earth has been roughly constant. The conventional wisdom is that the atmospheric greenhouse effect has been the stabilising influence;

but now it has been suggested that clouds could have done the job just as well.

The importance of the new calculations, by William Rossow, Ann Henderson-Sellers and Stephen Weinreich, of NASA's Goddard Space Flight Center in New York, is twofold. First, it seems that there is no need to invoke such a drastically different composition for the early Earth's atmosphere – no need for large quantities of ammonia or superdensities of carbon dioxide – as has been supposed. And, secondly, the evidence shows up the very large range of error in all computer models of climate that do not take proper account of cloud.

The clouds used in the NASA team's calculations come in two varieties. Low, thick cloud blocks incoming heat from the Sun and causes the Earth's surface to cool, while high, thin cloud traps heat that would otherwise be lost to space and warms the Earth through a "cirrus greenhouse" effect. When the Sun was cooler, there was less evaporation from the oceans, and so less thick cloud. In addition, the absence of oxygen and ozone from the early atmosphere produced a much cooler stratosphere, which allowed convection to penetrate higher, encouraging the formation of high, thin cloud. With the addition of just a little carbon dioxide to produce its own contribution to the greenhouse effect, the result is that the surface temperature of the model early Earth is kept comfortably above freezing (*Science*, vol. 217, p. 1245).

These results are by no means conclusive, since nobody knows just what amounts of each sort of cloud to plug in to the models. Rather, they show that all reconstructions of the early atmosphere based on climate studies contain very large uncertainties, and "conclusions about the early atmosphere based on such models must remain tentative".

"MONITOR", 23/30 December, 1982

PART TWO

The Changing Climate

Whether or not the homeostasis is maintained by Gaia, conditions on Earth have varied in the past few hundred million years over a range that may be modest by geological standards but is certainly sufficient to bring dramatic changes by any human standards. The most notable of these changes are the shifts in climate that sometimes bring ice ages over a large part of the Earth, but there are also lesser climatic shifts, more rapid but still slow compared with a human lifetime, that have influenced the rise and fall of civilisations on Earth. These long-term changes are not, perhaps, a problem to concern us greatly here and now. But as a background to the changes in the balance of the weather machine that are now being brought about by human activity, they provide an important reminder of just how extreme conditions can still be and yet remain within the bounds of what is, for Gaia, "normal".

The articles presented in this section begin with an appraisal of the role of climatic research in Britain, and are followed by contributions that treat the puzzle of climatic changes on time-scales from the very large – literally astronomical – down to those important over a few decades, centuries or millenia. Only the last of these are likely to affect us in our own lifetimes. But as we shall see, the background of long, slow climatic changes underlying the events we may live to see provides little in the way of comfort.

6

Climate and the Earth's albedo

WILLIAM BURROUGHS

The albedo – the proportion of sunlight our planet reflects back into space – has a crucial influence on the climate, but we are only beginning to understand its effect and how it varies

When the astronauts on Apollo 8 looked back at Earth on their way to the Moon, they saw a brilliant blue and white planet set against an inky backdrop – an image that was to captivate the public when the photographs were published. This image did, however, contain a more basic physical truth: it provided some measure of the complex processes that contribute to the Earth's albedo – the proportion of the incident Solar radiation reflected or scattered back into space.

Although the albedo is a fundamental parameter in controlling the Earth's climate, it was only with the advent of meteorological satellites that a value for it was obtained. And the way in which the albedo is made up of components that vary with time, from place to place across the globe, is still inadequately understood. Yet, without such understanding a proper analysis of the global energy balance and climatic change is not possible.

Measuring the Earth's albedo is difficult. To produce an accurate figure requires the measurement of the amount of sunlight reflected at the appropriate wavelengths over the entire planet – as continuous observations from satellites can now provide. But when it comes to a breakdown of the various contributions to the global albedo, the complexities of the physical processes involved require considerable simplification to give a sensible picture. Only recently have estimates been prepared that provide a reasonable insight into these complex questions.

The local value of the albedo depends on, among other things, the nature of the surface, the scattering properties of the atmosphere above the surface, and the incident angle of the Solar radiation. The reflectivity of the surface depends, for instance, on the type of soil and vegetation cover, while over the oceans the height of waves and the angle of the Sun play a crucial role. In addition, the extent of snow and ice cover (the cryosphere) at any given time makes a large contribution to the total albedo. But above all the part played by clouds dominates, as the values of albedo for various surfaces show (Figure 6.1).

The individual components that make up the Earth's albedo combine in an intricate set of feedback mechanisms to form an integrated whole. The measurements of the Earth's Radiation Budget Experiment obtained on the Nimbus 6 Satellite between July 1975 and December 1976, give a figure for the Earth's albedo of 0.31. The satellite also measured the overall radiation balance of the global atmospheric system. It found that the annual cycle of mean monthly long-wave radiation from the planet matches

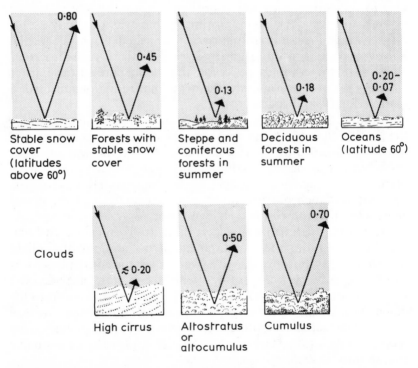

Figure 6.1 *Representative values of the albedo of various surfaces. Note each category covers a range of conditions which depend on latitude, type of soil, wetness and so on*

changes in Solar radiation; and monthly variations in outgoing long-wave radiation, due to changes in global cloudiness and snow and ice cover, are generally compensated by simultaneous variations in the planetary albedo.

When it comes to a breakdown of the global figure for the albedo there still remain considerable doubts. As a general rule, about half the planet is covered by clouds at any time and, because of their higher albedo, they make up about three-quarters of the global value. And there is some disagreement about the precise contribution made by the surface. Recent estimates for its average value have varied from 0.15 to 0.17, with the case for the lower figure apparently better justified. The differences arise from the precise treatment of the annual Solar radiation budget, and the correction for summer melt-water in areas covered by snow and ice.

While global observations provide some reliable measure of the current value of the albedo, there are other tantalising questions that we can ask. There is already considerable evidence of significant fluctuations in the extent of the cryosphere from year to year; what role do these changes play in climatic shifts on this timescale and over longer periods? Have human activities over the past 6000 years had an appreciable impact on the surface albedo?

Fluctuations in the cryosphere have long been postulated as an important influence in long-term climatic changes, by means of a simple feedback mechanism. Increased snow cover will lead to more sunlight being reflected back into space, leading to further global cooling which in turn leads to increased snow cover and so on. But without proper treatment of the changes in cloudiness that occur at the same time, such analysis is trivial. The role of the cryosphere's growth in precipitating the ice ages, for instance, must be subject to cautious analysis.

On a shorter timescale, satellite imagery now provides a reliable record of interannual variations in snow and ice cover. Over the past 14 years these have shown significant and sustained shifts. Although the early measurements are open to some qualification, the general trend was for an increase in continental snow cover over the period. These changes have been dominated by the snow cover over Eurasia, which is particularly variable. The most noticeable features were sharp increases in 1971 and 1976, and a marked reversal in 1979–1980 (Figure 6.2). These changes have some intriguing implications for long-range weather forecasting. For instance, the sharp increase in 1971 may have been a contributory

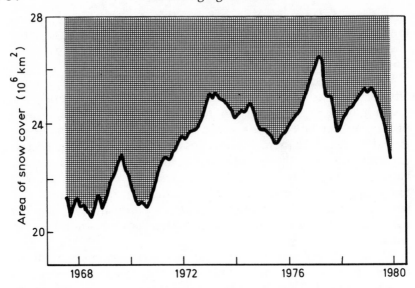

Figure 6.2 *Twelve-month running mean of monthly snow cover in the northern hemisphere*

factor to the extremes of weather in 1972, such as the drought in the Soviet Union, which led to a poor harvest. Similarly the sudden large and sustained increase in October 1976 may have had much to do with the subsequent patterns of blocking anticyclones, which produced the extraordinarily severe winter in the United States. These examples show that changes in snow cover, in particular over Eurasia, are an important guide in long-range weather fore-casting.

Man's role in affecting the planetary albedo may be direct – by altering the face of the land – and possibly indirect, in affecting the atmosphere, and hence cloudiness, by the release of pollutants. I will concentrate on surface effects as no comprehensive estimates have been made of the atmospheric consequences.

The most important aspect of surface changes is the long-term impact of agriculture and the associated clearance of forests. Over the past 6000 years Man has cleared a large proportion of the forests in the mid-latitudes of the northern hemisphere and has also overgrazed the northern sub-tropics of the Old World. From the time of Plato there have been frequent references to the way in which the forests have been removed from the landscape. These modifications to the Earth's surface have led to a change in its overall albedo and, in regions where winter snow is prevalent, to the way the albedo varies from season to season (see Table 6.1). Estimates suggest that about five per cent of the Earth's surface – 17 per cent of the continents – has been modified.

These anthropogenic changes could significantly affect the overall radiation budget, and modify regional climate. After making suitable allowances for cloud cover, their cumulative effect on the surface albedo is estimated to increase the global figure by roughly half a per cent, say from 0.305 to 0.31. Various climatic modelling exercises suggest that this could be sufficient to produce a global cooling of up to 1 K, which might be sufficient to explain much of the reduction in temperature that has taken place over the past 6000 years since the post-glacial climatic high. These effects, which have accelerated in the past century, may be as important as the much more widely publicised impact of carbon dioxide (*New Scientist*, vol. 90, p. 82).

Permanent changes

The possible impact on climatic patterns is equally intriguing. In particular, desertification, the most important anthropogenic effect, may have led to permanent shifts in regional climate. For instance, overgrazing is believed to have contributed to the problems of the Sahel and the steady expansion of the Sahara. In this

Table 6.1 *How Man changes the albedo*

Process	Land-type change	Change in albedo	Percentage of Earth's surface affected
Desertification	Savanna to desert	0.16–0.35	1.8
Temperate deforestation	Forest to field/grassland		1.6
	Summer	0.12–0.15	
	Winter	0.25–0.60	
Tropical deforestation	Forest to field/savanna	0.07–0.16	1.4
Urbanisation	Field/forest to city	0.17–0.15	0.2
Salinisation	Open field to salt flat	0.10–0.25 to 0.5	0.1

region, estimates indicate that the large increase in the albedo between savanna and desert (see Table 6.1) may have led to a significant climatic positive feedback mechanism. This is because the increased reflection of Solar radiation produces greater atmospheric stability, resulting in reduced rainfall (Figure 6.3), thus reinforcing desertification.

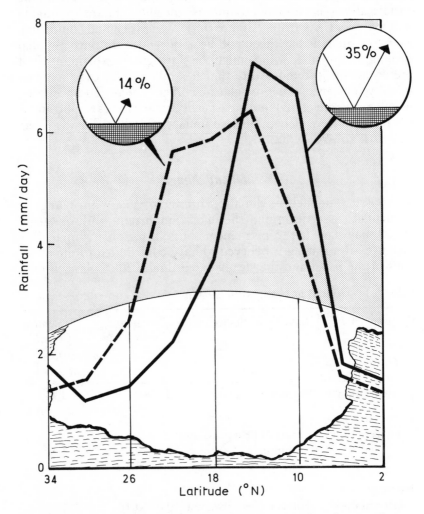

Figure 6.3 *Rainfall during July over North Africa, calculated from global general circulation models for different values of the albedo of the Sahara*

How do these perturbations fit into the context of the overall picture, which is dominated by clouds? The changes that have taken place on the surface, notably in snow and ice cover and in desertification may have led to compensating shifts in cloudiness. So we need to make adequate allowances for such changes.

Unfortunately, we are not in a position to make such allowances – we do not have any reliable measurements of the changes in global cloudiness. Furthermore, even the most sophisticated models of global climate contain only the simplest treatment of clouds. The models are far from being able to handle changes in not only the extent of cloud cover, but also in the type of clouds and the altitude at which they occur in different types of weather. This is doubly important. First, clouds have a major impact on the albedo. Because of their global distribution, an increase in cloud cover of one per cent will lead to an increase in the albedo of about half a per cent, and hence to a global cooling of about 1 K. Secondly, clouds also radically alter the radiative properties of the atmosphere at long wavelengths.

The correct treatment of clouds and the underlying shifts in surface albedo represents an immense challenge to computer modelling of the climate. Without a reliable and comprehensive treatment of these effects, one must exercise great care in calculating other perturbations of the climatic system (for example, the build-up of carbon dioxide in the atmosphere). In particular, more work needs to be done on a conclusion that has emerged from simple models – that changes in cloud cover may act as a vital stabilising element in preventing an erratic response to fluctuations in other contributions to the global climate. Until we understand this type of response more fully, we must exercise great caution in attributing past climatic variations to specific natural or anthropogenic changes in certain parameters.

On the regional scale and over shorter periods we need to understand how observed changes in the albedo may be of use in long-range weather forecasting. There is sufficient evidence to suggest that this may be a fruitful line of study. This will require improved modelling work together with a longer series of observations so that evidence of the consequences of anomalous autumnal snow cover, for instance, can be inferred from the atmospheric circulation patterns of the subsequent winter.

In the meantime, the way in which the various elements of the surface albedo act on their own and in concert with clouds remains one of the fascinating unsolved aspects of climatic change.

The views from space present a harmonious picture of the Earth in radiative balance. What we do not know is how this balance changes over time as a consequence of fluctuations in part or all of the planetary albedo.

16 July, 1981

7

The cause of ice ages

NIGEL CALDER

The picture of the ice ages, which periodically bury the sites of Boston, Birmingham and Berlin under great thicknesses of unmelted snow, has changed dramatically and ominously during the past few years. What American historian Thomas Kuhn calls a paradigm shift has occurred, where "paradigm" is a fancy word for picture or model. In the old picture which dated back to 1909 there were just four or five great eruptions of the northern ice in recent geological times, with long warm periods in between. Now we know that there were more like 20 major episodes of icing, and that the warm interglacials were very short-lived. Barring inadvertent or deliberate human action that might keep the world warmer, the natural trends are already taking the Earth out of the present interglacial and into the next ice age.

The greatest prize is a clear understanding of the cause of the comings and goings of the ice. From among dozens of ingenious theories, invoking such diverse mechanisms as sliding ice, volcanoes or cosmic dust-clouds, one emerged triumphant: the so-called Milankovitch hypothesis. The Earth changes its attitude and orbit with respect to the Sun, and as a result the sunshine falling on the northern hemisphere in summer waxes and wanes in a cyclical fashion, causing ice sheets to melt back or to grow.

The people principally responsible for the new picture of ice ages and their cause are the geologists and palaeontologists who devoted years of painstaking analysis to the climatic record preserved in the ocean bed.

Three of the most prominent among them give details in the current issue of *Science* (vol. 194, p. 1121) of a definitive test of the Milankovitch theory. Its publication provides an opportunity to outline the story of how scientists succeeded in charting past climates and interpreting the drastic changes correctly, in the face of misleading received ideas and severe technical difficulties.

One of the proponents of the "astronomical" theory of ice ages was Alfred Wegener of Germany, whose posthumous hand thus appears in a second great triumph after the confirmation of his continental drift. But Wegener perished on the Greenland ice sheet in 1930 and Milutin Milankovitch of Yugoslavia was left as the principal and persistent advocate of the hypothesis to which his name became firmly attached. All along, it had the supreme attraction of an undeniable cause in search of an effect.

Ice ages are primarily a phenomenon of the northern hemisphere, where huge continental platforms stand ready in sub-polar and middle latitudes to carry the great ice sheets; the southern hemisphere has lacked them ever since the break-up of Gondwanaland, so sea-ice rather than land-ice is its ice-age style. Astronomers told how the eccentricity of the Earth's orbit changed in calculable ways, how the planet slowly rolled, altering the tilt or obliquity of the axis relative to the sunlight, and how the "wobble" or precession of the Earth's axis (the time-honoured precession of the equinoxes) made the time of closest approach to the Sun fall at different seasons.

At one extreme, these cyclical changes would put a well tilted Earth as close as possible to the Sun during the northern summer. In other periods the intensity of sunshine falling on the northern lands would be markedly less, where the Earth was more nearly upright and the summer came when the Earth was at its farthest from the Sun.

With hindsight you can say that the Milankovitch theory was always very much better than the "facts" it was meant to explain. Early enthusiasts who thought the theory deserved to be right were forced into all kinds of games with the component cycles, with seasons, and with terrestrial latitudes, in their efforts to fit the theory into the Procrustean bed of false data. In the end, tortured arguments were quite unnecessary: the Milankovitch theory worked in its pristine form. The record of past climates gradually improved until at last it corresponded with the astronomical cycles.

Ocean records of past climates

Cesare Emiliani set the slow revolution in train in 1955. He was a young marine palaeontologist working in Harold Urey's isotope laboratory at Chicago. Two postwar techniques were available to him: improved methods of weighing molecules and the oceanographers' piston corers that were beginning to recover cores, or columns of mud, from the floor of the deep ocean. (The continuing saga of ships and men cruising the world to sample the ocean beds deserves more telling than I can offer here.) Using a core from the Caribbean, Emiliani picked out fossils of small marine animals (foraminifera) from successive layers of mud and measured the proportion of heavy oxygen (oxygen-18) in them. He found the heavy oxygen changing in a striking cyclical pattern that seemed to reflect profound changes in the global environment. He interpreted a high proportion of heavy oxygen as a sign of cool conditions, and vice versa.

The outcome was a much spikier record of changing climate than the four-ice-age theory would allow. Even in the truncated record of that first core, there were seven periods of deep cold, and the peak warm periods were very much shorter than the 100 000 to 250 000 years of the standard theory. More than a decade passed before the experts accepted that the marine-fossil isotope record was to be taken at face value.

In Czechoslovakia in the early 1960s, George Kukla and his colleagues found evidence for at least ten ice ages, in bands of light-coloured dusty soil (loess). They were deposited when that region was a Gobi-like desert, hemmed between the Scandinavian and Alpine ice. At first, Kukla's finding made little impression. From Britain came fresh evidence that the interglacials were indeed short. But the dating of the ice-age cycles was still presenting problems.

The break came in the late 1960s. It was a by-product of the general revolution then going on in the Earth sciences, in which the discovery of the reversals in the Earth's magnetism played an essential part. The last decisive swap-around of the north and south magnetic poles occurred 700 000 years ago. Neil Opdyke and his colleagues at the Lamont–Doherty Geological Observatory detected the reversal in the ocean-bed cores, eight ice ages down; and, at about the same time, the Czechs found the same geomagnetic event in their soil columns, also eight ice ages down. The match between land and sea was assured at last, and the first secure overall timescale was available for the ocean-bed cores. Difficulties remained because rates of sedimentation were never quite uniform and ages were not reliably proportional to the depths in the core. Judicious use of radioactive dating and other techniques gradually clarified the details of the timescale – notably in the precise dates for high sea level around 100 000 years ago, as exploited by Robley, Matthews and Wallace Broecker and their colleagues.

The stage was set for a definitive account of the ice ages and their cause. Techniques were improving all the time. Nicholas Shackleton of Cambridge had come on the scene with shrewder and better-instrumented methods for using oxygen isotopes as ice-age relics. He joined with Neil Opdyke in producing a detailed record of climatic changes over 870 000 years. Other centres, particularly Lamont and Brown University, were perfecting eco-logical methods of core interpretation that were to form the basis of the CLIMAP project for reconstructing global climates in the past – another stirring tale into which I must not digress. The astronomical calculations for the Milankovitch effect were being checked and refined, notably by Anandu Vernekar of Maryland. By the early 1970s, the Milankovitch bandwagon was beginning to roll in earnest.

The strong test of the Milankovitch effect is to show that the climatic features in the geological record go through precisely the same rhythms as do the antics of the Earth in orbit, with suffi-ciently close links in time (that is, in phase) to confirm a relation-ship of cause and effect. There should be no special pleading and no intervening theorising about the meteorological processes involved. The various astronomical cycles should be clear in the climatic record.

Thus, if the changing tilt of the Earth's axis (obliquity) affects the climate, then the climatic record ought to show the corres-ponding cycle of about 40 000 years coming through regardless of other fluctuations. Similarly the wobble (precession of the equi-noxes) should be apparent with a period of about 20 000 years, and the changes in the orbit (eccentricity) with a period of 90 000 to 100 000 years. These "signals" showed up very clearly as soon as the time scale was put right.

John Imbrie of Brown joined with Shackleton in making a frequency analysis of the 870 000-year Shackleton–Opdyke core. The 100 000-year cycle was dominant; the other cycles were visible too although less prominently.

By 1974, the endorsement of Milankovitch by Imbrie and other American ice-age researchers was already strong enough for Alec Nisbett and me, in our work on *The Weather Machine* for BBC TV. After studying the data critically, we adopted the theory as *the* explanation of the ice ages. John Gribbin criticised us at the time for doing so; the Meteorological Office, to whose director-general Gribbin now ascribes the Milankovitch revival (see Chapter 8), was also condemning the programme's treatment of ice ages and saying that the causes of ice ages were unknown.

James Hays of Lamont–Doherty Geological Observatory had sought Imbrie's and Shackleton's help in a more thorough investigation of the shorter-period fluctuations, connected with the roll and wobble. In August 1975, this Hays–Imbrie–Shackleton partnership outlined the results at a climate conference of the World Meteorological Organisation in Norwich. They made it clear that Milankovitch was right. According to Gribbin such studies "can only confirm that the cycles are present – they cannot reveal whether the changes in energy input are related to the changes in ice cover". But that is exactly what they do reveal. The energy input is known from the astronomical calculations, and the wonder of the modern heavy-oxygen technique is that it tells you the volume of the Earth's ice cover. The relationship between the two emerged strongly – as reported at Norwich and now published in full by Hays, Imbrie and Shackleton in *Science*.

How do you find out how much ice there was in the world, from a handful of small shells collected from the ocean bed, far from the ice sheets themselves? The ice sheets are made from snow, which comes from evaporated water. Molecules of water that incorporate heavy oxygen atoms evaporate more sluggishly than ordinary molecules do. So a growing ice sheet removes a disproportionate amount of ordinary oxygen from ocean water and leaves it enriched in heavy-oxygen atoms. Fossil animals preserve a record of the oxygen-isotope ratio in the water and hence of the amount of ice in the world at the time they were alive. One chooses animals that were not unduly exposed to vagaries of climate at the sea surface – either bottom-dwelling animals or, as in this recent study, an animal that lived fairly deep in the water (the foraminifera *Globigerina bulloides*).

A dramatic match with Milankovitch

Lamont has a library of thousands of ocean-bed cores from which Hays, Imbrie and Shackleton chose carefully. They settled on a pair of cores from the southern Indian Ocean east of the island of Kerguelen. One core gave a good record for the past 300 000 years, while for the other the upper part of the record was spoilt, but there was an excellent sequence from 100 000 to about

450 000 years ago. The two cores could be patched together to span almost half a million years. They both had a fairly high accumulation rate and were recovered far from any continent. These cores from the southern hemisphere carried information about climatic changes at both ends of the Earth. While the oxygen-isotope measurements would tell of the growth and recession of the ice sheets far away in Canada and Europe, the investigators could also follow the local sea-surface temperature.

To tell how the sea-surface temperatures east of Kerguelen had changed over many thousands of years, Hays and Imbrie used a technique developed by themselves and their colleagues, notably Nilva Kipp of Brown University. It can be likened to assessing the climate of a land area by counting the number of reindeer and camels. Applied to the statistics of small marine animals – for instance, the various species of radiolaria – it becomes a very sensitive climatic thermometer, able to detect changes of a third of a degree in the mean summer sea-surface temperature. One particular radiolarian (*Cycladophora davisiana*) gave another climatic indicator. This animal apparently prospers where water of low salinity overlies very cold water. It almost disappears in the warmest periods of the interglacials, but becomes prominent in the depths of an ice age.

The three climatic indicators were assessed at intervals of 10 cm throughout the 15 m or so of the "patched" cores. After all the analysis and preparation a computer was set to look for the appropriate frequencies of roll and wobble, in the geological time-series. The Milankovitch "signals" duly appeared. To check that they were no illusion, the investigators carried out various statistical tests, making sure, for instance, that they were not seeing harmonics of other signals. Then they were able to declare unambiguously that "changes in the Earth's orbital geometry are the fundamental cause of the succession of Quaternary ice ages".

We now take the relevant components of the Earth's motion one by one.

Roll. The obliquity signal with a period of about 42 000 years was gratifyingly consistent and sensible for the past 300 000 years. The conspicuous climatic ups and downs lagged about 8000 years behind the rhythm of the changing tilt of the Earth. In the older part of the record, the consistency was less good because the presumed timescale was less secure. In a further operation they called "tune-up", Hays, Imbrie and Shackleton adjusted the timescale slightly (well within the uncertainties of the dating) and obtained the same phase relationships going back to 425 000 years – a period spanning four major glaciations and 10 cycles of the roll.

Wobble. A 23 000-year cycle corresponding with the precession of the equinoxes also appeared strongly in the geological record. As you might expect for the higher frequency, the uncertainties about dating produced relatively greater uncertainties in the phase relationships, but over the past 300 000 years the climatic factors plainly changed closely in step with the wobble, with considerably less time-lag than in the case of roll. For older events, another factor intruded: the Earth's orbit remained nearly circular during the period 350 000 to 450 000 years ago, so you would expect the effect of the wobble of the Earth's axis to be less marked and the signal correspondingly weaker. Nevertheless the "tune-up" adjustments to the older timescale improved the phase relationships at this frequency too. The most delicate and impressive of all tests for the Milankovitch theory comes with closer examination of the astronomy and the fact that the precession of the equinoxes resolves itself into two frequency components with periods of 23 000 and 19 000 years, the latter being weaker. In the Hays–Imbrie–Shackleton analysis both signals emerged clearly, in the oxygen-isotope records and in the changing sea-surface temperatures.

Eccentricity. The slower changes in the eccentricity of the Earth's orbit modulate the effects of the other Milankovitch processes. For instance when the Earth's orbit is very nearly circular, scant relief comes when the northern summer coincides with the point of closest approach to the Sun. Hays, Imbrie and Shackleton found the modulation occurring more strongly than you might expect from the simplest point of view. In fact eccentricity came out as a major factor in its own right, with the coldest periods of the ice ages coinciding dramatically with the periods of near-circularity in the Earth's orbit.

To move on from the research to its implications: thoughts about ice ages are completely inverted. Ask not why the ice forms, but why it briefly recedes sometimes. The normal or average condition of the Earth at present is with a great burden of ice sitting on the northern lands – extending far beyond the present confines of the glaciers and the Greenland ice sheet, and making many of our favourite places uninhabitable. But the plate movements that set Antarctica in chilly isolation at the South Pole and crowded the northern continents around the Arctic Ocean tuned the Earth's geography to respond with almost ridiculous sensitivity to relatively small changes in the northern summer sunshine. Hays, Imbrie and Shackleton concur with an interpretation that I used simple-mindedly a couple of years ago, namely that it is easier to melt ice than to make it. An occasional surge of summer heat destroys much ice. When the orbit is nearly circular, this relief is less marked and the climate tends to grind on downwards into ever-deeper glaciation.

We live at a time of low eccentricity, and the relief at the end of the last ice age required a conspiracy of all three Milankovitch factors. A meagre improvement in eccentricity coincided with a phase of the wobble that made June the month of closest approach to the Sun; also with the phase of maximum roll, putting the summer Sun a little higher in the sky. This favourable conjunction dragged the Earth from an ice maximum 18 000 years ago to an ice minimum 6000 years ago. But all the factors have since reversed: the tilt and eccentricity are both diminishing again and the precession of the equinoxes has brought the month of closest approach to January. Fluctuations in the southern hemisphere sea-surface temperature in summer run a few thousand years ahead of the changes in the northern ice. The Hays–Imbrie–Shackleton curves show a rise from 8 °C in the depths of the last ice age, to 14 °C about 9000 years ago. Since then it has already fallen again to 10 °C.

The time has come to stop arguing about the history and the cause of the ice ages, and to start discussing how our species is going to hold back the next one. We have about 60 000 years of adverse "orbital geometry" ahead of us.

9 December, 1976

8

Milankovitch comes in from the cold

JOHN GRIBBIN

A new, and classically simple, reassessment of a celebrated model of climatic change forcefully reinstates its validity

The idea that ice ages – and perhaps smaller fluctuations in climate – could be caused by changes in the amount or distribution of Solar radiation reaching the Earth has many obvious attractions. Until last year, however, models based on this premise had signally failed to convince most climatologists. Now all that has changed. The first blow to established views came with the suggestion from a group at the US National Center for Atmospheric Research (NCAR) that the Solar "constant" may in fact be a variable – the Solar "parameter" (see *New Scientist*, vol. 69, p. 22). Although this proposal can explain many features of recent climatic change in a persuasive manner, it is still regarded as almost heretical by established authorities in both astronomy and climatology.

However, when such heretical ideas are being aired in scientifically conservative circles it is clear that fairly desperate solutions are needed to explain the known variations of climate; also, of course, by their very outrageousness such ideas make less outrageous theories look more respectable. This, perhaps, is one of the reasons for which the "Milankovitch model" of climatic change, which links major climatic changes to changes in the orientation of the Earth and the ellipticity of its orbit, has received renewed attention, culminating in the publication of a paper supporting the theory by no less an authority than the Director-General of the UK Meteorological Office, Professor B. J. Mason (*Quarterly Journal of the Royal Meteorological Society*, vol. 102, p. 473).

Long-term changes in Earth's motion

Mason's investigation of the Milankovitch model stems from the award to him of the 1975 Symons Memorial Gold Medal for "his outstanding contributions to the development of the science of meteorology." The work now published in detail was the subject of his Symons Memorial Lecture, delivered in March of this year. But the model itself is of some antiquity, even though unproven until recently. The Yugoslav Milutin Milankovitch published his classic papers in the 1930s, but the basic concept pre-dates even those papers by several decades. Indeed, the model is almost unique in having survived for so long without either being disproved or gaining acceptance.

Standard works (such as Arthur Holmes's *Principles of Physical Geology*, Nelson, 1965) have long acknowledged the existence of the model and spelled out the basics of the proposed mechanism. Three separate cyclic changes in the Earth's movements combine to produce the overall variations in the Solar radiation falling on the Earth, which are the key to the theory. The longest is a cycle of between 90 000 and 100 000 years over which the orbit of the Earth around the Sun "stretches" from more circular to more elliptical and back; next there is a cycle of some 40 000 years over which the tilt of the Earth's spin axis relative to the plane of its orbit (the obliquity of the ecliptic) changes, with the Earth nodding up and down relative to the Sun; and, finally, the pull of Sun and Moon on the Earth's equatorial bulge causes our planet to wobble like a spinning top, producing the precession of the equinoxes with a period of 21 000 years. These effects combine to produce changes in the amount of heat arriving at different latitudes in different seasons – but they do *not* affect the integrated flux of heat received by the whole planet in the course of a year.

One of the fascinations of the resulting model of ice ages is that it is intimately related to the Earth's present geography. In qualitative terms, it is easy to see that cool summers in the north might allow snow to lie permanently over wide areas, allowing the build-up of ice sheets; while warm summers would hinder snow accumulation and melt the ice. But just which are the critical seasons? And are the relative changes in insolation sufficient to explain the observed changes in snow and ice cover over the past few hundred thousand years? These are the questions that even the most ardent supporters of the Milankovitch theory were previously unable to answer. It is ironic that Professor Mason, far from being such an ardent supporter, said in his Symons Lecture that he tackled the problem more with the expectation of proving the theory wrong than in the hope of proving it right!

Most recent assaults on the problem have leaned towards the sophisticated modelling of how changes in the Solar input affect the balance of the Earth's climate. It is hardly surprising that no great progress has been made in view of the complexity of the feedback mechanisms involved. For instance, George Kukla, of the Lamont–Doherty Geological Observatory in New York State, pinpointed autumn as the season in which changes in the irradiation of North America and Eurasia produce the greatest changes in the Earth's surface temperature (*Nature*, vol. 253, p. 680). And Johannes Weertman, of Northwestern University in Illinois, has calculated the effect of the Milankovitch Solar radiation variations on the flow of ice sheets. Again, the balance of evidence favours the view that these variations are sufficient to trigger ice ages (*Nature*, vol. 261, p.17).

Through work of this kind, there has seemed to be some slow but steady progress towards the establishment of the Milankovitch model – but no one piece of work has produced clear, compelling evidence that the model *must* be right.

The reason for which Mason's contribution to this widespread debate is likely to be remembered as the turning point – the moment when the Milankovitch model "came in from the cold" – is that he has produced an argument of elegant simplicity that cuts to the heart of the problem and comes up with the right answers. In the best traditions of "back of the envelope" calculations, the basis of Mason's argument needs no understanding of sophisticated mathematics, and no aid from electronic computers.

The magnitude of the Milankovitch variations in insolation at a chosen range of latitudes, and the timing of the variations, can be determined very accurately and compared with the geological record (and other evidence) of climatic changes. Indeed, in many ways the calculation of the astronomical influences over past millennia has long been more precise than the available geological evidence. Until the past decade there was no way of establishing a good correlation between the two curves since the accepted geological record was, as we now know, not just incomplete but actually wrongly interpreted in many cases. This is one area where elaborate mathematical techniques and computers can help. A power spectrum of a series of temperature measurements that cover the past 600 000 years suggests the presence of cycles at

100 000, 40 000 and 20 000 years. These, of course, would be just the Milankovitch cycles. But this evidence (and similar studies made at Lamont–Doherty and in Cambridge) can only confirm that the cycles are present – they cannot reveal whether the changes in energy input are related to the changes in ice cover.

Latent heat calculations

Mason has now put together various pieces of evidence relating to changes in global ice cover, northern-hemisphere air temperature, and total insolation north of 45 °N (an arbitrary cut-off latitude) over the past 150 000 years. Mason's results show the close correlation between the major advances and recessions of the ice and the 40 000-year cycle of variations in insolation; but the question remains of whether the energy change involved is sufficient to explain this relationship.

It is, of course, simple to calculate how much heat is needed to melt a given volume of ice, and how much heat is given up when a certain volume of water freezes. And that is what Mason has done. According to him, using Milankovitch's original data, between 83 000 and 18 000 years ago, when the ice began to retreat, the overall deficiency in insolation was 4.5×10^{25} calories, 1 000 calories for each gram of ice formed. A. D. Vernekar's figures (*Meteorological Monographs*, vol. 12, no. 34, 1972) give a total deficiency of 2.5×10^{25} calories. But, either way, this estimate lies very close to the 677 cal g associated with cooling a gram of water vapour until it freezes. From 18 000 years ago to the present, the corresponding excess of insolation at high latitudes given by this simple calculation was between 4.2×10^{24} and 1.0×10^{24} calories. The amount of heat needed to melt the volume of ice that we know was melting over this time comes out to be 3.2×10^{24} calories! Even given the simplicity of the argument any "coincidence" that stretches across 24 orders of magnitude to provide such precise agreement cannot be dismissed lightly.

Of course, there is more to Mason's revival of the Milankovitch model than this. Models of how the feedback between ice, ocean and atmosphere operates, and investigations of the effect of the changing reflectance of the Earth, are being studied at the Meteorological Office, as elsewhere. Andrew Gilchrist, in particular, has already achieved some success by incorporating the Milankovitch effect into a general circulation model of the atmosphere. But the almost embarrassing simplicity of the key calculation in Mason's investigation goes much further than establishing the respectability of this model of the changing climate. Scarcely "O"-level mathematics was needed to find the right answer, once the right question had been asked. It is in seeing so clearly the right question to ask that Mason has provided such a remarkable insight to this particular problem. It should prove a valuable lesson to the growing band of scientists who delight in the number-crunching use of electronic computers without always choosing the best numbers to crunch.

30 September, 1976 © John Gribbin, 1976; all rights reserved

9

Fire and ice

PETER FRANCIS

Great volcanic eruptions that eject much dust are known to upset the weather pattern temporarily. But recently evidence has come to light of extensive volcanism on a global scale during the Pleistocene period. Can it be causally linked to the Ice Age itself?

The intriguing notion that the great glaciers and ice-caps which held much of the world in their frigid grip during the Ice Age could have been the result of volcanic heat and fire is not a new one. Probably the first person to link volcanic eruptions and climatic variations was the great American polymath, Benjamin Franklin. While serving in Paris in 1783 as the first diplomatic representative of the newly formed United States of America he wrote:

> During several of the summer months of the year 1783, when the effects of the Sun's rays to heat the Earth should have been the greatest, there existed a constant fog over all Europe and great part of North America. This fog was of a permanent nature; it was dry and the rays of the Sun seemed to have little effect towards dissipating it, as they easily do a moist fog. . . . Of course, their summer effect in heating the Earth was exceedingly diminished. Hence, the surface was early frozen. Hence, the first snows on it remained unmelted. . .
>
> Hence, perhaps, the winter of 1783–84 was more severe than any that happened for many years.

It can scarcely be a coincidence that 1783 also saw the largest volcanic eruption of historic times, that of Laki in Iceland. During the five months or so that this eruption lasted, about seven cubic kilometres of basalt lavas were extruded. Franklin had only rather vague information about the eruption, but he did ascribe the fog that hung over so much of Europe to "the vast quantity of smoke, long continuing to issue during the summer from Hekla in Iceland. . .".

Since the days of Franklin, the subject has captured the imagination of several distinguished scientists, notably W. J. Humphrey and H. S. Wexler in the United States, and Professor H. H. Lamb, now at the University of East Anglia, who has made a meticulous compilation (*Philosophical Transactions of the Royal Society* A, vol. 266, p. 425) of all recorded volcanic eruptions from 1500 to the present day, and attempted to assess their importance in producing a "dust veil". From Lamb's work, and that of his predecessors, it is quite clear that individual major eruptions can cause significant, but temporary, effects on the atmosphere.

Everyone has heard of the great eruption of the Indonesian volcano Krakatoa in 1883, the explosions from which reverberated around the entire Indian Ocean, and were heard as far away as Rodriguez Island, nearly 5000 km distant. It is less widely known that this stupendous eruption hurled several cubic kilometres of ash and dust into the stratosphere. Much of this material rained down again in the immediate area of the volcano, but the finer dust formed a cloud which drifted westwards during the following weeks. The eruption occurred on 26 August; by 10 September the dust cloud had drifted *right around the world*, and was once more approaching Indonesia. It did not stop there, though, and in effect made several more trips around the world, becoming more diffuse and widespread all the while. Initially, the dust cloud was confined to the equatorial regions, but eventually it spread out to cover most of the globe.

Its effects were obvious. All around the world there was for a period of many months a succession of magnificent sunsets, sunsets so glorious that the phenomenon was even alluded to in a poem by Tennyson:

Had the fierce ashes of some fiery peak
Been hurl'd so high they ranged aboutthe globe?
For day by day, thro' many a blood red eve,
In that four-hundredth summer after Christ,
The wrathful sunset glared against a cross. . .

(*St Telemachus*)

More prosaically, but much more importantly, the haze of volcanic dust in the atmosphere caused a world-wide drop in the level of Solar radiation reaching the Earth. Similar effects have been recorded after several other major eruptions since Krakatoa, most recently after the eruption of Agung volcano, Bali, in 1963. Prior to Krakatoa, of course, there was no means of recording Solar radiation levels, but some attempts have been made to demonstrate links between eruptions and climatic variations by "secondary" methods, principally studying historical records to identify years characterised by short summers, food shortages and poor wine harvests, which followed major eruptions. A conspicuous example is that of 1816, sometimes called the "year without a summer", subsequent to the eruption of Tambora in Indonesia in 1815. During that miserable year there were only three or four days without rain in Merionethshire between May and October and severe food shortages affected large areas. Little is known about the eruption, but some reports have suggested that it was bigger even than Krakatoa, and that there were remarkable sunsets and luminous twilights in London for six months afterwards.

It's not difficult to see how major eruptions could influence weather. Largish dust particles will effectively block out Solar radiation, while smaller ones will scatter it. A dust veil, too, may

Figure 9.1 *Surtsey erupts near Iceland on 22 November 1963. The heavy curtain of ash falling from the volcanic column gives some idea of the immense amounts of debris that a volcano can carry into the atmosphere (Credit: Professor S. Thorarinsson)*

cause a "reverse greenhouse effect", favouring the transmission of *outgoing* radiation, rather than incoming. It's a long step, though, from demonstrating that eruptions can temporarily influence weather patterns, to showing that they have played a part in the onset of the Ice Age, or even of glacial advances.

Fantasy hardens into fact

Sadly, discussing the notoriously unpredictable vagaries of the weather always brings out the country yokel in us. Many a respectable scientist, who would not be seen dead in rustic smock and wellington boots, is all too ready, when the subject of the weather comes up, to lean (metaphorically) nonchalantly against his lab bench, start scratching his head with a biro taken from the top pocket of his white coat, and assert: "Argh, now you mark my words, 'tis all that dust in the air that do cause many a bad 'arvest. Whoiy, Oi remember . . .". And so on.

A great deal of nonsense has been written by such scientist-yokels trying to demonstrate links between episodes of volcanism and glacial advances, from the evidence available, and all have made the same mistake. Weather records have been kept in detail only for some 150 years, and in rough form for a few hundred years before that. Our knowledge of pre-historic climatic variations comes almost exclusively from fossils (notably pollens) dated by radio-carbon methods, which inevitably often have large error ranges. Furthermore, our record of volcanic eruptions over the period covering the Ice Age to the present day is so scanty as to be almost negligible. Therefore, in trying to make correlations between the two phenomena, one is comparing one set of rather poorly known data with another set of extremely poorly known data.

This limitation has not prevented some yokels (most of them definitely *not* volcanologists) from looking at such records of volcanic activity as do exist, and from them postulating worldwide "waves" of volcanic activity that are supposed to have affected areas as far apart as Japan, New Zealand and South America. These "waves" are alleged to be associated with episodes when glaciers began advancing in response to a deterioration in climate. Those who argue most strongly for such correlations, however, do their cause a great disservice, because they make the mistake of interpreting data too literally. To take a case in point, just because there are *n* radio-carbon-dated volcanic episodes in South America does *not* mean that there were *n* "waves" of volcanic activity in South America, a continent in which there are probably less than a dozen radio-carbon dates on *any* volcanic events. Future work might reveal 2*n* episodes, or even n^2. Inadequacies in the existing data apart, preservation of volcanic events in the geological record is a chancy process to start with, so it's unwise to start looking for "waves" of volcanic activity in any area that has not been meticulously worked over, and it's even more unwise to start identifying the same "waves" in countries on the other side of the globe.

It's a pity that much recent work has been of this rather rustic, simplistic type, since the problems of climatic modification are becoming more and more important to society, with many an ominous rumour of the approach of a new ice age. Those who have argued that the last ice age was at least in part caused by volcanic activity have always come to grief on their inability to demonstrate that it was preceded by a major volcanic episode, and this in turn resulted from the difficulty mentioned earlier; the non-preservation of large parts of the geological record.

This situation has changed dramatically recently, with the publication of an important paper by J. P. Kennett and R. C. Thunell of Rhode Island University, Kingston (*Science*, vol. 187, p. 497). Kennett and Thunell were not faced with the problem of trying to correlate patchy, incomplete parts of the record of volcanic eruptions that is preserved on dry land. Instead, they examined the drill cores obtained by the Deep Sea Drilling Project (DSDP) from sites on the ocean floors all over the world. The deep ocean basins may not seem at first sight to be the best places to look for records of volcanic activity, but in fact they are almost ideal.

Dust particles drifting downwind from a major explosive volcanic eruption will shower down a steady rain of ash particles, which will eventually settle through the water, and accumulate on the ocean floor. Once there, there is little erosion to disturb them, and ashes from successive eruptions will be preserved in the simplest possible layer-cake stratigraphy, sandwiched between layers of non-volcanic sediments, mainly muds and oozes. The only snags in this near-ideal situation are occasional hiatuses or breaks in the sedimentation (which would make it difficult to distinguish between different volcanic events), disturbances of the sediments by busy-body burrowing organisms, and, more important, the possibility that chemical alterations may take place, blurring the identity of the ash layers. The most important of these is the conversion of the glassy ash particles to cherts over the passage of time.

Kennett and Thunell examined sediment cores from 320 DSDP holes all round the world, and identified volcanic ash horizons in 84 of them. When they plotted up the *number* of ash layers against the age of the sediments, they found that there was a very obvious increase during the Quaternary period – roughly the last two million years. When broken down into smaller areas, the data reveal that the same surge in activity can be identified in every area sampled.

This, then, appears to be strong evidence for a genuine world-wide "wave" of volcanic activity, far more convincing than earlier suggestions. And, of course, it is just the right age, since the widespread continental glaciations of the Ice Age in the northern hemisphere are thought to have commenced about 2.4 My ago.

Although it is tempting to jump to the conclusion that the cause of the Ice Age can now be confidently identified in a world-wide wave of volcanic activity, the case is still very far from proven, for a number of reasons. First, there could be some kind of mechanism that we don't yet know about that favours the preservation of young ashes on the sea floor. Second, Kennett and Thunell counted only the *number* of ash layers; this gives no guide to the *magnitudes* of the eruptions, and thus to the amount of dust that might have been present in the atmosphere. It seems likely that one really big eruption has a much more profound effect than many smaller ones, since smaller ones are unable to throw ash high enough into the air for it to have much effect. Third, Kennett and Thunell counted a total of 270 ash horizons deposited during the Quaternary. If each horizon is the result of a single eruption, this represents a rate of only one eruption every 7000 years. This is not a very high figure, particularly since some geologists think that eruptions of the size of Krakatoa may occur as often as once a century. On top of all these reservations, of course, there are many other completely different ideas about what causes ice ages, most of them concerned with rather esoteric geophysical variations.

Problems with land volcanoes

Before discarding the possibility, it is worthwhile turning back to the evidence of volcanoes on dry land to see if there is anything to substantiate the apparent outburst of volcanic activity during the

Quaternary. Here, though, we come right up against the old problem, the incomplete geological record. It is, in fact, remarkably difficult to demonstrate that the global rate of volcanic activity has varied from one million-year period to another. It's quite easy to do this for small areas; quite the reverse for the whole globe.

The problem becomes rather easier if one considers only eruptions that produce large quantities of ash. The kind that come to mind immediately are those typified by the AD 79 eruption of Vesuvius, and Krakatoa, both of which erupted several cubic kilometres of ash. The 1912 eruption of Katmai in Alaska closely resembled these, but it also gave rise to the kind of pyroclastic flow known as an ignimbrite (a fluidised flow of hot, solid pumice fragments). Most ignimbrites are more easily preserved in the geological record than air-fall ashes, which are loose and friable, and therefore easily eroded away. So, if one looks around the world for areas or periods of time in which ignimbrites were produced in large volumes, one might be getting towards identifying periods when large quantities of dust were being ejected into the atmosphere.

This, unfortunately, is where we enter the realms of speculation since there isn't nearly enough data to demonstrate a major increase in ignimbrite eruptions during the last two million years. What is becoming apparent, though, is that there has been a vast amount of ignimbrite erupted over the last 20 My. In the Central Andes alone, ignimbrites younger than 20 My cover at least 150 000 km^2, and at least one of these has a volume of 100 km^3. Huge volumes of ignimbrite were also erupted over a broadly comparable period in Central America, Mexico, and the southwestern USA, while other ignimbrites have been erupted more recently in Sumatra, Japan, Kamchatka and New Zealand.

Eruptions that individually yielded tens of cubic kilometres of ignimbrite almost certainly had a more profound effect on world weather than a humble Krakatoa, but this still leaves us a long way from demonstrating that volcanic eruptions of *any* kind caused or contributed to the Ice Age. It's possible, though, that if there was an unusually large number of very dusty ignimbrite eruptions during the last 20 My, their cumulative effect could have been such as to cause a climatic deterioration in which some other, external, agency was able to tip the balance, and "break the ice", so to speak.

Future work may conceivably demonstrate a cast-iron link

between volcanism and glaciation. If this could be proved, it might make the causal relationship between the two even more fascinating, because it has already been suggested that an ice age, conversely, could cause volcanic activity. This isn't as daft as it sounds. During an ice age, huge volumes of water are removed from the oceans and locked up in the form of ice in the polar regions. This lowers the level of the oceans perceptibly, perhaps by as much as a hundred metres, and may upset the isostatic equilibrium of the ocean basins by "unloading" them. That, in turn, may trigger off movements deep in the Earth's interior, sufficient to cause widespread volcanic activity. This is not a tongue-in-cheek argument, since there are many who believe that a lot of earthquakes, and some volcanic eruptions, of the present day are caused by tidal stresses of a magnitude similar to those that might be caused by unloading the ocean basins.

Whatever new facts emerge in the future, and whether ice ages can be shown to cause volcanic activity or vice versa, we can still be perfectly certain that scientists all over the world will be ready to lean against their lab benches, scratch their heads thoughtfully, and ruminate about the weather.

3 July, 1975

PART THREE

Cause for Concern

Changes of climate which scarcely leave a trace in the geological record are sufficient to disturb the balance of our agriculture and economy. When *New Scientist* was born in 1957, climatologists were concerned about a slight warming of the globe that had set in during the nineteenth century and persisted up to the 1950s; but almost immediately they realised that this trend had reversed, and that the world was cooling once again. But the debate about the reasons for these changes, and their likely significance for Mankind, remained one for the specialists until the 1970s. Then, the first wave of concern about drought in the Sahel region of Africa brought home to a wider audience, for the first time, the truth that far from having "conquered" climate with our technology, the rapid expansion of human population and an increasing dependence on fertilisers and mechanisation to produce maximum yields when conditions were just right had left large numbers of people at greater risk from small shifts in the weather patterns than ever before. Predictions that the world might "run out" of food by 1976 did not come true, but they helped to focus attention on a real problem, one which, as recent tragic events across the affected region of Africa have shown, is still very much with us. To millions of people, in spite of the bulging granaries of Europe and North America, it seems we *have* run out of food.

While scientists struggled to interpret the pattern of changing climate, their work began to become part of political debate. Some of the best indicators of climatic changes in the recent past (the past 1000 years or so) turned out to be tree rings and ice cores drilled from the polar glaciers. The records showed that the changes we are living through are nothing unusual, and may even recur with a semi-regular pattern over the centuries. What is different now is that the population explosion and the way we have chosen to exploit the world's resources, especially in agriculture, have set us too rigidly in a pattern where one kind of weather brings surpluses to the world's granaries, but any slight shift away from the optimum brings disasters in its wake.

10

The changing climate

H. H. LAMB

There has been an important warming-up of the world since the mid-nineteenth century. But there are good reasons to doubt whether this trend is continuing. 1959 has given Britain a brilliant summer, but has been the severest ice year north of Iceland for a very long time

Is the climate changing? The short answer is that climate is always changing to a greater or lesser extent. It is subject to many external influences, solar and terrestrial, which themselves vary. The basic astronomical variations are cyclic, with periods ranging from a few years to many thousands of years; but the other variations in the environment are mostly irregular and non-periodic.

Climate should not be expected to remain static, since the controlling influences are never quite the same. The changes that so obviously distinguish one year from another are part and parcel of the longer-term variations. These affect, for instance, the frequency of anticyclones producing fine days as well as those more persistent (or recurrent) anticyclones that give us fine summers and cold winters. Changes in the course and strength of the main streams of the atmospheric circulation are implied. As a result, the frequencies of fine summers and severe winters vary enough from decade to decade and century to century for the changes to be quite noticeable. Moreover, the national pocket is affected through harvest failures, drainage problems, coast erosion, etc.

Cycles or periodicities possibly play some part in these variations, but it seems to be a minor part. One cannot fasten on to some particular periodicity, such as the eleven-year sunspot cycle, and base a forecast of a good or bad summer on that alone. Other things – for instance, the extent of snow and ice, which reflect (that is, lose) the Solar radiation back to space, or the distribution of heat stored in the oceans – are liable to have effects too big to be ignored.

The situation is confused both by the multiplicity of influences at work and by the fact that many of them are themselves produced by the weather of the current and previous seasons. In some cases very long "lag effects" of seasons gone by are involved. We might consider the ice caps left over from the ice age as the extreme examples of lag effects; but in reality the economy of these ice sheets is not far from balanced at the present time. It seems certain that there have been periods within the recent past when the Greeland ice cap was growing, although it has been wasting during the present century; and the question of whether the great Antarctic ice cap is growing or declining is now under debate in the light of observations made during the International Geophysical Year.

There has been an important warming-up of most of the world since the mid-nineteenth century, a rise of annual mean temperature amounting by now to over 1 °C. The Arctic ice has retreated and so have the Alpine glaciers. Flora and fauna, forests and fish populations in the oceans, have all tended to shift their zones of occupation polewards in consequence. At some places near the ice margin in the Arctic the average winter temperatures have risen by 4 or 5 °C and the open season for shipping has lengthened accordingly.

It is important to know whether this warming trend is likely to continue, as well as to estimate the possible effects on climate of disturbances caused or contrived by the activity of man. But before any forecast can be given it is essential to get beyond the purely statistical type of analysis of climatic figures to an understanding of the physical processes at work; further, we must identify both the magnitudes and the patterns of their effects.

The verdict, whether it be a forecast of the undisturbed climatic trend or an assessment of the effects of possible man-made disturbances, affects every aspect of human life. And the stakes are heavy. Are we on the verge of opening up vast new lands for settlement in the Arctic? Is it reasonable to extend the area of cultivation of southern fruits or forest trees or grains? Will subtropical lands become increasingly arid? These are questions to which governments, agricultural planners, hydroelectric engineers and others would like to know the answers.

Botanists, fishery research institutes, foresters, glaciologists and others at home or abroad have all been able to produce accounts of how their particular concerns have been affected by the climatic changes of the last decades or the last century or two. An earlier change of climate caused the decline of the vineyards that prospered in many parts of England in the early Middle Ages. Many have attributed this decline purely to economic and historical changes, especially more exacting standards of taste and the increasing import of southern wines. But the decline is so closely paralleled by that of the yields of central European and other northern vineyards that it must be basically attributable to cooler and more uncertain summers. The sites occupied by former English vineyards include some places that are now notorious for late Spring and early Summer frosts. To explain this we are probably driven to the conclusion that the ocean between Britain and Iceland was several degrees warmer 700 to 1000 years ago than it is today, and of this there is supporting evidence from archaeology in Greenland and from the long records of ice around the coasts of Iceland.

Clearly, there is much to be gained from coordination of research in different, and otherwise unrelated, fields in order to piece together the climatic history of our era. The resulting record would be of use to all. And there is much that could be learnt from the meteorology of the significant climatic changes that occurred, particularly the changes from the optimum climate around AD 1000 to the much colder period 1550–1850. The latter has been called the Little Ice Age, because the Alpine and northern glaciers generally reached their most advanced limits since the end of the last great ice age ten thousand years ago.

Professor Gordon Manley prepared data on how the normal summer and winter temperatures in central England, represented by forty-years-running means for July and January, have varied over most of the period since the invention of the thermometer. (Forty years is certainly long enough to dominate the impressions of a human lifetime.) These show that the temperatures in the height of summer have not varied significantly, but that the winter climate of England between 1740 and 1850 was equivalent to that of the borders of France and Germany today. They show, too, that all the years since 1939 have apparently taken us past the peak of mild winters into a somewhat colder regime.

I am at present investigating the climatic changes of the period since the basic meteorological instruments were invented in terms of the distribution of barometric pressure and the prevailing patterns of wind circulation. Data on the average pressure for January over most of the world between 1900 and 1939, and between 1790 and 1829, show how much the normal patterns of one 40-year epoch may differ from another. The general vigour of the atmospheric circulation in winter, at least over the North Atlantic and Europe, has been materially greater in the present century. This is shown by a deeper and more conspicuous Iceland "low" and the stronger pressure gradients for westerly winds sweeping Atlantic air into the heart of Europe. The evidence so far available points to a similar intensification of the atmospheric circulation over widely separated parts of the world, certainly from 1850 to 1920, and in other seasons of the year as well. The weaker circulation for the 1790–1829 data corresponds to a period of colder winters in Britain and Europe.

Because the water currents in the ocean surface are largely wind driven, it is not surprising to find evidence that the supply of Gulf Stream water – on which the mildness of the British climate most directly depends – was weaker about 1800 than it is today. It also followed a more southerly track, in keeping with evidence that the main depression track was a few degrees of latitude farther south, as was the ice limit on northern waters. Data show the discrepancy between the sea surface temperatures observed in early surveys and more modern values.

Such a great weakening of the circulation of air and oceans as we observe around 1800 should have assignable causes. I hope that some of these may be identified by study of the mean circulation maps for individual years. Factors that have to be considered include:

(1) possible variations of the Sun's output of energy, for instance during the eleven-year and longer sunspot cycles;
(2) variations in the atmosphere's transparency to Solar radiation due to carbon dioxide content (increasing strongly since the industrial revolution), cloudiness, volcanic dust and now possibly dust from nuclear explosions;
(3) changes in the Earth's surface conditions – such as distribution and amount of heat stored in the oceans, extent of ice and snow.

In the case of (1) only minute variations, confined to the ultra-violet, have been detected with certainty, although various meteorological studies have suggested that sunspots and Solar flares do have some effect. Here the observations from artificial Earth satellites may shed new light, because without them the real strength of the Solar beam remains unknown. Some of it is absorbed in the upper atmosphere in the process of converting oxygen into ozone, and we await the first reliable observations of the beam before it encounters the atmosphere. Comparable observations of the initial intensity of the beam at all phases of the Sunspot cycle are needed.

Studies of atmospheric behaviour in the years immediately after the great eruptions of Krakatoa in 1883 and Katmai in 1912 strongly suggest that volcanic dust is also important. It has been estimated that after several great eruptions in 1783–85, world surface temperatures generally fell by 2 °C, for a year or two. Great volcanic outbursts appear to have been commoner in the seventeenth, eighteenth and nineteenth centuries than since. Coincidences of multiple volcanic eruptions with the worst phases of the Little Ice Age lend colour to the suggestion that persistent veils of fine dust particles suspended in the upper atmosphere may seriously affect the amount of Solar energy penetrating.

One aspect of the latest trends is that in the last twenty years the frequency of snow lying in lowland districts of the British Isles has increased since the optimum years of the 1920s and 1930s, with obvious effects upon the cost of keeping communications open. Taken together with the undeniable evidence of charts that the atmospheric circulation has once more become weaker since 1940, we must begin to doubt whether the general climatic improvement of the past 100 to 150 years is continuing. Nor should the recent fine summer be allowed to instil uninformed optimism, because 1959 is reported as the severest ice year north of Iceland for a very long time. As a matter of fact there are suggestions that the ice distribution on the Atlantic favoured an atmospheric circulation pattern that gives dry weather in north-west Europe.

Climatic forecasting cannot properly be undertaken until we understand much more about the mechanisms we are now exploring. Furthermore, the forecast might at any time be upset by an unpredictable burst of Solar activity or of great volcanic activity on this planet. Forecasting what the next few decades will bring is not just round the corner, although enlightened estimates of the probable climatic trend in the absence of external disturbances may become possible.

Perhaps we shall see gradiose attempts at alteration of climate, for instance by shattering or melting the Arctic pack-ice, before we reach the stage of being able to make reliable forecasts. Such undertakings might alter the climate over great regions of the

Earth, opening up new lands here and having harmful results there. Not all the results would be predictable and not all would be good. Yet there might be possibilities of increasing the total quantity of food that the world could produce for its ever-growing population. Meanwhile there is much to be learnt about the mechanism of climate – the general circulation of the atmosphere – and its inter-relationships in different parts of the world.

22 October, 1959

THE COLDEST ENGLISH WINTER SINCE 1740?

Scattered instrumental records by amateurs in various parts of England provide a legacy of reasonably reliable data, from long before official meteorology began. Between them they provide a sequence representative of the English Midlands going back to before 1740, as described by Professor Gordon Manley ten years ago in the *Quarterly Journal* of the Royal Meteorological Society. According to Professor Manley it now becomes evident that the severity of the present winter in England, if represented by the departure of temperature in December, January and February below the average, exceeds that of any preceding winter since 1740. December fell about 2.5 °C, January 6.0 °C and February probably 4.0 °C below the average, giving a mean departure of 4.1 °C. In 1740 it was 4.6 °C.

Last month ranks as the coldest January since 1814 and, as February now appears likely to give a mean below the freezing point, it is noteworthy that such a succession has only been recorded in 1740 and in 1878–1879. It was very nearly matched in 1838 and 1895. In 1895, however, February was considerably colder than January; this probably explains why Lake Windermere became more thoroughly frozen than has so far been reported this year.

The gradient of temperature from south to north has been unusual. Thanks to the prevalence of easterly winds using the short sea route, and the persistence of the heavy snow cover over much of the South and Midlands, Tynemouth, for example, has had considerably higher temperatures than Plymouth.

Frost has penetrated more than two feet deep in parts of Cambridgeshire – much as in 1895. Records of frequency of snow cover are very rarely available before 1912 so exact comparisons are not easily made. The mean number of such days, N, over the lower-lying Midlands is about 10 and statistics suggest that the limit of expectation lies close to N + 50. Professor Manley points out that this figure could now be equalled or surpassed, as March is yet to come and statistical indications support the likelihood that it will be chilly.

West of the Pennines and the Southern Uplands snow cover has been much less persistent, and a good deal of sunshine has been enjoyed. There is not yet any report to hand of minima below −22 °C, or of "trees split by the frost" as in 1879, when locally in Berwickshire the temperature fell to −28 °C.

Persistent westward displacement of all the normal surface pressure distribution round the Arctic Basin, combined with what looks like a very backward tilt of the upper wave pattern awaits its explanation by the experts. The repeated development of the Icelandic anticyclone has been conspicuous. Warm water in the North Pacific might plausibly be suggested, but that may not be the whole story in the light of what we hear from Russia. This winter promises to provoke as many meteorological papers as 1947; news of the behaviour of the recently emphasised "polar night westerlies" at a very high altitude will be eagerly awaited.

"NOTES AND COMMENTS", *28 February, 1963*

11

The ice drifts back to Iceland

LEO KRISTJANSSON

A climatic trend may be merely a nuisance, but there are many situations where such a trend will produce menacing or even catastrophic effects; examples we all recognise include flood-prone areas, and killing frost seasons. And in Iceland, an excited conference of more than fifty local historians, geoscientists and applied scientists recently discussed the problems posed by the return of a most unwelcome visitor accompanying the cooling climate – the Arctic drift ice. This ice had hardly been seen from Iceland since the 1920s until 1965 and 1968, when it blocked shipping and fishing at the north coast of the island for several months.

The excitement, and worry, of the whole population of Iceland stem from reasons best explained by the historians at the conference: along with disastrous volcanic outbursts, disease and colonial rule, frequent cold spells and "ice years" kept their ancestors between bare survival and extinction for several centuries. During the last cold spell, from 1870 to 1918, thousands emigrated to America.

Not surprisingly, historical scientific records from these years are unreliable. Moreover Iceland still very much represents a missing piece in the palaeoclimate jigsaw painstakingly assembled by the meteorologist H. H. Lamb and others on both sides of the Atlantic. Now, the geoscientists are taking steps to fill this gap, by studying records left in nature itself since the first occurrence of glacial action in Iceland over three million years ago. Thus, a detailed temperature record has recently been obtained by oxygen isotope analysis from a deep core through the Greenland ice sheet representing 100 000 years. And layers of volcanic ash in Icelandic soils are proving to be of great help in dating botanical and archaeological remains which may be indicative of past climatic conditions.

At the Reykjavik conference, the behaviour of the Arctic ice was studied mainly through summaries and analyses of routine reports, but more spectacular modern techniques also received much attention. These included the drifting of the manned ice island ARLIS II along the coast of Greenland in 1964–1965, satellite photographs of the ice limit now received directly in Iceland, and infra-red reconnaissance of sea temperatures from aircraft.

But the new techniques have not significantly altered earlier concepts about the Arctic ice. In contrast to Antarctic or Baltic ice, it consists of floes a few metres deep and tens of metres across, which are constantly being created, broken up, melted and joined at the mercy of winds, currents and temperatures. The major current to the Arctic is the warm Gulf Stream, which pushes the edge of the ice to beyond Norway. It is balanced by the outflow of the East Greeland Current which carries the ice with it along the Greenland coast. Increases in ice production up north, reduced strength of the current itself, or persistent westerly to northerly winds, may move the ice limit to Iceland – usually for weeks, and sometimes for months, in the spring.

The large number of causes contributing to climatic development, from transport by ocean currents to the physics of ice crystallisation, makes it almost as difficult for the scientist to forecast the climate as for the historian to record it. But many believe that the cooling trend in air and sea temperatures in most of the North Atlantic and Arctic will continue for a few more years at least; Soviet work indicates that a polar air circulation pattern resembling that of 1900–1928 has been establishing itself since 1960. An increase in the extent of polar air masses would, in any case, deflect the depressions crossing the Atlantic farther to the south than before, bringing unsettled weather to western Europe.

Only one meteorologist, therefore, ventured to forecast how long the ice is going to stay at the coast of Iceland this year. From an empirical correlation formula, employing Jan Mayen summer temperatures and pressure gradients between Iceland and Greenland in previous years, P. Bergthorsson told the conference he is expecting a three to four months' ice period in 1969. With the ice only a few tens of miles off in the beginning of February, he may well turn out to be right.

Of course, everybody's hoping he's wrong, and the "applieds" at the Reykjavik conference explained why. The Icelanders' standard of living, although among the highest in the world, is in many respects just as vulnerable as that of their ancestors. For the farmer, a drop of 1 °C in summer temperature still means a 15 per cent reduction in crop yields. The fishermen, who in previous fishing seasons could lie in wait for the Norwegian herring as it migrated in huge schools to eastern Iceland, have in the past two seasons had to chase it all the way to Jan Mayen and Spitsbergen as it avoids the increasingly cold waters around Iceland. The two recent devaluations of the Icelandic currency (from 120 kronur to the £1 to 210 to the £1) are largely caused by the consequent drop in herring exports.

Living with the ice, perhaps for months every year from now on, will present many problems for the fifth of the population of Iceland that inhabits villages and farm communities on the north coast. Shipping then being blocked by ice, and roads usually being blocked by snow, stockpiles of essentials like cattle grain and fuel (and coffee!) will have to be kept there. There is also a danger of damage to harbours, ships and fishing gear by the ice, danger of stray polar bears (one has been shot in Iceland this year, only about the twentieth to be killed there this century) and so on – not to speak of inconveniences or the depressing effect of living by a silent, cold, white sea for long periods of time. Coast Guard aircraft are now making detailed weekly surveys of the ice limit, so that fishing and shipping can keep out of dangerous or threatened waters. Following tragic experiences of Icelandic as well as British trawlers, much attention is being paid to safety measures such as the prevention of over-icing at sea, and all fishing vessels are now required by law to radio their position to shore stations daily.

6 March, 1969

CLIMATIC RECORDS UNFROZEN FROM THE GREENLAND ICE

The massive bodies of ice that cover parts of the Earth's surface preserve within them records of climatic changes during the past 100 000 years. In a new investigation a Danish–American team of researchers has now determined in considerable detail the temperature changes throughout the time span represented by a long core taken from the Greeland ice-cap (*Science*, vol. 166, p. 377).

W. Dansgaard, S. J. Johnsen and J. Moller of the University of Copenhagen, and C. C. Langway Junior of the US Army Terrestrial Science Center, carried out mass spectroscopic studies of oxygen isotopes from sections of a 1390-metre-long ice core extracted from the Greeland ice sheet at Camp Century. The abundance of oxygen-18 relative to oxygen-16 at the same depth along the core depended on the temperature of precipitation; decreasing temperature of formation led to decreasing content of oxygen-18 in rain or snow. Dansgaard and his colleagues were able to correlate changes in temperature of formation along the ice core with geological time using a theoretical model for ice flow in the glacier.

Their results compared favourably with other methods of determining times of climatic changes, such as carbon-14 dating of pollen, and analysis of ocean sediments. The ice core data showed more detail and revealed climatic oscillations of 120, 940 and 13 000 years. The first two can be associated with fluctuations in Solar radiation. This is corroborated through studies of carbon-14 production which is affected by radiation from the Sun. The amount of carbon-14 absorbed by plants follows the same time oscillations as the oxygen-18 abundance. The cyclic climatic change of 13 000 years can be attributed to the Earth's precession around the Sun. The time of year when the Earth is closest to the Sun changed from June to December about every 13 000 years, and consequently affected the surface temperature.

The workers admit that their theoretical calculations of the ice flow may not be precise but do provide reasonable answers. The ice core data seem to allow far greater, and more direct, climatological detail than any previous known methods.

"MONITOR", 30 October, 1969

12

Where Poseidon courts Aeolus

GERALD WICK

Although the oceans play a large role in determining our weather and climate, oceanographers and meteorologists seldom collaborate. To overcome this deficiency, an interdisciplinary team of Earth scientists is embarking on a unique experiment, NORPAX, that may lead to improved long-range weather forecasting

The key to the North American climate, and perhaps that of Europe, may lie in the North Pacific Ocean. Meteorological and oceanographic data gathered over the past 20 years indicate strong correlations between temperature fluctuations in the North Pacific Ocean and persisting climate regimes in the Northern Hemisphere. The implications of this discovery are so great that the United States National Science Foundation (NSF)/International Decade of Ocean Exploration (IDOE) and the Office of Naval Research (ONR) have just allocated $1.4 million for the first year of a long-term research programme designed to unravel the mechanisms that determine the large-scale air/sea interactions over the North Pacific. The Scripps Institution of Oceanography, La Jolla, California, has been selected to coordinate and manage the multi-university programme. In July the same national agencies gave $3.2 million to General Dynamics for buoy construction. These sums of money make the research programme, called NORPAX (North Pacific Experiment), one of the largest combined physical oceanographic and meteorological experiments in the world. With accelerated funding, NORPAX is expected to grow in the coming years.

As long as 80 years ago, Lt John Pillsbury, an American naval officer and oceanographer, recognised that interactions between ocean currents and atmospheric patterns could affect the weather over continents. He wrote in his 1891 book The Gulf Stream: ". . .

The moisture and varying temperature of the land depends largely upon the positions of these currents in the ocean, and it is thought that when we know the laws of the latter we will, with the aid of meteorology, be able to say to the farmers hundreds of miles distant from the sea, 'you will have an abnormal amount of rain during next summer', or 'the winter will be cold and clear', and by these predictions they can plant a crop to suit the circumstances or provide an unusual amount of food for their stock. . . . From a study of these great forces, then, we derive our greatest benefits, and any amount of well directed effort to gain a complete mastery of their laws will revert directly to the good of the human race."

The years 1957–1958 brought a new awareness to ocean-ographers and meteorologists of the interactions between the sea and the atmosphere. In those years, there was a general warming of the ocean water over large areas of the North Pacific basin. The strength of some oceanic currents diminished and their courses were altered. Atmospheric flow patterns were disrupted; the distri-bution of many biological species was severely modified and bio-logical communities were dislocated. Warm water penetrated into the North Pacific allowing some subtropical marine species to migrate all of the way to Alaska. In those years, a large area of anomalously warm water in the North Pacific diverted the jet stream to the north. Through complex downstream responses, the northern displacement of the jet stream over the Eastern Pacific Ocean resulted in a southerly dip over North America allowing the cold polar winds to exert their influence over the eastern part of the continent. As the jet stream moves southward, cold Arctic air enters through the troughs. Conversely, warm tropical air flows northward where the jet stream moves northward. Thus North America entered a new winter regime that persisted until 1971. In 1972 the water temperature patterns, for unknown reasons, reverted as did the temperature patterns over the continent.

The first documented case of climatic regimes that persist for about a decade is the Biblical "seven years of fat and seven years of lean" of Joseph's time. However, as we seem to have lost our ability to interpret dreams, the long-range weather predictors need to look to other signposts for the future. Judging from the Biblical example, the value of long-range weather forecasting is clear. Management of water resources, agriculture and certain industries are highly dependent upon the weather. An understanding of the ocean dynamics is also important for commercial and military organisations. Furthermore, a detailed knowledge of climatic fluc-tuations is essential for the evaluation of Man's impact on the environment. Considerable effort is being expended to establish natural "baselines" to compare with man-made effects on the environment. A knowledge of natural fluctuations is equally important to ensure that the "baselines" are not established during unrepresentative periods and that we are not over-emphasising or under-emphasising the environmental changes induced by Man.

The oceanic heat engine

Although the relatively sudden climatic fluctuations are well documented, their origin still remains a mystery. One body of opinion believes that extraterrestrial events, such as Solar cycles, trigger new climatic regimes ranging from short-lived droughts through long-lived ice ages. Jerome Namias, one of the co-principal investigators with NORPAX, believes that we should look closer to home for the causes of climatic fluctuations. Namias, formerly a major figure with the US National Weather Service and now at Scripps, thinks that we should study all internal effects before going to extraterrestrial arguments. The important factors affecting climatic change are the boundary conditions in the ocean such as heat sources, currents and oceanic mixing. Continents can also contribute to climatic change through such variables as abnormal snow cover and soil conditions. Abnormal snow cover can upset the heat balance by increasing the reflected radiation up to five times that of the Earth's normal surface condition. Extra moisture in the soil will require atmospheric heat for evaporation that could otherwise be used to raise air temperature. Namias has shown that these conditions can be instrumental in influencing the weather patterns. But the sluggishness of the ocean and its vast surface area make it the prime candidate for determining climatic regimes.

Compared with the atmosphere, the oceans have a "long-term" memory. Once a particular circulation is established in the ocean, it can take several years for a new regime to set in. A possible, but as yet only partially verified, mechanism is as follows: ocean patterns that are set up during one winter may be covered over by warm water in the summer and thus would be unaffected by the winds. Then the next winter these oceanic patterns will surface and influence the atmospheric circulation into the previous winter's regime.

Although most of the research on the air/sea interaction has centred on correlations between sea surface temperatures and atmospheric circulation, the important quantity is the actual heat flux between the oceans and the atmosphere, not the sea surface temperature itself. The heat flux basically depends upon the temperature difference between the air and the sea and upon the wind conditions. Also the duration of the flux depends upon the depth of the temperature anomaly. Thus, it is possible for the surface warming of the summer to obscure the deeper colder water, which may eventually exert a greater influence on the atmosphere. During the experimental phase, the NORPAX investigators will strive to measure the heat content and ocean/atmosphere heat flux.

It is possible to calculate the atmospheric circulation from the sea surface temperature anomalies when they correspond, as they often do, to the actual heat flow to the atmosphere. (The anomalies are the deviations from long-time averages of the ocean conditions. Twenty years is often taken as the time period. These anomalies often cover a million square km and are at least 4 °C higher than the surrounding water.) The uneven heat distribution in the ocean causes perturbations in the major atmospheric circulation. It is also possible to calculate the oceanic circulation from atmospheric conditions because the winds drive the ocean currents. There is an intimate relationship between the sea and overlying air and attempts to unscramble their individual significance may be as fruitless as asking the question: "Which came first the chicken or the egg?" Clearly both the atmosphere and the ocean must be considered as one system. Yet the sheer mass and sluggishness of the ocean lead the NORPAX investigators to believe that the sea is the harbinger of our climatic fate. Although very similar physical processes determine the dynamics of the ocean and the atmosphere, the sluggishness of the ocean arises from its larger density (1000 times that of the atmosphere), its larger total mass (1 300 000 times greater) and its larger heat capacity (2000 times greater).

Alternative theories

Namias believes that the North Pacific's temperature anomalies are the major influence on the climate. Through atmospheric "teleconnections" it can affect climate throughout the northern hemisphere, and perhaps in the southern hemisphere as well. A different emphasis is stressed by Professor Jacob Bjerknes, a well known meteorologist from the University of California, Los Angeles, and a co-principal investigator for NORPAX. Bjerknes thinks that temperature anomalies along the equator are more important. According to his ideas, the equatorial waters drive atmospheric circulation determining North Pacific conditions. One of the major initial objectives of NORPAX will be to test these two hypotheses. During its first phase, NORPAX investigators will check the patterns of anomalies and describe what is happening. Perhaps later they will gain the insight to develop accurate models improving on their present crude models of ocean/atmosphere circulation and thermal characterisation.

The roots of NORPAX sprouted about 14 years ago when Professor John Isaacs, Scripps Institution of Oceanography, realised that the changes being studied in the California Current were associated with very-large-scale changes over most of the North Pacific. He believes that long-range weather forecasting will never be realised unless data are simultaneously collected over the *entire* ocean. The present NORPAX programme grew out of Isaac's effort. He and his associates at Scripps started in the 1950s developing buoys that they felt were suitable to withstand the severe winter storms in the North Pacific. An array of the buoys, called bumblebee buoys due to their shape and colour pattern, could conceivably gather the necessary data. They had demonstrated their durability by withstanding hurricane force winds and swell 10–15 m over water depths of 7000 m. These buoys have been used for the past few years to monitor ocean temperatures from surface to 300 m, and to collect meteorological data. The existing buoys will be used to supplement the NORPAX experimental effort.

The bulk of the buoy data will come from General Dynamics' buoys which have radio equipment for telemetering data to Scripps for analysis. General Dynamics is in the forefront of buoy technology (a sorely neglected field) with their 13-m (40-foot) diameter pie-shaped "monster" buoys – so nicknamed because of their size. General Dynamics has completed two monster buoys for NORPAX, "Dana" and "Alpha". The first prototype, "Bravo", had withstood a hurricane off the Florida coast in 1965. The monster buoys are equipped with sensors to monitor wind speed, humidity, precipitation, barometric pressure, Solar radiation, compass bearing, wave height, sea-water temperature at several depths, salinity, and water pressure. These data can be stored in two computer memories, one with a capacity of 24 hours, the other with a full year's storage capacity. The monster buoys have a telemetry range of up to 4000 km and will be used to interrogate and command smaller buoys with a 1000 km telemetry range. The small buoys, also developed by General Dynamics, have similar hull shape and instrumentation to the monster buoys. They will be deployed in clusters surrounding monster buoys and island stations.

A novel feature on the monster buoys is the power source needed to provide electricity for the instruments. After considering all sorts of exotic power sources, the General Dynamics engineers settled on diesel fuel generators which charge nickel–cadmium batteries. Each buoy has two generators and sufficient diesel fuel generators to last for two years' operation. The generators can automatically change their oil on command.

A complex data flow

As the buoys are currently the most expensive item on the budget, it is tempting to label NORPAX a buoy experiment. But project manager Dr Tim Barnett, of Scripps, emphasises that the buoys are only a part of the total data acquisition. Other prime sources include historical records, standard meteorological data, instrumented island stations, weather ships, ships of opportunity (merchant ships crossing the areas of interest), aircraft and spacecraft.

The general scientific programme is manned by a multi-university team. Present participation includes oceanographers and meteorologists from the University of California, both the San Diego (Scripps) and Los Angeles campuses, and the University of Hawaii. Proposals are invited from scientists at other universities and from foreign countries. Data, both historical and current, are being exchanged with Canada, Japan, Russia, Great Britain, and Australia. It is anticipated that scientists from these five countries and from Germany will eventually participate in NORPAX.

Once the data are acquired, it will be no easy matter to catalogue and analyse them. Data from the instrumented ships, buoys, islands, aircraft and spacecraft will flow through appropriate agencies on their way to the master data library at Scripps. Co-operating agencies include the US Navy, the National Marine Fisheries Service, Environmental Data Service, National Aeronautics and Space Administration (NASA), National Weather Service, and the National Oceanic and Atmospheric Administration

(NOAA). Those using the data will include these same agencies, the Department of Defense and, of course, the participating scientists. International programmes, such as GARP (Global Atmospheric Research Programme) and IGOSS (Integrated Global Ocean Station System) could also benefit from interaction with NORPAX.

NORPAX opens up a completely new field of research. No previous experiments have considered the air/sea interactions on such a large scale. Although NORPAX seems to be an excellent opportunity to improve long-range weather and ocean forecasting, it is not receiving an especially enthusiastic welcome, particularly in some sections of the oceanographic community. Antagonists claim that the scientific objectives are not well defined and that the programme can be done more easily and with less expense by other techniques. Obviously the big issue is the cost of NORPAX. At present, the onus is on the NORPAX investigators to show their colleagues that the money is well spent. We cannot tell in advance if their efforts will live up to their expectations, but it is certain that the whole oceanographic and meteorological community will be keeping a close watch on their progress.

18 January, 1973

CURRENT DROUGHTS MAY MARK A GLOBAL WEATHER SHIFT

Too little and too late has typified the monsoon in northern India this year, following repeated failures of the rains in recent years. This story now seems to be part of a general modification of the climatic pattern of the northern hemisphere, with all the climatic zones shifted slightly to the south. Dr Derek Winstanley has related the southward displacement of the monsoon region to similar latitudinal shifts in the other climatic zones, and suggests in *Nature* (vol. 244, p. 464) how these changes relate to changing circulation patterns over the entire northern hemisphere.

Dr Winstanley's interest in the problem stems from his work at the Anti-Locust Research Centre, London. Although he has now left the centre, in 1970 he published an analysis of the causes of devastating rainfall which caused extensive flooding in North Africa in September 1969. The relevance of this to locusts is that the rains permitted prolonged and successful breeding of the desert locust in the following winter and spring.

The immediate cause of the rain was the movement of a strong cyclonic storm over the central Mediterranean; and this, in turn, was but a link in an apparently anomalous general circulation pattern of the northern hemisphere in the autumn of 1969 (*Weather*, vol. 25, p. 390).

It now looks as if that situation was not so anomalous after all, but merely a strong indication of future trends. The schoolboy mnemonic for remembering the features of a so-called Mediterranean climate is "warm, wet westerlies in winter" – but in the years up to the early 1960s these warm wet westerlies visited only the northern Mediterranean. Since then, however, the troughs that bring the rain in winter and spring have moved south. As a result of this shift in the circumpolar westerly wind pattern, the rainfall in north Africa and the Middle East during the late 1960s was the highest ever recorded.

If one climatic zone shifts, the whole pattern moves. In Britain, for example, there has been a decline in the frequency of westerly winds. Lone Atlantic yacht-sailors and others have reported changes in wind patterns and an increase in ice cover of the sub-Arctic ocean.

Further to the south, from Mauritania to north-west India, the summer monsoon rainfall has decreased by more than 50 per cent since 1957, says Dr Winstanley. Rainfall data from eight stations situated at the northern edge of what was the monsoon belt suggest that the region is now the southern edge of an arid belt. That is why we have heard so much lately of drought and economic disaster in India, Chad, Niger, Upper Volta, Dohomey, Mali, Senegal and Mauritania.

According to Dr Winstanley, "It is probable that the abnormal southward extent of the troughs in the circumpolar westerlies has restricted the northward extent and intensity of the tropical circulation systems controlling the monsoon". The trend may well be a semi-permanent feature of the climate of these regions in the immediate future. And, although the increased rainfall in the subtropical regions of Africa and the Middle East may help in reclaiming some deserts, this discovery will be little comfort to the inhabitants of regions that are now well on the way to becoming new deserts.

"MONITOR", 28 June, 1973

13

The drought that won't go away

DEREK WINSTANLEY

The Sahel drought made headlines in the early 1970s, but faded from the news as soon as a little rain appeared. Now, the drought is back, confirming the gloomy predictions of some climatologists. Will the lessons learned by experience last time around help to alleviate the suffering now?

In 1972 and 1973 you could hardly open a newspaper without being faced with pictures of people and cattle dying in their thousands in the sub-Sahara zone of Africa. Thanks to higher rainfall and massive amounts of international aid the situation

Figure 13.1 *Drought and over-grazing hit the Saharan fringe province of Kordofan, Sudan (Credit: Earthscan/Mark Edwards)*

Figure 13.2 *Herdsmen buy water from government stocks (Credit: Earthscan/Mark Edwards)*

improved over the subsequent two years. The news media no longer had a disaster to cover and to most people the 24 million inhabitants of the Sahelian countries slipped back into the obscurity from which they had temporarily emerged – after all, who had heard of Mauretania or Upper Volta before the drought? Today there are more than two million additional mouths to feed in these countries, but attention has shifted to other climatic abnormalities, the recent droughts and harsh winters in Britain and the United States.

Unfortunately, the rains that drenched the Sahelian countries for most of the half-century before they gained independence in the early 1960s have not returned. Rainfall in 1974 and 1975 was still 10 per cent below "normal" and in 1976 it was more than 30 per cent below "normal". Again in 1977 and now this year there have been large water shortages.

The main feature of the abnormal rainfall distribution is that the severity of the drought is primarily a function of latitude: in the semi-desert area at about 18 °N rainfall over the period 1968–1976 has been 50 per cent below normal, but the situation improves southwards. Taking the example of The Gambia, rainfall over this nine-year period has averaged 20–30 per cent below normal. This pronounced latitudinal shift presumably reflects the changes in the large-scale atmospheric circulation mechanisms that control rainfall distribution.

Another way of looking at the drought situation is to examine the geographical distribution of rainfall over this nine-year period together with the normal distribution of rainfall. It then becomes clear that the isohets are displaced southwards by only one degree of latitude in the north and a mere half a degree over The Gambia; this is sufficient to cause large percentage decreases. The reason for this is that the rainfall gradient in this part of the world is so strong: moving south from Mauritania to The Gambia rainfall increases by 100 mm every 60 km.

These changes suggest that climatologists who warned five years ago that the "normal" pattern had changed were correct. But it is a combination of increasing human and animal pressure on the land and of these natural climatic oscillations that has accelerated the process of "desertification" in this part of the world. Whether or not climatic conditions will continue to contribute to this process in the longer term is another matter.

The significance of the rains to a country like The Gambia can be gauged from the fact that 85 per cent of the population of 525 000 is engaged in agriculture. The economy is dominated by peanut cultivation and peanuts account for 95 per cent of exports by value. In 1965, when The Gambia achieved independence from Britain, considerable doubt was expressed as to whether the new nation could survive. In fact real domestic products rose an average of 4.7 per cent over the next ten years with an annual real growth in per capita output of 1.9 per cent.

Falls in peanut production due to the drought in the early 1970s were offset by the doubling of the world price for peanuts, and the increased export revenue balanced the price increase of imported goods. As peanut prices now show signs of sliding back, a drop in production caused by the drought is more likely to have a disastrous effect on the economy than in the early 1970s. An inevitable balance-of-trade deficit caused by a decrease in the value of exports and the need for higher food imports will be a severe setback for this West African democracy. The drought emphasises further the need for crop diversification and increased food production, but retards the implementation of measures to achieve these objectives.

During the 16 years since independence, rainfall in the Sahelian countries has averaged 20 per cent lower than in the preceding 30 years – the so-called climatological "normal" period. Clearly, great caution must be exercised when planning for the future, for even the climate of the 30 years directly preceding the present can be very misleading in obtaining an estimate of rainfall during the years ahead.

In Britain the closest parallels to the drought and heatwaves that reached a peak in the summer of 1976 are to be found in the first half of the eighteenth century – more than 200 years ago. Historical records indicate that this was a period with frequent famines in the sub-Sahara zone and it is possible that one has to go back over 200 years to find a parallel to the present climatic situation in the sub-Sahara zone.

In the six years from 1971 to 1976 annual rainfall over England and Wales was 10 per cent lower than in the climatological "normal" period 1931–1960. In the 16 years from 1735 to 1750 rainfall was 14 per cent lower than in 1931–1960. There is, therefore, a well documented precedence for a longer period of even drier conditions in Britain. This is not intended as a gloomy prognostication for the next 10 years, but is intended merely to strengthen the argument that it is possible that rainfall in the sub-Sahara zone from the 1920s through the 1950s was abnormally high, as it was in Britain. In the perspective of a longer climatic record it is possible that drier conditions could be more "normal".

The economic and social impact of drought tends to be greater the lower the level of development of the country, the greater the dependence on agriculture and the more concentrated the seasonal rainfall. In the case of The Gambia, where life expectancy at birth is still only about 34 years and the average per capita income is £50, the impact is severe. The Gambia is an archetypal example of the poor countries in the sub-Sahara zone that are affected by this changed rainfall pattern.

In the early 1970s, many governments of these countries were unwilling to seek international aid at an early stage of the drought, because they regarded the famines as something to be hushed up, an indication of the failure of their domestic policies. Will they be more willing to seek aid now, with the realisation that global forces are contributing to their hardship? Or must the poorest inhabitants of those countries suffer once again while their leaders pretend that nothing is amiss?

19 October, 1978

FOOD AID FORTHCOMING?

If promises are anything to go by, food aid for drought-affected Sahel states such as Gambia may be forthcoming more rapidly now than last time around. In the 1977–1978 season, rainfall across Gambia at the start of the planting season (June 1977) was low and variable, between 60 and 80 per cent of "normal"; in July it remained 40–70 per cent of normal, with officially declared drought by mid-August affecting millet, maize and upland rice crops. Recovery with good September rains helped to prevent a major crisis, but the FAO Office for Special Relief Operations estimated a need for 6000 tonnes of rice, 9000 tonnes of coarse grain and some milk powder to make up the deficit. By 21 July 1978, pledged aid amounted to 17 644 tonnes from a variety of sources. This is no guarantee that either the quantity or quality of actual food aid will be appropriate to the country's needs, but suggests a much more rapid response to the prospect of a food shortage than occurred in the early 1970s.

19 October, 1978

14

Africa's drought may last many years

MICHAEL CROSS

Evidence that a long-term change in Africa's climate may have caused the present famine has emerged from a new study by British meteorologists. The work means that governments and aid agencies may have to revise radically their strategies for repairing the damage done to African agriculture, and in helping farmers to avoid disasters in the future.

The Sahel region of West and Central Africa is now going through its second great drought in 15 years. The first, in the early 1970s, caused one of the worst famines on record. Last year, aid agencies reported that a similar disaster again threatens many African countries south of the Sahara (*New Scientist*, 29 November 1984, p. 10).

Despite the history of famine, most agricultural planners have discounted the idea that an inexorable shift in the climate is to blame. They point out that in many African countries, the amount of rain has remained high, even during "drought" years.

However, Dr Mike Dennett, an agricultural meteorologist at the University of Reading, yesterday unveiled results that suggest this accepted wisdom does not tell the whole story. He told a meeting of the Royal Meteorological Society that a new analysis of rainfall statistics in the Sahel shows that the region has been getting steadily drier for the past 20 years. The change is most dramatic in August, the wettest month.

Dennett's work will appear in the *Journal of Climatology* later this year. It is based upon new analysis of figures taken month by month at up to 50 weather stations across the western Sahel.

Annual rainfall figures showed "the well known features of a relatively high and stable rainfall in the 1950s and 1960s, followed by lower conditions". The amount of rain in June and July, the early rainy season, was above the mean during the 1950s and below during the 1970s. But there was no consistent downward trend. Rainfall in August, however, "has continued to decline consistently throughout the period".

Since 1968, the amount of rain that has fallen in August has been an average of 27 per cent below the mean from 1931 to 1960. Figures from September show a similar, but less dramatic, trend, Dennett said.

According to Dennett, these figures mean that the "view put forward in the mid-1970s that there was no evidence of a climatic shift . . . now needs some modification. It is clear that rainfall during August has been consistently low for the past 16 years, giving average conditions during August drier than any other comparable period during the instrumental record".

Why is the change taking place? According to Dr Peter Rown-tree of the Meteorological Office, who opened yesterday's meeting, preliminary experiments have shown a clear link between reducing the soil's capacity to store water and a reduction in rainfall. Such a drastic fall in the storage capacity comes when soil is stripped of vegetation, usually by over-grazing. The evidence that this is happening in the west of the Sahel is strong.

Because there is little evidence from tree rings in the Sahel, research on long-term trends depends on often unreliable historical documents. Only proven evidence that the climate has been

Figure 14.1 *The consequences for soil erosion (Credit: Earthscan/Mark Edwards)*

stable would tell researchers how drastic a change the present run of dry years represents.

If rainfall during the most important month has been getting worse for the past 20 years, why has famine not followed a similar pattern? Dennett suggests that in the years between 1975 and 1981, when the Sahel was apparently recovering from the drought, rain early in the season allowed some crops to germinate.

Also, farmers have switched from growing sorghum to millet, which has a shorter growing season. Such respites may be temporary. Dennett points out that farmers in the Sahel now depend more than ever on temperamental rains early in the season. "If early rains fail, as they did to some extent in 1982 and 1983, severe social and economic problems will result."

If forecasters can predict years of poor rainfall, does this mean that drought will follow? Not necessarily. Famines develop in a complicated way, and a lack of rain is only part of the cause.

Scientists at the International Livestock Centre for Africa, in Addis Ababa, have applied a computer model to predicting famines. The model collates meteorological data and predicts the amount of water available for crops to grow. Scientists can then estimate how long each area's growing season will be, and work out the amount of food that farmers will be able to produce.

Ethiopia's rain, like that of the Sahel, falls mainly in an intense rainy season which lasts from June to August. Usually, far too much rain falls at this time. Large amounts run off sloping fields, eroding the topsoil. And when the skies clear in September, crops have to mature on the water trapped in what soil there is left.

In normal years, the drought-prone areas of northern Ethiopia have enough moisture to support a growing season of 90 days. This is barely enough.

In good years, the "short rains" of February and March soften the soil, and allow time for the crops to grow. Unfortunately, the short rains are unreliable and often fail completely. When this happens, farmers cannot begin to prepare their land until the main rains start. They lose between 10 and 30 days preparing a suitable seedbed.

The International Livestock Centre's computer has collated more than 30 years of rainfall data from different Ethiopian provinces. The data clearly show the link between poor rainfall, short growing seasons and famine. For example, in the Asmara area the famine years of 1971–1974 had no short rains, and the growing season fell to about 70 days.

In 1982, Asmara had a good season. But in 1983 the short rains were light, and the main growing season again dropped to about 70 days. Widespread crop failures followed.

The Centre's scientists conclude that famines happen when the short rains fail for two or more years and the main growing seasons are so short as to make crop failure inevitable.

According to the team, the computer could provide early warnings of famine by late June every year. But whether anyone would be able to do anything about it is another matter.

17 January, 1985

THE NEXT ICE AGE MAY BE CLOSER
THAN YOU THINK

A shift from present-day climatic conditions into a full ice age requires a decrease of no more than 0.13 per cent in the amount of heat reaching the Earth from the Sun, the insolation. Peter Fong, of Emory University in Atlanta, Georgia, makes this startling claim in the pages of the journal *Climatic Change*, where it appears with a footnote from the Editor cautioning that the work has generated "strong, but mixed, reactions from three referees", and that it is being published "in order to spur debate" (vol. 4, p. 199). That it seems certain to do.

The basis for Fong's claim is a new calculation of the dynamics of the Earth's polar ice sheets, taking due account of the latent heat of melting and freezing of the great ice masses, their geometry, and the way they change the reflectivity of the Earth's surface (its albedo) as they advance and retreat. The main features of climatic change over an ice age are the advance and retreat of the ice sheets, and the changes in average ocean surface temperature. Fong points out that the standard computer models of climate, the general circulation models, are tuned to atmospheric changes and cannot be applied to this problem, which operates on a timescale of hundreds of thousands of years, rather than hundreds of days, and so he has developed a different kind of model to focus on the ice age problem.

Although his conclusion is surprising, it explains rather well one of the great puzzles in climatic research today. Studies of sediments from deep ocean cores have established beyond doubt that the great ice sheets ebb and flow during an ice age in step with changes in the Earth's orbit around the Sun, and its orientation in space. These are the so-called Milankovitch cycles. But the longest of these cycles shows up far more strongly in the deep-sea records than anyone expected. This is a rhythm roughly 100 000 years long which seems to be the most fundamental ice-age rhythm today. During the past million years, we have had a pattern of 100 000-year long ice ages separated by 10 000-year long interglacials.

The astronomical rhythm that matches this climatic cycle is a change in the ellipticity of the Earth's orbit, from more nearly circular to more elongated and back again. But this change produces only a modest change in the amount of heat reaching the Earth's surface in different seasons – covering a range of merely 0.18 per cent.

Conventional theories say that this is only one tenth of the change needed to produce the pattern of Ice Ages and interglacials; Fong's calculations suggest that we may have to think again.

"MONITOR", 22 July, 1982

15

Australia's drought and the southern climate

MARCEL VAN DIJK, DAVID MERCER AND JIM PETERSON

The Australian drought is part of a hemisphere-wide pattern of unusual climatic phenomena

---

Fires that ravaged parts of eastern Australia in recent weeks were the culmination of the worst drought this century. By March 1983 it had persisted for 11 months. The drought has its origins in a persistent pattern of atmospheric circulation that has affected the whole of the southern hemisphere, bringing drought also to South Africa and parts of South America, and probably related to the return of El Niño, a surge of warm ocean water off the western seaboard of South America (see below). Although there is no certain cause of the hemispheric pattern, it has been related by some researchers to the eruption last year of El Chichón in Mexico, and by others to a recurring cycle of drought and flood in the southern hemisphere. Quite possibly, however, the fluctuations may be no more than the results of random changes in atmospheric activity which, occasionally, bring large deviations from normal conditions.

The drought persisted in eastern Australia during 1982 and the cumulative effect up to the end of January 1983 is shown in Figure 15.2. By the end of June 1982 serious or severe deficiencies in rainfall had developed over most of New South Wales, central and south-western Queensland and northern Victoria. By the end of August rainfall deficiencies of three to five months duration had become established over much of South Australia, almost all of Victoria and New South Wales, Tasmania and southern Queensland. The failure of winter rains was followed by abnormally small rainfall in spring and by the end of 1982 the severe conditions

Figure 15.1   *Melbourne, 1 February 1983: overshadowed by a plume of smoke from a bushfire at Mt Macedon, 80 km to the north-west. A week later came the hottest February day on record and the sky was blackened again by dust storms (Credit: David Mercer)*

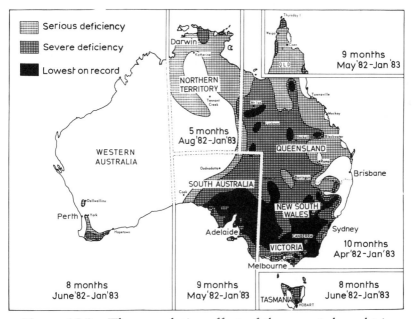

Figure 15.2   *The cumulative effect of the recent drought in south-eastern Australia*

extended over most of eastern and southern Australia. The only state that has so far escaped severe drought is Western Australia.

The effects of the drought have been exacerbated by a history of agricultural problems. From 1850 to 1900, as European immigrants settled much of Australia they introduced millions of cattle and sheep to what was often very marginal country and left behind a woeful legacy of rabbits and feral animals such as donkeys, camels, goats and pigs. Together with over-grazing by over-stocking, this led to a serious and continuing degradation of the land. About a third of the continent and more than half the country's farmlands are, as a result, now affected by soil erosion, and conservative estimates put the cost of "repair" at a billion dollars.

In the 1940s, a pattern of meteorological events similar to those of recent months resulted in millions of tonnes of top-soil being blown away in a series of devastating dust storms, and these storms are now being repeated. In Melbourne on the afternoon of 8 February 1983, the sky was completely blacked out for a while. The temperature in Melbourne before the storm was 43.2 °C, the highest ever recorded there in February.

Coming at a time of deep economic recession, the drought has affected the whole economy of Australia. The problems are typified by farmers growing rice and cotton on irrigated land in New South Wales. These are potentially lucrative crops, but they involve enormous inputs of capital and expensive investment in irrigation. Because of the drought, cotton farmers in north-western New South Wales are receiving only 10 per cent of their normal allocation of water from irrigation projects, while the cost of water has risen by as much as 30 per cent. Recent projections suggest a 36 per cent decline in this year's rice crop and a 22 per cent fall in cotton yield.

The situation is even more serious for beef and sugar production in Queensland and the Northern Territory, usually two of the country's most profitable exports. Cattle are in poor condition and many have been slaughtered; meanwhile, the wheat crop from the latest harvest was only 8.7 million tonnes, compared with 16.5 million tonnes in 1981/82. The bushfires of 16 February 1983 (ironically, Ash Wednesday) were simply the latest in a growing list of catastrophes.

Blocking the rain systems

So what caused all the problems? It would certainly be easier to mitigate the effects of such a drought if long-range forecasting could be made more effective, and although there is as yet no secure basis for the kind of forecasting required, an analysis of the causes of the latest drought offers some hope of explanations that may have predictive value in future. The meteorological factors that produce abnormal patterns of atmospheric circulation and suppress rainfall over eastern Australia are difficult to isolate. Very simply, persistent high pressure over eastern Australia and across to New Zealand has blocked the passage of rain-bearing low-pressure systems and their associated cold fronts northward out of

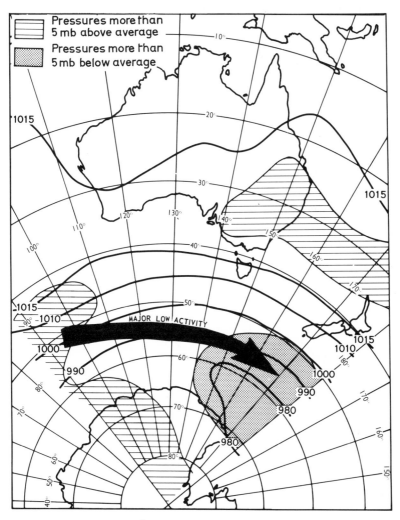

Figure 15.3 *The blocking high – November 1982*

the Antarctic (Figure 15.3). Superficially, this is a "blocking high" of the kind that brought prolonged drought to England and parts of continental Europe in 1976. The pattern at sea-level shown in Figure 15.3 also persisted in the upper atmosphere, with a high-pressure ridge helping to steer cyclones along trajectories much further south than usual.

There seems to be a link between these phenomena and the distribution of irregularities in atmospheric pressure and sea surface temperature across a large part of the southern hemisphere at low latitudes. The abnormally high pressures over Australia during the latest drought are part of a changing pattern called the "southern oscillation", a seesawing of pressure between the Australian region and the central Pacific Ocean. At one extreme of the southern oscillation the pressure over Australia is low and that over the Pacific is high; at the other extreme, as in 1982, the situation is reversed. During this drought the amplitude of this

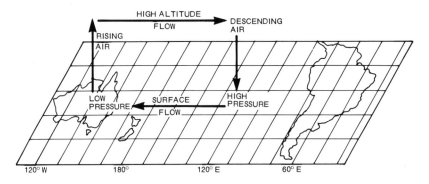

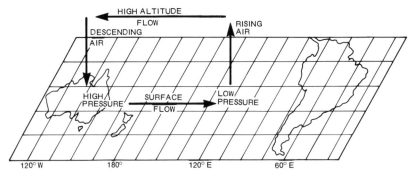

Figure 15.4   *The two modes of Walker circulation that form the southern oscillation*

effect has been bigger than at any time since reliable pressure records for the region were first taken 50 years ago.

The southern oscillation reverses irregularly, but typically at intervals of from two to five years. It has its own associated pattern of atmospheric circulation, named after Sir Gilbert Walker who identified it early in this century (Figure 15.4), and it is also associated with changes in the pattern of surface temperature. At present, with Walker circulation flowing west to east at low level there is warm surface water in the eastern Pacific and cool surface water in the west. The temperature pattern also reverses when the pattern of atmospheric pressure of the southern oscillation reverses. Patterns of air pressure, surface winds and sea surface temperatures are all interlinked. The sea surface temperatures of the Pacific switched from one state to the other as the Australian drought set in. Figure 15.5 shows the state in November 1982.

The warming in the eastern Pacific is known locally as El Niño, and the strong El Niño of 1983 has had severe effects on the local anchoveta fisheries off Peru (*New Scientist*, 10 March, p. 632). Unusually, however, the latest El Niño developed during May, rather than the usual season which is about five months later (see Below).

Indeed, there is a lack of knowledge about the causal mechanisms of climatic variability in general. Droughts in South Africa (see Below), changes in the southern oscillation, El Niño and other

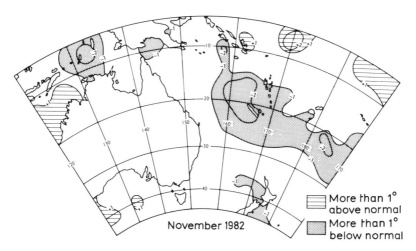

Figure 15.5 *Sea surface temperatures change in step with the southern oscillation*

facets of the circulation in the southern hemisphere are surely interlinked, but the complexity of the energy exchange between the ocean and the atmosphere is such that computer models cannot yet provide reliable forecasts of changes in phenomena such as the southern oscillation.

Meanwhile, the present Australian drought can be put in perspective by comparison with the five major droughts that hit the region in the previous 100 years, which is as far back as we have accurate meteorological records in Australia. The present drought is already one of the worst to affect south-eastern Australia in that time, and if it persists until May it will match anything in the record. That record also shows clear long-term trends, as well as fluctuations in rainfall and temperature. In a broad band of inland Australia covering Victoria, New South Wales and Queensland, average annual rainfall increased by 100 to 150 mm between 1946 and 1974. Does the present drought herald a reversal of that trend, or is it just an unusually large erratic fluctuation away from the norm? Either way, the best hope of predicting such events, and mitigating their impact, lies in a better understanding of the southern oscillation and its role in the circulation of the southern hemisphere.

7 April, 1983

THE ANALYSIS OF BAD TIMES

As well as the Australian drought, the southern hemisphere has experienced a series of extreme climatic events in the past year. Over the Pacific Ocean, the most significant change was the sudden onset of the pattern known as El Niño in May last year. This warm water flow in the eastern Pacific usually occurs near Christmas time, although its arrival is unpredictable and it does not come every year. In 1982 it arrived five months early and, in addition, was one of the strongest events of this kind observed in the present century. The effects of the fluctuation persisted throughout the year and into 1983, bringing 108 mm of rainfall at Guayaquil in Ecuador in November, compared with a normal figure of 8 mm, and 614 mm (normally 214 mm) at the same site in January 1983, compared with a record of 701 mm in January 1973, the only higher figure ever recorded there. Widespread flooding, loss of life, property damage and economic disruption has occurred across one-third of Ecuador.

As explained in the text these events are part of a pattern of distinctive changes in the temperature of the sea surface and pressure in the southern hemisphere. On past occasions, the warming of the eastern Pacific has been followed by a warming of the tropical Atlantic, and this typical sequence of events was completed in January 1983 as warm conditions ("positive sea surface temperature anomalies") began to be reported across the equatorial Atlantic.

Another feature of past episodes of warming in the eastern and equatorial Pacific has been the occurrence of droughts in the southern part of Africa and in north-east South America, and once again the present event shows no deviation from the pattern. Countries such as Botswana, Mozambique, Namibia, Swaziland, Zimbabwe, Zambia and the Republic of South Africa have all been affected. Since October last year, South Africa has been in the grip of serious drought, with agricultural production expected to decline by at least 700 million Rand. In January 1983, the water content of reservoirs in South Africa had fallen to 50 per cent of its level at the same time last year, and the 1982 maize crop was 40 per cent lower than the record of 40 million tonnes harvested in 1981. Last November, Zimbabwe ordered rice from North Korea because drought had disrupted the usual source of supply in Malawi, while Mozambique has been receiving aid in the form of rice from Japan.

These are just a few examples. The pattern of the connected climatic events in the southern hemisphere is nothing unusual, but its timing is and so is the strength of the phenomenon. Why should the southern oscillation have flipped, bringing El Niño in May rather than October or November? The temptation to link the change with the disruption to equatorial atmospheric conditions produced by the El Chichón eruption in April is strong, and lends weight to the argument of researchers at the University of East Anglia that the major effect of the volcano on climate occurred soon after the eruption. A related possibility is that the El Niño of 1982 was not the usual primary pulse of that event, but an unusually strong secondary pulse. Such secondary pulses have been observed at about this time of year after very strong El Niños in 1956, 1957 and 1972 – but this 1982 "secondary" would have been stronger than the "primary" it belongs to, again raising the question "why?"

But while the exact timing of this pattern of events was unusual, the return of the overall pattern in the early 1980s comes as little surprise to some researchers, who have been warning for several years that a new drought cycle was due. R. G. Vines, of CSIRO in Melbourne, is among the theorists who have analysed rainfall patterns over South Africa, Australia and New Zealand and found evidence of cyclic patterns including recurring severe droughts at roughly 20-year intervals. Such claims are always contentious in climatic circles, and opponents of the work claim that the cycles are not statistically significant, and criticise Vines's claim that the patterns correlate with changes in the Sun's activity. However, it is surely worth noting that in September 1980 the *South African Journal of Science* carried an article by Vines (vol. 76, p. 404) in which he considered the prospect of extended drought conditions in South Africa in the mid-1980s. "If the fluctuations in rainfall . . . continue as they have over approximately the past 90 years" he said "the development of drought at that time is to be expected (*as it is also in south-eastern Australia and New Zealand*)" (my italics).

7 April, 1983

16

Suicide in the desert

DEBORA MACKENZIE

Food stopped arriving at the Ethiopian port of Assab last week. Western donors are quoted as saying they had slackened the pace of relief shipments that will be needed to keep eight million Ethiopians from starving in the coming year, because of reports that Assab was overcrowded with food.

But the World Food Programme's emergency director Trevor Page said last month that there was no serious overcrowding or wastage at Assab. He warned that gaps in food shipments could mean starvation for thousands (*New Scientist*, 1 November, p. 3). Such a gap may now have developed.

The matter illustrates what many relief workers are starting to realise, that the prevention of mass starvation in Africa depends critically on timely assessment of food shortages. As the drought drags on, workers all over Africa are trying to come to grips with the data of disaster in time to keep the Ethiopian catastrophe from spreading to much of the continent.

The appropriate application of communication and transport technology can make all the difference between villages with failed crops, but enough food and seed to make it to the next planting season, and camps full of starving refugees. Luis Nunez of the League of Red Cross Societies says that despite the virtual failure of crops, two Red Cross organisers have managed to help 110 000 people in Senegal to avoid famine.

Meanwhile, crop failure in neighbouring Mauritania is driving 255 000 people to seek assistance, which 12 Red Cross workers can barely provide.

The difference, says Nunez, is that in Senegal food was distributed at the first signs of crop failure by well organised local authorities. It was not given to individuals, but to communities. Leaders of extended family groups of up to 60 people are given cards entitling them to rations from this store. Hence, says Nunez, many people have not left their homes to seek food in disease-ridden refugee camps.

In Mauritania the problem of getting relief to people early enough was complicated by a large nomadic population, which usually does not seek aid until faced with starvation. But the situation in Mali shows that even nomads can be reached early enough.

Across the Niger river from Timbuktu, where refugees from other areas of Mali are starting to accumulate, a group of Tamachek nomads took up village life a year ago, when they had lost most, but not all, of their cattle to drought.

Nock Ag Altia, a Tamachek leader, told French reporters that "it is not dishonourable to settle. It is dishonourable to lose all our animals, and have nothing to feed our families. We need material aid, but not camps".

With £18 000 from local aid workers, the Tamachek built a dam on the Niger marshes, and this year harvested 180 tonnes of rice from 76 hectares. Instead of selling it, they decided themselves to set up a long-term store, says Michel Sidibe of the French agency, Terre des Hommes.

But the difficulty of communication in Mali is shown by the fact that until this group was shown on French TV last week, the Red Cross officials supervising famine relief in Mali knew nothing about the project.

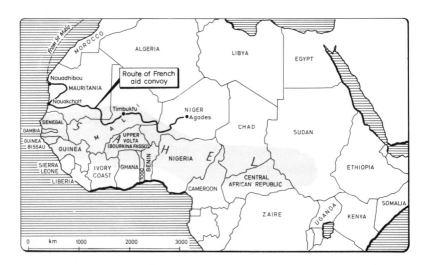

Figure 16.1   *The desert trail of death – and hope*

Workers farther north in Gao tell a different story. There, Tamacheks did not encounter aid until their last animals were dead. Desperate, and traditionally too proud to seek gifts of food, whole families are committing suicide in the desert, according to Nunez.

"In Mali we were a little late" says Nunez. The Red Cross is feeding 100 000 people at 180 centres in Gao province. "The problem was that people migrated much earlier than we expected, because they remembered the 1973 drought, when they moved too late" he says. This time, "the aid people all moved too late". If agencies had known things were getting bad when the people did, they might have moved in time.

But, says Nunez, "the big problem is that no one knows how many people there are, or where they are". The price of a goat had dropped to £2 in September, but on 30 September, the UN Food and Agriculture Organisation's report on Africa was still saying that despite "reports of severe malnutrition in Mali . . . crop production estimates and findings of the assessment missions . . . will be available only after several weeks, thus estimates of food air requirements for 1984/85 . . . have not yet been made."

Nunez outlines the difficulties. In December 1983 the Red Cross said Mali was not badly off, but the position could get worse. Last March, the rains failed. The Red Cross predicted the food problem would deteriorate in June. In July, it launched an appeal. The first food started arriving in early October, and cost $300 a tonne to ship overland from Togo.

Paul Dahan, in charge of the Red Cross's Sahel emergency unit, plans to speed the process by setting up a relief centre in Niamey, Niger, staffed with experts in both food aid and assistance in long-term projects. The centre will be linked by radio to national relief authorities in Mauritania, Mali, Chad, Sudan, Niger and Bourkina Fasso (Upper Volta), says Dahan, and will have a light plane to inspect and assess reported emergencies quickly.

To respond to them, he plans to provide a warehouse with buffer stocks of food and blankets. To keep supplies moving in from rich countries, he says the Niger authorities will provide a 24-hour computerised telephone and telefax link between Niamey and Geneva.

The famine is also worsening in Bourkina Fasso, with 640 000 people threatened in Yatenga province, and little aid on the way. So far, says Dahan, not many people have migrated. If other organisations move quickly, he says, some of the population may be kept from having to flee to camps.

Estimates of the people at risk from famine in Bourkina Fasso have risen with reports that 600 000 Burana people in the hitherto unaffected south have lost 70 per cent of their livestock, with a bull now fetching one-sixth its usual value in grain.

Oxfam and Norwegian church groups are distributing food in an effort to keep refugee camps from developing, but they say they will need 50 000 tonnes of grain to get through next year.

The drought in Chad has displaced more than 200 000 people, according to an official of the United Nations who has just returned from Africa. Djibril Diallo of the United Nations Development Programme said on Monday that the problem could only get worse. "Chad is just at the harvest period . . . if people are beginning to run away now because of crop failure, what happens when the dry season comes in two or three months?" According to Diallo the government of Chad is trying to contain the crisis by setting up four feeding centres around Ndjamena, the capital.

He visited one centre set up on fertile land exposed when the level of Lake Chad dropped. The World Food Programme is supplying food for some 15 000 people there in exchange for development work. But supplies of food – dished out at the rate of 4 kg of grain to each father and each mother every two weeks – "are getting very low". The main problem is transporting supplies into landlocked Chad. Food has to come in through Nigeria and Cameroon, but the infrastructures of both countries are overloaded.

One side effect of the drought has been to threaten communications across the river Chari, to the west of Ndjamena. All food from the outside must cross this river, but Diallo said that by January it would be too shallow for the ferry. The government is appealing through the UN for urgent funds to build a bridge.

Although the warning may have come early enough, aid groups will have trouble responding. In Ethiopia the UN's Kurt Janssen says that of the minimum of 800 000 tonnes needed to get the country through the next harvest, half has been promised, and a quarter delivered.

But the mouths to feed in the south keep multiplying. 700 000 Somali refugees have moved back into Ethiopia, whose government has announced that 2.5 million people will be resettled in the south from the stricken north next year. Aid officials, seeing the political implications of moving people out of the rebel-held northern area, have reacted warily to the plan.

It is not known if southern agriculture can support the influx.

Steve Davey of the Red Cross, who had just returned from Ethiopia, says "programmes to sustain proper land use", and prevent the erosion that cripples the north, "may be easier in the south and west, while Wollo [in the north] may be easier to reclaim with fewer people in it." As it is, he says, "Wollo now is about finished for agriculture."

29 November, 1984

PART FOUR

The Human Impact: Ozone

At the same time that our vulnerability to natural changes in climate began to become clear in the early 1970s, there was a growing realisation that human activities were now taking place on such a scale that they might begin to disturb the natural balance of the weather machine, and create new climatic conditions, unprecedented since life emerged onto the land. Early complacency that Nature – Gaia – could cope with the worst we could throw at her was followed by a pendulum swing of almost hysterical fear, especially in the United States, that Mankind might be about to destroy "the environment". The first supposed threat of this kind to emerge into the arena of public debate and influence politicians was the idea that the ozone layer, essential to the well being of life on the land surface of our planet, might be destroyed or severely damaged by unchecked use of chlorofluorocarbons, gases widely used in the early and middle 1970s as the propellants in aerosol spray cans. The argument raged throughout the decade. *New Scientist* never took sides on the issue, but tried to maintain a voice of sweet reason, reporting equally the claims and counter-claims from opposite sides of what became a sometimes bitter wrangle. On 2 October 1975 the magazine even devoted a special issue to the problems of the spray can and the ozone layer. By the end of the 1970s, the "threat to the ozone layer" seemed to have been more imagined than real. But in 1984 a new variation on the theme emerged, one that will undoubtedly cause more head scratching for the experts in the years ahead.

17

Aerosol sprays and the ozone shield

SHERRY ROWLAND

During the past few years, several potential man-made threats to the stability of the ozone layer have been widely discussed – the stratospheric flight of fleets of supersonic aircraft (SSTs), the atmospheric testing of nuclear weapons, and now the accumulation in the atmosphere of the chlorofluoromethane gases, CF_2CL_2 and $CFCL_3$. Both substances are commonly used as propellants in aerosol sprays, and CF_2Cl_2 is the most widely used refrigerant gas. Annual world-wide production of the two gases is now approaching one megaton. The common thread of all of these hazards is the release in the stratosphere of free radicals capable of attacking ozone and its precursor, atomic oxygen, by catalytic chain processes through which a single free radical can remove hundreds or even thousands of ozone molecules before being itself removed. With the SSTs and nuclear weapons, the free radical chains involve catalysis by NO_x – the nitrogen oxides, NO and NO_2. Chlorofluoromethanes are themselves highly inert chemically, and do not react directly with ozone or with ordinary oxygen atoms. However, after absorption of short-wavelength ultra-violet radiation (1900–2250 Å), each chlorofluoromethane decomposes with the release of free radical atomic chlorine, which attacks ozone through the catalytic chain reactions:

$$Cl + O_3 \rightarrow ClO + O_2 \qquad (1)$$

$$ClO + O \rightarrow Cl + O_2 \qquad (2)$$

The release of these chain carriers does not await the deployment either of large SST fleets or the explosion of large numbers of nuclear weapons in the atmosphere, but is already occurring as a by-product of current consumer technology.

Several recent appraisals of chlorofluoromethanes in the environment have been extensively discussed in the US and around the world, and led to the appointment by the US National Academy of Sciences of an *Ad Hoc* Panel on Stratospheric Effects of Chloro-fluoromethanes. At its meeting in late October this five-member panel concluded that the problem is serious, and should be given immediate attention by the Academy itself. Consideration of the panel recommendations is already underway.

The chlorofluoromethane threat to the ozone layer was origi-nally outlined in an article in *Nature* in June by Mario J. Molina and the author (vol. 249, p. 810). The key steps in the analysis are listed below.

(1) These gases have long atmospheric lifetimes because their chemical and biological inertness, as well as their relative insolubility in water, prevent rapid removal by tropospheric processes.

(2) Although unable to decompose by absorption of Solar radia-tion penetrating to the troposphere, each can decompose above 25 km because of a partial stratospheric "window" allowing ultra-violet radiation in the 1900–2250 Å range to reach into the middle stratosphere.

(3) Ultra-violet photolysis of these molecules releases Cl atoms in the stratosphere, and initiates the free radical chains.

(4) The 1972 world production rates (0.5 Mta^{-1} for CF_2Cl_2 and 0.3 Mta^{-1} for $CFCl_3$) were already large enough to have major effects on the ozone level when the atmosphere becomes saturated with them.

The long atmospheric residence time has been established experimentally by direct measurement of tropospheric concentra-tions in remote areas throughout the world. The problem is inter-national in scope not only because the atmosphere mixes globally, but also because industrial production has spread to many coun-tries. Originally manufactured under the DuPont trademark Freon, these chemicals are now made and distributed under a variety of identifying names in all major industrial countries of the world.

Long-term effects

Both ozone and molecular oxygen can also absorb 1900–2250 Å radiation, and the chlorofluoromethanes must diffuse upward above most of the ozone and oxygen before encountering such radiation in any appreciable strength. Vertical diffusion in the stratosphere is relatively slow, and Molina and I estimated that these molecules would survive in the Earth's atmosphere for an average of 40 to 150 years prior to stratospheric photolysis. Usage of these materials has doubled every five to seven years since 1950, and the amounts now in the atmosphere are far short of the concentrations to be expected in the future, even without further increases in production. We calculated that the concentrations of these compounds, assuming usage held at the 1972 rates, would be 15 to 20 times larger in the twenty-first century than it is now. Such greatly increased concentrations of chlorofluoromethanes would then be sufficient for ClO_x catalysis to replace catalysis by natural NO_x as the dominant removal process for ozone above 30 km. The calculations also outlined some special aspects of this environmental problem – the effects on the ozone layer will continue to increase rapidly with time; there is a delay period of some years before the observation of the maximum effects; and any changes in the ozone layer will continue to be observable through most of the next century because of the long atmospheric lifetimes.

Chlorine atoms are also able to react with molecules such as CH_4, H_2 and H_2O_2 and with the free radical HO_2 to form HCl, although the reaction with ozone is a thousand times more probable than all of these other reactions together throughout most of the stratosphere. The HCl formed by these reactions can itself be attacked by free OH radicals with the formation and the re-release of the Cl atoms to begin the chains anew. In the stratosphere, the sequence of reactions (1) plus (2) requires less than two minutes, and will continue until the chain is temporarily terminated by the formation of HCl, or permanently ended by downward diffusion of the chlorine species (HCl, ClO or Cl) into the weathering processes of the troposphere. At all altitudes, the concentration of HCl is calculated to exceed that of Cl plus ClO, with ozone removal occurring ony during the Cl/ClO parts of the chemical cycle.

This overall photochemical/kinetic sequence has now been examined in greater detail for the chlorofluoromethanes by ourselves at Irvine, and by three additional research groups: P. Crutzen of the US National Center for Atmospheric Research (on leave from the University of Stockholm); Ralph Cicerone, Richard Stolarski and Stacy Walters of the University of Michigan; and S. C. Wofsy, M. B. McElroy and N. Sze of Harvard. The latter three groups were among the many involved in the Climatic Impact

Assessment Program (CIAP), a three-year major investigation of the stratosphere with emphasis on the potential impact on the ozone layer of the NO_x programme, these three groups had already begun consideration of stratospheric chlorine from other possible sources, and were readily able to include the chlorofluoromethanes in their calculations. Some of the other chlorine sources are natural (sea-salt; volcanic activity), while others are man-made (industrial release of HCl; the proposed US space shuttle). However, all are much less important stratospheric sources of chlorine atoms than Solar photolysis of the chlorofluoromethanes.

Ozone depletion estimates

Estimates have now been made by these four groups of the worldwide average ozone depletion and/or its growth with time for continuing atmospheric release of the chlorofluoromethanes. The calculated average ozone depletion for saturation at the 1972 usage rate has varied from 7 to 18 per cent. When more realistic projections of technological intentions – for example, a continuation of the 10 per cent growth per year since the 1950s – are put into the calculations, considerably higher eventual ozone depletion rates are predicted. These calculations indicate that the ClO_x now in the stratosphere from photodissociation of CF_2Cl_2 and $CFCl_2$ is already causing approximately a one per cent average depletion in the ozone shield, a amount that is completely undetectable because of the natural variability in ozone concentration at individual stations. Predictions for the near future indicate three to six per cent depletion effects in the 1980s depending to some extent on the pattern of usage in the next decade.

Even if further release of the compounds to the atmosphere were to cease immediately, the calculated ozone depletion would still rise to double its present value five to ten years from now, after ClO_x species have diffused upward to the critical 30–50 km altitudes. Any maximum effect on ozone occurs about a decade or so after further release has been discontinued because of the built-in time delay for diffusion to the high stratosphere. Furthermore, the tropospheric reservoir will continue to diffuse molecules into the stratosphere to be photo-dissociated with a half-life for CF_2Cl_2 removal of about 70–100 years. Therefore, any level of ozone depletion once reached will be maintained well into the next century even with no further atmospheric release – a ten per cent depletion in the year 2010 would carry a four to five per cent effect into the twenty-second century.

The discrepancies among these various calculations lie chiefly in the assumptions made about rates of vertical circulation in the stratosphere, a subject of active concern among aeronomists. The search for other chemicals sinks or reactions has not yet turned up any with more than minor influence on the overall description of stratospheric chlorine chemistry. The laboratory measurements of the pertinent chemical reaction rates appear to be in reasonable order. Fortuitously, fundamental studies of Cl and ClO chemistry, including reactions 1 and 2 as well as some others of interest, were begun a few years ago by Dr M. A. A. Clyne and his collaborators at Queen Mary College, London. Their determinations of accurate kinetic rate constants for these reactions appeared almost simulataneously with the discovery of their relevance to stratospheric chemistry. The intensive CIAP has also greatly increased both the knowledge of stratospheric chemistry, and the ability to describe this chemistry with models capable of quantitative predictions of reasonable accuracy.

Ozone is continually formed in the stratosphere by the action of sunlight on molecular oxygen, which is split into two atoms of oxygen, each of which then adds to another molecule of oxygen to form ozone, O_3. The amount of ozone present in the atmosphere is determined by the balance between this process of formation and its destruction by chemical reactions among the reative species present. Ozone averages less than one part per million in the entire atmosphere, and is found almost entirely in the stratosphere at altitudes between 10 and 40 km. This thin layer of ozone is involved in two important atmospheric phenomena. First, it intercepts much of the Solar ultra-violet radiation and prevents it from reaching the surface of the Earth – between 2400 and 3000 Å, ozone is essentially the only atmospheric material acting as an absorber. Second, the absorption of this radiation, plus some in the visible and infra-red parts of the spectrum, raises the temperature of the stratosphere such that the 50 km temperature is usually 60–70 °C warmer than the temperatures characteristic of the 10–20 km level (about 210 °C). The resulting temperature structure is important in influencing the circulation patterns for the stratosphere.

Thinning of the ozone layer would permit increased penetration to the surface of ultra-violet radiation, particularly in the biologically important region near 2900–3000 Å. Current estimates from the CIAP indicate that a five per cent average depletion in ozone would result in 40 000 additional cases of skin cancer per year in the US alone. In addition, there are other possible biological effects of increased ultra-violet radiation which cannot readily be either calculated or dismissed as negligible – effects on plants, insects, plankton, absorption in DNA molecules, etc.

Substantial changes in either the amount of ozone or in its distribution would introduce changes in the stratospheric temperature structure, and probably in stratospheric circulation. Whether such changes in the stratosphere would influence tropospheric circulation patterns and perhaps lead to some climatic changes is quite uncertain. The CIAP has included attempts to evaluate these additional possible biological and climatic effects, but the current basic data and theory seem insufficient for any definite conclusions to be reached within the next few years.

The concern for chlorofluoromethanes in the stratosphere can be traced to their detection in the troposphere in urban England in 1971 by James Lovelock, then at the University of Reading. A subsequent shipboard survey by Lovelock through the North and South Atlantic disclosed that $CFCl_3$ had become a conveniently measurable component of the entire world troposphere. Its potential value as a tracer for atmospheric and oceanic circulation patterns has led to numerous additional measurements of $CFCL_3$ concentrations by Lovelock, by a group from the US Naval Research Laboratory, and by others. These measurements have confirmed not only that $CFCl_3$ is everywhere, but also that its concentration is rising rapidly – the $CFCl_3$ concentration was 35 per cent higher in February 1974 than in November 1972, in NRL measurements of East Pacific surface air. Although CF_2Cl_2 has also been detected in even larger amounts, the sensitivity of detection for this molecule by electron capture gas chromatography is about 50 times less than for $CFCl_3$ and the data for CF_2Cl_2 are thus both less numerous and less precise. The concentrations of each compound are now approximately one part in 10^{10} in the troposphere. The atmospheric longevity of $CFCl_3$ can be estimated separately by a comparison of the amount of this compound actually manufactured to date with the amount present in the troposphere, as almost all of it is released within a few months of production. The tropospheric concentrations correspond to a minimum lifetime longer than 20 years.

Most ClO_x catalysed removal of ozone is calculated to occur between 30 and 50 km. However, no concentration measurements for any Cl-containing species have yet been successful above about 20 km and requests for more comprehensive data generally focus on *in situ* stratospheric measurements of Cl, ClO, HCl, CF_2Cl_2 and/or $CFCl_3$. The predicted stratospheric profiles for both FC_2Cl_2 and $CFCl_3$ show a rapid fall-off in concentration above the tropopause as a consequence of the Solar photo-dissociation sink, with only small amounts left at 30 km or higher. Measurements by Lovelock in the low stratosphere do show a fall-off in $CFCl_3$ immediately above the tropopause, suggesting the reality of the proposed ultra-violet sink. Attempts to detect HCl in the stratosphere have not yet been successful, while no searches have yet been made for ClO or Cl. It may be several years before such measurements can be made successfully above 25 km.

Several other halogenated molecules are detectable in the troposphere, especially in urban regions, reflecting their release by Man. Of these the most potent stratospheric threat is probably carbon tetrachloride, CCl_4, originally widely used as a cleaning agent, and measurably present in the stratosphere in concentrations also of about one part in 10^{16}. Estimates of the stratospheric effect from photo-dissociation of CCl_4 indicate that there is an additional one per cent average global depletion of ozone from this source. However, the direct release of CCl_4 to the atmosphere now occurs in quantities much less than those of CF_2Cl_2 and $CFCl_3$, and the atmospheric concentration is probably near the saturation level for the current release rate of CCl_4. Lovelock has suggested that CCl_4 might even be of natural origin, which would also imply saturation. Consequently, substantial increases in calculated ozone depletion from CCl_4 are not expected in the future barring a major increase in its technological release to the atmosphere.

Other chlorinated molecules such as CH_3CCl_3, $CHCl = CCl_2$ and $CCl_2 = CCl_2$, among others, are also released to the atmosphere in quantities approaching 0.1 megaton/year or more. However, there is evidence that these molecules have short lifetimes in the troposphere, and are consequently much less important as potential stratospheric problems. The molecules containing carbon–carbon double bonds can react rapidly with OH radicals in the troposphere and be removed by this process and probably by other reactions as well. Similarly, compounds containing carbon–hydrogen bonds are also susceptible to attack through reaction with OH to form water and should also have relatively short tropospheric lifetimes. The presence of these bonds in halocarbon molecules and such as $CHFCl_2$, CHF_2Cl and CH_2FCl should likewise make them vulnerable to attack and removal by OH radicals in the troposphere. These three compounds are all available commercially, but are used in rather small quantities. In some uses, especially refrigeration, it may be possible to substitute one of these hydrogen-containing compounds for CF_2Cl_2 or $CFCl_2$ with far less stratospheric hazard.

A modest research programme into potential environmental problems with the chlorofluromethanes has been supported for several years by the Manufacturing Chemists' Association, and has thus far concentrated primarily on tropospheric measurements, on their photochemical properties, and on possible tropospheric sinks. Work at the University of California, Riverside, has shown no measurable loss of the chlorofluoromethanes in simulated urban smoggy atmospheres, as well as no indication of biological interactions. Both CF_2Cl_2 and $CFCl_3$ have been shown by other research at Riverside to react rapidly with excited single-state oxygen atoms, and removal by this route constitutes a small additional stratospheric sink for the chlorofluoromethanes. The MCA programme is being expanded to include stratospheric measurements, but a spokesman has indicated that no experiments in the middle or upper stratosphere are expected for several years. The indications are strong, however, that substantial increases can be expected in the near future in US government support for stratospheric chlorine research.

5 December, 1974

US ACTION ON CHLOROFLUOROMETHANES

The annual production in the United States of the two principal chlorofluoromethanes rose from about 740 million lb in 1972 to over 810 million lb in 1973. A large fraction of this total is discharged into the atmosphere from aerosol sprays. On the basis of the evidence summarised in Professor Rowland's article that such compounds pose a threat to the ozone layer, the Natural Resources Defense Council has petitioned the Consumer Product Safety Commission to declare the chlorofluoromethanes to be "banned hazardous substances", thus prohibiting their manufacture and distribution.

The Commission, a body set up two years ago in response to growing demands for national consumer safety standards, is an independent regulatory agency whose job it is to formulate and enforce new product safety standards and, where necessary, to remove dangerous products from the American market-place. The Commission must grant or deny the Council's petition within 120 days of its date of filing.

In a separate development, the same week as the Council's petition, the National Academy of Sciences announced on 21 November that it was to convene a special panel "to evaluate critically the existing relevant data and calculations and to recommend further research". The panel is to set out "the scientific basis for a public decision" within a year. This panel will replace the NAS *Ad Hoc* Committee, of which Professor Rowland is a member and which, as he admits, "contains too many district attorneys and not enough judges".

Reaction from the aerosol industry has been low-keyed so far. The Aerosol Education Bureau has issued a statement, quoting Dr Raymond McCarthy, head of the Freon Products Division of DuPont, the biggest manufacturer of the chlorofluoromethanes, in which it was announced that several major studies coordinated by the Manufacturing Chemists' Association will be commissioned to check into the "hypothesis'.

According to D. McCarthy, "until the first results of the industry research are obtained, the available facts do not rank as proof. All we have now are assumptions without experimental evidence. It would be an injustice if a few claims, which even the critics agree are hypotheses, were to be the basis of regulatory or consumer reaction".

Rowland is unimpressed by the industry's stance. He points out that while it has been aware of his calculations since February, it has been unable to demonstrate any flaws. All the available evidence – which he agrees is incomplete – points to an effect in the stratosphere of the propellant gases; the industry has not evidence to the contrary. Rowland himself gave up using aerosol products a year ago.

5 December, 1974

BRITISH VIEWPOINTS

In *Nature* of 22 November (p. 292), there was a paper by James Lovelock, whose earlier work Rowland cites. In this paper, "Atmospheric halocarbons and stratospheric ozone", Lovelock, in referring to his earlier work, wrote: "In our paper on the distribution of halocarbons over the Atlantic we unwisely commented: 'The presence of these compounds (the fluorochlorocarbons) constitutes no conceivable hazard'. It may be as unwise to assume that we are now at an early stage of a serious global pollution incidence". However, when I spoke to him last week, Lovelock pointed out that this paper had been sent to *Nature* in July, and that he was now not so confident about the latter statement.

Commenting on Rowland's article, he said that he felt it might not go far enough in some directions. Lovelock earlier this year went to Cape Town to measure the concentrations of various compounds in the atmosphere, because "there is no possibility of species getting to Cape Town if they don't get into the stratosphere". He found lots of methylchloroform there, and believes that to have travelled from industrialised regions to Cape Town it must be a long-lived species. Similarly, he feels that methyl chloride may be present in the atmosphere in large quantities, formed by the reaction between methyl iodide (manufactured by sea-weeds) and sea-water; however, present apparatus can detect methyl chloride only at high levels. One of the problems, Lovelock points out, is the way in which research is currently limited to substances one can measure with adequate sensitivity.

A spokesman for the British Aerosol Manufacturers' Association at the end of last week echoed the comments of the American association (as reported in the preceding section), and said that he felt the current situation had been well summed up by Professor Richard Scorer in his recent letter to *New Scientist* (10 October, p. 140). The spokesman estimated that about two-thirds of the propellant gas used in aerosol in Britain was chlorofluorocarbons, and that the total annual usage was probably about one-tenth that in the United States.

5 December, 1974

18

Chlorofluoromethanes and stratospheric ozone – a scientific status report

SHERRY ROWLAND

The chlorofluoromethane compounds, CCl_2F_2 and CCl_3F, are essentially inert in the lower atmosphere, but eventually rise into the stratosphere and are dissociated by Solar ultra-violet radiation with the release of chlorine atoms. These chlorine atoms then catalyse a chain reaction resulting in partial depletion of ozone in the stratosphere. If ozone were to be depleted, the environmental effects would include an increase in human skin cancer, uncertain effects on other biological species, and uncertain effects on the world's climate. That is a brief summary of the "fluorocarbon ozone depletion" theory postulated by Dr Mario Molina and me in the 28 June 1974 issue of *Nature* on the basis of calculations that were described more completely by us in *Reviews of Geophysics and Space Physics* in February 1975. A description was also published in the *New Scientist* on 5 December 1974.

These scientific deductions have been described by their detractors as "hypothesis", "speculation", and "utter nonsense". Nevertheless they have formed the backbone for passage of laws concerning the further atmospheric release of these compounds in the states of Oregon and New York; for consideration in the US Congress and very recently by international organisations; and were stated, in June 1975, to be "a legitimate cause for concern" by a 14-agency scientific task-force of the US government.

In early 1974 no successful measurements of any chlorine-containing compounds had been reported in the stratosphere and relatively few in the troposphere. Some of the other input into the original theory was also based on a minimum of evidence, although Dr Molina and I felt it was adequate. Of course, the possibility existed that some important pieces of stratospheric chemistry, either known or unknown, had been omitted from the calculations and that their discovery and inclusion would alter and perhaps invalidate the estimates of ozone depletion.

Both our group and numerous other scientific groups have been examining these details for the past 15 months, and a substantial amount of new information is available. This article summarises the scientific evidence accumulated during this intensive period of research as it affects several basic postulates of the theory. The environmental consequences of ozone depletion had already been the subject of intensive investigation because of concern for nitrogen oxides released into the stratosphere by high-altitude aircraft. The reports of these investigations are now becoming available.

(1) The molecules CCl_3F and CCl_2F_2 are essentially inert toward environmental reactions in the lower atmosphere and are accumulating there.

Measurements of tropospheric concentrations of CCl_3F by Peter Wilkniss *et al* of the US Naval Research Laboratory and by James Lovelock have shown a steady increase, with a present concentration of about one part in 10^{10}. Although more difficult to measure, CCl_2F_2 has been established to be present at about two parts in 10^{10}. There are no indications of a natural source for either compound.

About 90 per cent of CCl_3F is released to the atmosphere within six months of manufacture, and a comparison of present observed concentrations versus total world manufacture to date indicates almost all of it is still in the atmosphere. A lower limit of about 30 years can be placed on the atmospheric lifetime of CCl_3F. Similar comparisons cannot be made for CCl_2F_2 because much of this compound is used as a refrigerant, with an uncertain time delay before release to the atmosphere.

No quantitatively important tropospheric removal reactions have been identified, and all off the evidence is consistent with a stratospheric sink being of prime importance.

(2) Both chlorofluoromethane gases rise into the stratosphere and are decomposed at altitudes between roughly 15 and 40 km. CCl_3F decomposes at a lower altitude than CCl_2F_2 because the former reacts more readily with Solar ultra-violet radiation.

The mixing ratio of CCl_3F versus altitude was predicted in July

1974. Atmospheric samples have been returned to the ground for measurement after collection with high-altitude aircraft, balloons and a rocket. For the concentrations of CCl_3F versus altitude measured by two separate research groups, the agreement between theory and observation is good. CCl_2F_2 is observed to penetrate further upward into the stratosphere, as anticipated, but was not found at 50 km in the sample collected by rocket. These stratospheric measurements demonstrate that these molecules *do* decompose in the region of intense Solar ultra-violet radiation.

(3) CCl_3F and CCl_2F_2 are decomposed by ultra-violet radiation in the 190–215 nm band, with the release of Cl atoms.

Four separate research groups have now shown that one Cl atom splits away immediately each time a quantum of ultra-violet radiation is absorbed. Furthermore, products are found in laboratory experiments that indicate that a second chlorine atom is detached during the reaction with O_2 of the residual free radical (e.g. $CClF_2$ from CCl_2F_2). It is therefore certain that chlorine atoms are being released in the stratosphere by the photo-decomposition of CCl_3F and CCl_2F_2.

(4) The important chemical reactions for chlorine in the stratosphere are those summarised in the diagram:

$$HCl \underset{CH_4,H_2}{\overset{OH}{\rightleftarrows}} Cl \underset{O,NO}{\overset{O_3}{\rightleftarrows}} ClO$$

Accurate knowledge is required of the concentration of O_3 O, NO, OH, CH_4, and H_2; *and* of the reaction rates for these six reactions at stratospheric temperatures. New measurements of the reaction rates have been attained for all six of these reactions, often by several separate research groups. The most important fact to note is that the original estimates of reaction rates were all correct within a factor of two, i.e. no major errors had been made in the original measurements. For quantitative estimates, of course, factors of two are important and the new measurements provide more accurate input data for such calculations. The reaction of Cl with O_3 is slower than previously believed (less O_3 depletion); that of Cl with CH_4 probably faster (less O_3 depletion); that of OH and HCl certainly faster (more O_3 depletion). The best estimates for the other reaction rates are approximately as measured earlier.

The concentrations of O_3, CH_4, H_2 and NO had all been rather satisfactorily measured earlier. However, neither O nor OH had been adequately measured in the stratosphere by the summer of 1974. James Anderson of the University of Michigan has now measured both O and OH in separate experiments in mid-stratosphere. The measured O atom concentrations are in good agreement with those used in the model calculations. The OH concentrations have previously been estimated within a threefold range of values in similar model calculations. The initial quantitative estimates of ozone depletion used the low OH value from this range. The OH concentration measured by Anderson is in the middle-to-high part of this range (more O_3 depletion).

(5) Gaseous HCl is the predominant chlorine-containing decomposition product at most stratospheric altitudes, but increases in mixing ratio with increasing altitude.

When all of the rate constants and molecular concentrations are combined with one another, the distribution of chlorine among HCl, ClO and Cl can be estimated at each altitude. An approximate calculated distribution of HCl, ClO and Cl from CCl_2F_2 has been obtained. The most important features of this estimate are:

(1) HCl is the predominant chlorine species throughout;
(2) the mixing ratio of HCl *increases* with altitude;
(3) ClO is expected above 25 km; and
(4) Cl, which reacts very rapidly with the relatively abundant O_3, is always in low concentration.

During the past year Allan Lazrus of the National Center for Atmospheric Research (NCAR) has measured HCl profiles by reaction with a base-coated filter carried aloft by aircraft or balloon. The HCl mixing ratio increases with altitude, indicating a stratospheric source of chlorine atoms above 20 km. The mixing ratio of HCl is about one part in 10^9 at 25 km and above.

C. B. Farmer of the Jet Propulsion Laboratory has also found similar amounts of HCl and a mixing ratio increasing with altitude by direct spectroscopic detection – thereby confirming that the chlorine found on the Lazrus filters was indeed present in the stratosphere as gaseous HCl. Both experimenters have found much lower levels of HCl at the bottom of the stratosphere indicating that direct injection of chloride through the tropopause plays a very minor role. Such injection has been postulated for chlorine in sea-salt (which Lazrus would have caught on the filters as well) and from volcanoes.

Lazrus has also used neutral filters in his aircraft and balloon experiments. Below 20 km these filters collect the particles of sulphuric acid present in the stratosphere, but retain negligible amounts of chlorine. Above 25 km, however, the neutral filters also collect some chlorine, indicating the presence of another species in addition to HCl. This species has not been positively identified, but its chemical reactivity is consistent with a free radical such as ClO. The presence of other stable chloro-acids (e.g. perchloric acid, $HOClO_3$) in appreciable quantity has been ruled out experimentally by the coincidence in the Lazrus experiments between measured total chlorine (neutron activation analysis) and HCl (colorimetric analysis for $Cl-$).

(6) No quantitatively important stratospheric chlorine chemistry has been omitted.

The proof of the absence of unknown additional reactions is always difficult because of the nebulous nature of the procedure. Various ion-molecule reactions have been suggested despite the low concentration of stratospheric ions and the relatively low reactivity of the cluster ions that predominate, and other possibilities have occasionally been put forth.

However, since HCl, ClO and Cl are all rapidly interconnected by the chemical reactions shown above, any as-yet-undiscovered reaction that might drain off ClO or Cl into some as-yet-unidentified product would of necessity *also* rapidly drain off the HCl as well. The very presence of HCl at the 1 in 10^9 level is strong proof that no massive alternate stratospheric sink exists for the chain carriers ClO and Cl.

The amounts of HCl anticipated at various altitudes can be estimated from the sums given for each of the stratospherically important organochlorine compounds. The four major contributors to stratospheric HCl at present are methyl chloride (CH_3Cl), carbon tetrachloride (CCl_4) and the two chlorofluoromethanes (CCl_3F and CCl_2F_2). Perhaps the most frequently heard erroneous assumption in connection with this problem is that the presence of natural chlorine compounds (e.g. CH_3Cl) reduces or eliminates the effect of the addition of anthropogenic chlorine compounds such as CCl_3F or CCl_2F_2. The natural ozone balance is maintained through its creation by the action of solar UV on O_2, and its removal chiefly by NO_x catalysis but also by HO_x catalysis, direct reaction, and by a small amount of ClO_x catalysis. All of the calculations show that, whatever these removal processes, the injection of more NO_x (as by SSTs) or ClO_x (through CCl_2F_2 and CCl_3F) will result in a depletion of the average level of ozone. The amount of HCl found by Lazrus and by Farmer is in good agreement with that expected from the tropospheric chlorocarbon measurements of Lovelock, Rasmussen, Hantz, Wilkniss and their co-workers.

It should be recognised that there is still some disagreement in the appropriate instrumental calibrations, especially for OCl_2F_2, and in the global assay for CH_3Cl. In addition, the reaction of OH with HCl is so slow, especially below 25 km, that considerable fluctuation around the average concentrations might occur as air packets are transported considerable distances without equilib-

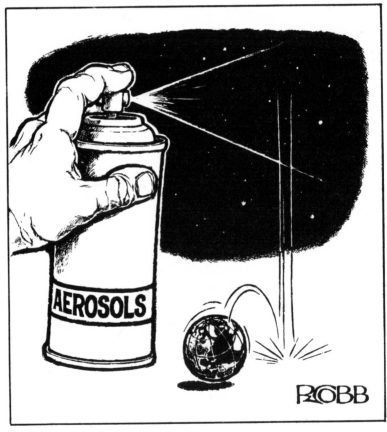

(Credit: R. Cobb, reproduced by courtesy LA Free Press)

ration. Despite these potential sources for discrepancies the agreement between estimated and measured HCl versus altitude is quite good.

When molecules such as CCl_2F_2 and CCl_3F are decomposed, new fluorine-containing species must also be formed in the stratosphere. Zander of Liege has now positively identified HF at 30 km and above, confirming the presence of the expected fluorine sink.

Calculations of ozone depletion

In summary, there now exists a substantial number of actual stratospheric data on several chlorine- and fluorine-containing species, all of it in good agreement with the original hypothesis. As these data have accumulated a fundamental change has taken place. In June 1974, we presented a plausible, detailed description of the stratospheric chlorine chemistry of the chlorofluoromethanes based on the known laboratory properties of CCl_2F_2 and CCl_3F, and on stratospheric observations involving Solar radiation and chemical compounds not containing chlorine. The existence of a chain reaction removing ozone in appreciable amounts through ClO_x catalysis is now a straightforward deduction not only from laboratory data but also from direct stratospheric observational data.

Semi-quantitative comparisons can be made of the relative rates of O_3 removal by the natural processes of NO_x catalysis, HO_x catalysis and direct reaction of O with O_3, and by anthropogenic removal through ClO_x catalysis. The ClO_x chain of reactions (1) and (2) has its NO_x chain counterpart in (3) and (4):

$$Cl + O_3 \rightarrow ClO + O_2 \tag{1}$$

$$ClO + O \rightarrow Cl + O_2 \tag{2}$$

$$NO + O_3 \rightarrow NO_2 + O_2 \tag{3}$$

$$NO_2 + O \rightarrow NO + O_2. \tag{4}$$

Good estimates of the importance of these two chains and of the direct reaction (5)

$$O_3 + O \rightarrow 2O_2 \tag{5}$$

can be made by calculating the relative rates of removal of O atoms by NO_2, O_3 and ClO. The concentrations of O, NO_2 and

O_3 are known by direct measurement and the steadily increasing concentrations of ClO can be readily predicted for the future from the measurements detailed above. Such a comparison clearly indicates a quantitatively important role for anthropogenic ClO_x catalysis as additional chlorofluoromethane molecules continue to be released to the atmosphere.

The procedure for quantitative calculation of the amounts of ozone that will be removed by such reactions have been thoroughly developed by more than a dozen research groups in the past few years for application to the stratospheric injection of NO_x in the exhaust of supersonic transport aircraft. The agreement among various calculations is now quite satisfactory when applied to a specified set of input data. Many of these same groups have now adapted these calculations to the ClO_x problem by inclusion of the appropriate chlorine equations. These quantitative evaluations are most sensitive to the rates of the six reactions listed under point (4) as they influence the fraction of time chlorine is found as HCl, ClO and Cl, respectively. The chain removal of O_3 is carried on by Cl. ClO, while bound as HCl, is temporarily inactive insofar as ozone depletion is concerned. Permanent removal of the chlorine occurs as the HCl/ClO/Cl equilibrium eventually drifts down to the troposphere and is removed by processes such as rainout.

The initial evaluations of ozone depletion a year ago led to an estimate of a present depletion of about 1 per cent, and a long-term steady-state depletion of 7–13 per cent for continued atmospheric release of the fluorocarbons at 1972 rates. As indicated above, some of the newly measured rate constants and concentrations tend to decrease ozone depletion and some tend to increase it. However, when these new data are all put into the calculation the increasing and decreasing trends have approximately cancelled one another and the original estimates are basically unchanged.

Fluorocarbon use has increased about 13 per cent per year for about two decades and continued to rise in 1973. In late 1974 and 1975, the rate of production levelled off and actually began to decrease, primarily as the result of the world-wide recession obut in the US also reflecting in part a decline in consumer demand for fluorocarbon-propelled aerosol sprays. Long-term atmospheric release at rates exceeding the 1972 levels would, of course, lead to still higher ozone depletions than those indicated above.

All of the calculations published so far have used a simple one-dimensional model in which motion is considered only in a vertical direction and average values of concentrations over latitude and longitude are used. In the comparable SST calculations the introduction of 2D (adding latitude) and 3D (adding longitude) models gave approximately the same average calculated ozone depletions for specified input data while providing data on variations with latitude and longitude. Preliminary results are now available from two multi-dimensional models and both indicate substantial ozone depletion effects at all latitudes. These initial calculations with multi-dimensional models have confirmed the general validity of the 1D calculations of average ozone-depletion, while indicating somewhat higher depletion than the 1D model results for comparable input data.

Two important timescales emerge from the 1D calculations. The time delay of a few years while rising through the stratosphere ensures that concentrations in the 30–50 km region (and therefore ozone depletion) will continue to increase for about a decade after further tropospheric release of the compounds has ceased. The calculated atmospheric lifetimes range from 40-150 years (and the observed one for CCl_3F is about 30 years), long enough that we already know that the compounds will still be present in the atmosphere for most of the twenty-first century.

The absorption cross sections of these molecules for ultra-violet radiation are somewhat temperature dependent, with less absorption than earlier calculated at stratospheric temperatures. When corrected for these temperature effects, however, the average atmospheric lifetimes of these molecules are only about ten per cent longer. Inclusion of the small contribution from $O(1D)$ (singlet oxygen) attack on CCl_2F_2 in the stratosphere, on the other hand, shortens the calculated average atmospheric lifetime by a few per cent.

Consequences of ozone depletion

The possible consequences of ozone depletion have been very intensively studied for the past few years in connection with evaluation of the environmental effects expected from supersonic aircraft. These concerns have been described in detail in the report of the Climatic Impact Committee of the US National Academy of Sciences, *Environmental Impact of Stratospheric Flight*, published earlier this year. Comparable reports from European countries are due to be published shortly.

The effects discussed in the NAS report include human skin

cancer; effects of increased ultra-violet on other biological systems; and climatic effects. Partial depletion of the ozone layer would permit increased penetration of ultra-violet radiation between 290 and 320 nm (2900–3200 Å), designated UV-B radiation. The NAS report concludes that "although the incidence of skin cancer is influenced by various factors, the evidence is good that the prime cause of the disease is UV-B radiation" and "a reasonable estimate of the percentage increase in skin cancer . . . may be made by assuming that a 1 per cent decrease of stratospheric ozone will cause roughly a 2 per cent increase in skin cancer. It should be noted, however, that while a 10 per cent decrease in stratospheric ozone gives about a 20 per cent increase in melanoma mortality, a 10 per cent decrease in stratospheric ozone appears to give more than a 20 per cent increase in the incidence of skin cancer – possibly a 30 per cent increase."

The consequences of increased UV-B radiation for other biological systems are as yet beyond calculation, largely through the absence of the appropriate experimentation. It would indeed be surprising, however, if Man were the only biological species on which increased UV-B had a deleterious effect.

Stratospheric ozone serves as the heat source for warming the upper stratosphere through its interception of UV radiation below 300 nm. If the ozone layer were depleted or shifted to lower altitude, the temperature structure of the stratosphere would be altered. The intuitive evaluations of the meteorologists range from "negligible" to "profound" concerning the effect of such stratospheric temperature variations on tropospheric climate. The NAS report says "as far as climatic change and agricultural effects are concerned, no clear-cut statement can be made concerning expected changes in temperature and rainfall. Nevertheless, a global change in surface temperature of a few tenths of a degree and an associated change of rainfall are not ruled out. Local changes may be larger, and the economic, social and political effects of such changes could be substantial." More precise information on the presence, absence and/or magnitude of such effects will probably require 10–20 years of study.

An additional possible climatic effect of the chlorofluorocarbons has just been recognised by V. Ramanathan, who has pointed out that the strong infra-red absorptions of CCl_3F and CCl_2F_2 fall in the "windows" through which infra-red emission from the Earth escapes into space. The greenhouse effect (see box) of incremental CO_2 (from the burning of fossil fuels) in retaining additional infra-red radiation in the troposphere has been discussed for decades. However, the CO_2 put in by Man (about 30 parts per million since 1890) is in addition to 290 ppm already there naturally, which was already removing almost all of the radiation that CO_2 can absorb. The chlorofluoromethane absorptions, falling in transport infra-red regions, are very much more effective per molecule in absorbing outgoing IR and Ramanathan has calculated that two parts in 10^9 of CCl_3F and CCl_2F_2 would be sufficient to retain the radiation needed for a 1 °C global warming.

2 October, 1975

"GREENHOUSE" THREAT?

While everyone else has been concerned with the effects of fluorocarbons on the ozone layer, Dr Veerabhadran Ramanathan of NASA's Langley Research Center has been calculating the consequences of an increase of the fluorocarbons content in the atmosphere on climate. The results of his calculations, due to be published in *Science*, are ominous. Fluorocarbons have a "greenhouse" effect that will warm the Earth by enough to cause significant climatic changes – including perhaps the melting of the polar ice-caps – if their concentration in the atmosphere increases from the present 0.1 parts per thousand million to one or two parts per thousand million.

Ramanathan has been working on the Earth's infra-red radiation balance for several years. Last year he became involved in calculating the effect on the Earth's heat balance of a thinning of the ozone layer – which itself has a greenhouse effect – predicted as a consequence of large-scale SST operations. His interest in ozone led him to fluorocarbons which, he realised, absorb infra-red strongly in the 8–12 μm region. In the cool temperatures of the troposphere, fluorocarbon molecules would absorb heat radiated from the Earth's surface and trap a substantial portion of it. Ramanathan is confident in his infra-red chemistry, but less confident in his speculations about the consequence of a warming of the troposphere.

2 October, 1975

19

The ozone layer

JOHN GRIBBIN

Ozone (O_3) is a blue gas with a distinctive odour familiar to anyone who has worked with electric sparks (or sniffed around the back of a colour TV set) or who has used ultra-violet radiation for sterilising in the "germicidal" band of wavelengths below 280 nm (2800 Å). Ironically, in view of its association with health, vitality and fresh sea breezes – and its importance as a shielding layer in the atmosphere – ozone is toxic to humans at a concentration as low as one part per million in air.

Historically, the presence of ozone in the atmosphere in significant quantities has been suspected for very nearly 100 years. The key evidence, which became available in the early days of spectroscopy, is that the spectrum of Solar radiation reaching the Earth's surface cuts off abruptly close to 290 nm. The first suggestion that this cut-off is due to absorption in the Earth's atmosphere was made in 1878. Two years later the so-called "Hartley bands" of absorption by ozone, extending from about 210 to 320 nm, were discovered and linked with this atmospheric absorption. Confirmation of the presence of the associated absorption processes in the terrestrial atmosphere came in 1890 with the detection of absorption in this range of wavelengths in the spectrum of Sirius.

For more than 20 years after these discoveries it seems to have been accepted that the absorbing ozone was present in the lower reaches of the atmosphere. Attempts were made to find the upward extent of the absorption by making observations from mountain tops, but these observations still showed the cut-off in the Solar spectrum, making it clear that the "ozonosphere" must be situated high in the atmosphere.

In 1917 observations of the rising and setting Sun were used to provide an indication of the distribution of ozone in the atmosphere. Because of the changes in the absorption spectrum that occur as the Sun is observed through successively longer columns of air as it sets (or shorter as it rises) it was possible 60 years ago to determine that ozone concentrates in a layer between 40 and 60 km above sea-level. More modern observations, using the same technique, give better limits of 10 to 50 km, with the concentration maximum at an altitude of about 25 km. This pattern has been confirmed by direct measurements from balloon-borne instruments and from spectra obtained using rockets and satellites.

The layered structure of the Earth's atmosphere and the place of the ozone layer in that structure can be seen best by considering the variation of temperature with altitude. The atmosphere is kept warm by the Sun. Some Solar radiation is reflected away into space at the top of the atmosphere, ultra-violet and infra-red frequencies are absorbed in the upper regions, but by far the bulk of this incident energy penetrates to the ground.

The warm ground provides heat to the atmosphere immediately above it, partly by conduction but mostly by radiation at infra-red frequencies, which are strongly absorbed by atmospheric water vapour and carbon dioxide. In turn, the lower atmosphere re-radiates part of this energy, some returning to the surface for another trip around the cycle, and some going upwards.

Atmospheric blanket

The net result is that the surface is rather warmer than it would be if it received the same heat from the Sun but had no atmospheric blanket – the well known "greenhouse effect". The heat also produces convection in the atmosphere, at least in the lower regions, and this plays a key role in determining the circulation patterns of weather and climate. But this convection is confined within a well defined layer, the troposphere, by the presence of ozone in the stratosphere above.

Through the troposphere, the layer of the atmosphere in which weather occurs, the temperature falls by about 6 °C for every kilometre increase in height. This fall slows down at around 10 km altitude, stops near 15 km, and from 20 to 50 km temperature increases from a minimum of roughly −60 °C at the bottom to a maximum of 0 °C at the top. This warming layer – the stratosphere – corresponds closely to the layer of ozone concentration, and the presence of the ozone is related to the warming. The temperature inversion inhibits convection, and this is what keeps the weather in its place in the troposphere.

An increase in temperature must mean that energy is being absorbed, and that energy can only be coming from the Sun. The photodissociation of molecular oxygen (O_2) by ultra-violet radiation provides the mechanism for absorbing energy, but the amount absorbed at different altitudes depends on how many molecules of oxygen there are to be dissociated and on how much of the Solar ultra-violet has penetrated to that layer without being absorbed in still higher layers. Consequently, the greatest concentration occurs where there is a balance between intense radiation (higher altitude) and denser oxygen concentration (lower altitude). The vagaries of the interactions also ensure that the atmosphere does not increase in temperature throughout the entire range from the base of the stratosphere upwards.

When an oxygen molecule absorbs Solar ultra-violet energy and dissociates, the resultant free oxygen atoms (O) can combine with other oxygen molecules to form ozone. The second step in the ozone production process depends on there being plenty of undissociated oxygen molecules around to combine with, and it seems to take place more efficiently in the presence of other molecules, which catalyse the reaction. So the greatest concentration of ozone is found between 20 and 30 km altitude. But the free atoms of oxygen may also recombine as ordinary molecular oxygen, or a single atom of oxygen can react with an ozone molecule to produce two atoms of molecular oxygen. The ozone itself is unstable against photodissociation by radiation below about 300 nm (this is the very feature that revealed the presence of the ozone layer in the first place), the effect being to produce one oxygen molecule and one free atom of oxygen from one ozone molecule.

In spite of these complexities, it is fairly straightforward to calculate the equilibrium balance, which gives the expected concentration of ozone as a function of altitude, and this agrees well with observations, at least for altitudes above 10 km. Because the pattern of reactions is fairly complex, the way in which ozone concentrations vary is not always obvious – this is one reason for which it is very difficult to assess the effect of Man's polluting activities on the ozone layer.

Variable equilibrium

Even the time taken for equilibrium to be reached if the balance is disturbed depends strongly on altitude. Although it only takes a few minutes to reach equilibrium at altitudes above 50 km it can take several days for the region below 30 km. Because of this, the lower region is never really in equilibrium, but is disturbed by the meteorological circulation. As the affected layer is also the region of greatest ozone concentration ground-based observers looking upward through the whole ozone layer see a strong correlation between changes in ozone concentration and meterological changes in circulation and weather patterns. More obviously, the change of Solar input with latitude and with the seasons affects the ozone concentration throughout the atmosphere; less obviously, however, even though ozone is produced by sunlight there is no tendency for it to go away at night.

The surprising observation that ozone concentration tends to increase slightly at night emphasises the dangers of drawing "obvious" conclusions about how other factors will affect the layer. The probable reason for this increase is that at altitudes above 40 km the equilibrium balance is shifted away from ozone by the presence of Solar ultra-violet radiation, so when the radiation is absent there is a tendency for ozone to persist. At lower altitudes there would be a tendency for ozone concentration to decrease at night – but as it takes days to reach a new equilibrium at those altitudes there is no chance for the effect to become noticeable.

Although ozone is mixed downwards into the troposphere in very small quantities, it is soon destroyed in the lower atmosphere, and is only found in measurable quantities at the surface of the Earth in photochemical smog.

Above the stratosphere, from 50 to 80 km altitude, is the mesosphere, another layer in which cooling dominates. The minimum mean atmospheric temperature of any layer (about $-100\,°C$) is reached at the top of the mesosphere, and from there on outwards temperature increases monotonically through the thermosphere. At these altitudes the heating mechanism is again primarily dissociation of oxygen molecules by Solar radiation, but the shortage of molecules and the energy of the radiation ensure that no ozone is produced; rather, the absorption of energy goes a stage further than dissociation of molecules, with at least half the oxygen atoms produced being energised into an excited state. There is increasing ionisation at higher altitudes, and greater numbers of free electrons, so the whole region above the stratosphere is also known as the ionosphere, subdivided into three layers (D, E and F) defined by the degree of concentration of free electrons. The structure of the ionosphere varies according to the input of energy from the

Sun, and is powerfully affected by the roughly 11-year cycle of Solar activity.

In a sense, the top of the thermosphere is at the temperature of interplanetary space, 1000 °C or more, but at such low densities the concept of temperature is no longer very useful. By about 500 km the atmosphere is so tenuous that collisions between its component molecules and atoms are so rare that it is meaningless to regard it as a continuous gas, and this is the point above which the components can leak away into space (the exosphere). At such altitudes, magnetic effects become more important for the ionised gases (or plasma), and the region where they interact with the Earth's magnetic field to form the radiation belts and magnetosphere forms the outer boundary of the atmosphere for all practical purposes.

Although the ozone layer is of particular importance to land-based life on the Earth, it is only one part of an atmosphere in which many components are balanced. Ozone is constantly being produced and destroyed by the interactions involving sunlight, and it is misleading to think of it as a finite resource, like oil, that can be destroyed once and for all. What could happen is that the balance of the set of equilibrium reactions that maintain the layer may be shifted, either in favour of less ozone or in favour of more (which could be equally damaging).

Like the ionosphere, the ozone layer is affected by the Solar cycle of activity, and it is debatable whether Man's effects are as large as natural variations; there certainly must be a very stable balance in favour of such a layer for it to have persisted for the 3000 My during which life has been releasing oxygen into the atmosphere, or even the 400 My for which life has existed on land.

2 October, 1975 © *John Gribbin, 1975; all rights reserved*

OZONE SINKS

According to the US National Academy of Sciences report, *Environmental Impact of Stratospheric Flight*, published earlier this year, there are three "fairly easily identifiable sinks of ozone". These are the Earth's surface, which is estimated to destroy about 1 per cent of the ozone produced globally; the reaction between oxygen atoms and ozone molecules (17 per cent); and breakdown of ozone by hydroxyl and hydroperoxyl radicals (11 per cent). Thus, "about 70 per cent of the ozone formed is unaccounted for by these sinks".

Because of the catalytic cycle of ozone destruction by nitrogen oxides, "within the uncertainty of the observed NO and NO_2 distributions, the NO_x system is capable of destroying 70 per cent of the ozone produced between 0 and 45 km" and it appears that this system is the most important sink for ozone in the stratosphere, and is therefore largely responsible for maintaining the balance between ozone generation and its destruction.

2 October, 1975

20

Ozone depletion and cancer

ARTHUR JONES

People around the world are concerned that chlorofluoromethanes released from aerosol spray cans pose a serious threat to their health, through depletion of the ozone layer. The primary concern about the ozone-layer depletion is that the ultra-violet ray intensity at the surface of the Earth would increase, bringing about more skin cancer fatalities among caucasians. According to the IMOS report, *Fluorocarbons and the environment*, issued earlier this year, "There is persuasive, although not absolutely conclusive, clinical and epidemiological evidence of a direct link between Solar radiation and the historically observed incidence of several generally non-fatal (non-melanoma) types of skin cancer in humans". I certainly do not find this evidence conclusive, and believe an alternative case can be made.

It is a long-known fact that ultra-violet intensity at the land surface increases with altitude above sea-level. In going from sea-level to the altitude of Denver, Colorado (1 mile, 1.61 km), the ultra-violet intensity at 295 nm increases by 125 per cent. The residents of Colorado (mean elevation 2.1 km) have always been subjected to UV intensities several times greater than those that might result, on the average, from the hypothesised ozone-layer depletion of 16 per cent (33 per cent increase in UV) by 2000 AD. In addition to the higher UV content of Colorado sunshine, the percentage of clear days (70 per cent) is above the national average.

Publications by the American Cancer Society show that Colorado has one of the lowest skin cancer fatality rates of all of the states, 1.69 deaths per 100 000 population compared with a national average of 2.40 per 100 000. The entire desert south-west has about 125 per cent greater UV intensity in sunshine, due to altitude, than does New England, yet the death rate from skin cancer in New England is 24 per cent higher than it is in the south-west.

On a world basis, many factors appear to play a more important role in skin cancer fatalities than UV intensity. In the equatorial regions, UV intensity at the land surface is higher because the Sun's rays pass through the ozone layer more perpendicularly than in more northerly or southerly latitudes. In spite of this, the lowest reported skin cancer death rates in the world come from Mauritius (0.2 per 100 000) and Nicaragua (0.2 per 100 000), even though they are located in near equatorial regions. On the other hand, Ireland (2.64 per 100 000) has the world's third-highest rate while England and Wales (1.50 per 100 000) is 27th. Mexico (0.65 per 100 000) is 38th.

Evidence is strong that UV intensity is not the principal factor in determining the skin cancer death rate. Genetic factors, skin pigmentation, behavioural characteristics, medical facilities, broad straw hats and suntan lotion all have some influence on skin cancer fatalities. An additional 4000–12 000 deaths per year from skin cancer in the US have been predicted for a 16 per cent depletion of the ozone layer. It should be remembered that present annual deaths in the US from this cause are 5000.

Some authors have recommended an immediate ban on the use of fluorocarbons without any direct evidence that they affect the ozone layer. To me the indirect evidence strongly suggests that these compounds are unlikely to have a significant effect on the Earth's ozone layer and, even if they did, an increase in skin cancer deaths would not necessarily result.

2 October, 1975

21

Will chlorofluorocarbons really affect the ozone shield?

ALAN EGGLETON, TONY COX AND DICK DERWENT

Recent studies on the effects of these aerosol propellants on strato-spheric ozone have centred on chlorine nitrate. If the predicted properties of this little known chemical prove correct, then chloro-fluorocarbons may cause a much smaller decrease in stratospheric ozone than previously calculated

Claims that chlorofluorocarbon aerosol propellants may be impairing the Earth's ozone layer are being reassessed in the light of new knowledge of stratospheric chemistry. Until now the picture has been as follows. Oxygen molecules are dissociated by ultra-violet radiation to form two oxygen atoms and these subsequently combine with further oxygen atoms to form ozone. The production of ozone, however, is balanced by its destruction.

The major ozone destruction process in the unperturbed natural stratosphere is the well known nitrogen oxide catalytic cycle:

$$NO + O_3 \rightarrow NO_2 + O_2$$
$$NO_2 + O \rightarrow NO + O_2.$$

Net result:

$$O_3 + O \rightarrow 2O_2.$$

Nitric acid forms a temporary sink for NO_x by the reaction:

$$NO_2 + HO \rightarrow HONO_2$$

but photolysis of the nitric acid restores NO_x to the cycle.

The chlorofluorocarbons–11 ($CFCl_3$) and –12 (CF_2Cl_2) used as aerosol propellants are inert gases, stable in the troposphere, which diffuse to the stratosphere where they are photolysed by short-wavelength ultra-violet radiation to yield chlorine atoms. These take part on the chlorine catalytic cycle:

$$Cl + O_3 \rightarrow ClO + O_2$$
$$ClO + O \rightarrow Cl + O_2$$

Net result:

$$O_3 + O \rightarrow 2O_2.$$

Similarly, there is also a temporary sink for free chlorine in the form of hydrogen chloride produced from methane:

$$CH_4 + Cl \rightarrow CH_3 + HCl$$

and restored to the cycle by hydroxyl radicals

$$HO + HCl \rightarrow H_2O + Cl.$$

This is very much a simplified picture and a full treatment has to take into account a much larger number of photo-chemical reactions. Further, to make quantitative estimates of ozone depletion, we must allow for the fact that chemical equilibrium is not established at all levels in the stratosphere, so atmospheric transport processes make an important contribution. Inclusion of all these processes requires a computer model of some complexity and so far most calculations have been made using one-dimensional models in which only the vertical motions in the atmosphere have been represented, expressed in terms of eddy diffusion coefficients.

Although there is still some disagreement over the best values to take for these eddy diffusion coefficients, which cannot be directly measured in the atmosphere, considerable progress has been made in refining the input data so that a "best estimate" can be obtained of an eventual ozone depletion of about eight per cent if chlorofluorocarbon emmisions continue indefinitely at present levels. Obviously, however, the validity of such calculations depends on having included all the relevant reactions of the significant species in the stratosphere. In particular, it is clear from a simple examination that the omission of any reactions leading to additional temporary sinks will over-estimate the ozone destruction resulting from either the nitrogen oxide or chlorine cycles.

One result that can be obtained from the computer model is the fraction of the free chlorine that is "locked up" in the temporary sink HCl. In the original calculations this turned out to be greater than 99 per cent in the lower and middle stratosphere, only falling to about 90 per cent in the upper stratosphere. Thus stratospheric HCl concentrations should be independent of Solar intensity with no seasonal changes.

What has changed matters, however, is that Allan Lazrus and colleagues of the National Center for Atmospheric Research at Boulder, Colorado, recently reported measurements of HCl in the stratosphere, obtained by sampling from aircraft and balloons over the United States, which showed concentrations about twice as high in the summer of 1975 as observed in the autumn of 1975 and the winter of 1976. This unexpected seasonal variation suggested the presence of another temporary chlorine sink that *was* affected by changes in Solar intensity.

Rowland has suggested that a rather unfamiliar compound, chlorine nitrate ($ClONO_2$) might constitute such a temporary sink. This compound, which can be prepared either by the reaction of chlorine dioxide (ClO_2) on nitrogen dioxide (NO_2) or chlorine monoxide (Cl_2O) on nitrogen pentoxide (N_2O_5), has been investigated in few laboratories and its reactions have not received much attention. It is a moderately stable gas with a boiling point of $-18\ °C$. The fundamental point for the present discussion is that chlorine nitrate can also be formed in the stratosphere by a "fast" reaction $ClO + NO_2 \rightarrow ClONO_2$, although quantitative measurements of the rate constant have not so far been reported in the literature.

To assess the importance of this compound for stratospheric chemistry Rowland made the not unreasonable assumption that this rate constant could be set equal to that for the thermodynamically similar reaction between hydroxyl radicals (OH) and NO_2. He also assumed that the only significant process for destruction of chlorine nitrate was ultra-violet photolysis, the rate of which can be estimated from known Solar intensities in the stratosphere and the ultra-violet absorption spectrum of the compound, assuming a quantum efficiency of one. Using these data, Rowland calculated that a substantial proportion of the free chlorine in the stratosphere was present as chlorine nitrate at altitudes below 35 km, but that above this height the increasing intensity of ultra-violet radiation reduced its concentration to negligible proportion at 45 km. He went on to calculate the consequent reduction in the ClO radical concentration and the reduction in the ozone destruction that resulted. He suggested that the introduction of chlorine nitrate would reduce estimates of the ozone depletion brought about by chlorofluorocarbons by a factor of between 0.7 and 0.85.

However, this somewhat simple method of calculation does not take into account the effect of chlorine nitrate on the nitrogen oxide destruction cycle. When we do this, a considerably different picture emerges.

We have previously carried out computer modelling of stratospheric chemistry and dynamics using a one-dimensional model at Harwell for the Department of the Environment (AERE Report R-8325, HMSO). Today we publish a further report (AERE R-8383, HMSO) in which these calculations are extended to include chlorine nitrate. First, to check the validity of using the rate constants from the $OH + NO_2$ reaction as rate constant for chlorine nitrate formation, we have made use of some thermodynamic data reported in 1974 on the standard enthalpy of formation of chlorine nitrate, which in turn permits calculation of the required rate constant of chlorine nitrate formation. This turns out to be close to the rate constant for the $OH + NO_2$ reaction used by Rowland and also to a kinetically similar reaction: $NO_3 + NO_2 \rightarrow N_2O_5$.

Under atmospheric conditions all three reactions are in the pressure-dependent region between second- and third-order kinetics where it is difficult to extrapolate laboratory values to the full range of temperature and pressure required. However, the values for $OH + NO_2$ have been determined over the full temperature and pressure range and we can use these to approximate the rate constants for $ClONO_2$ formation with some confidence.

For the destruction rates of chlorine nitrate we have used Rowland's photolysis coefficients plus the rate constant for thermal decomposition derived from the results of Martin. When we put these numbers into our computer model we arrived at figure for the fraction of free odd chlorine species (Cl, ClO, HCl and $ClONO_2$) present as chlorine nitrate for typical present-day atmospheric concentrations of chlorofluorocarbons and other chlorine compounds. To cover possible errors in our estimate of rate constants we have also made calculations for "medium" and "low" values of the rate of formation of chlorine nitrate, which are respectively 1/10 and 1/100 of the "high" values.

Our results for the "high" values are similar but not identical to those reported earlier by Rowland using his simpler computational method. They show a maximum in the mole fraction of chlorine nitrate at about 30 km which could approach a value of unity if the "high" values assumed for the rate constant turn out to be correct. Even with the lower rate constant values, significant amounts of chlorine nitrate are predicted to be present.

We did these calculations for a constant mean Solar intensity at 30 °N. When model calculations are carried out allowing for diurnal and seasonal variations in Solar intensity then we would expect the mole fraction of chlorine nitrate to show corresponding variations as its lifetime with respect to photolysis is short, varying from a few hours at 45 km to tens of hours at 15 km. As the total amount of free chlorine remains virtually constant, we would predict an inverse seasonal variation in HCl concentration, which constitutes the other major free chlorine reservoir. This is exactly what Lazrus observed. The magnitude of the seasonal fluctuation suggests that the true rate constants for chlorine nitrate formation are closest to the "medium" rate constant values we used.

We also calculated the ozone depletion predicted with chlorine nitrate. This was also carried out for "high", "medium", and "low" rate constant values and we assumed release of chlorofluoro-carbons–11 and –12 continuing indefinitely at 1973 product rates. We find that the predicted ozone depletion for the "medium" rate constants is roughly a quarter of that expected in the absence of chlorine nitrate; and if we use the "high" rate constants the calculations predict a significant increase in ozone concentration. This differs from Rowland's result because we included the effects on the nitrogen oxide cycle which are actually more significant than those on the chlorine cycle. A major part of the ozone destruction by chlorine species takes place in the region 35–45 km, where the formation of chlorine nitrate is less impor-tant than lower down. Destruction by nitrogen oxides, on the other hand, is most effective in the region 20–35 km where the ratio of chlorine nitrate to other free chlorine species reaches a maximum.

Clearly these results can only be considered tentative until we have experimental measurements of the important rate constants concerned. Several groups are working on the $ClO + NO_2$ reac-tion, but it will be some time before we have reaction rate data covering the complete range of pressure and temperature in the atmosphere. We still have to consider the possibility of further reactions leading to the destruction of chlorine nitrate in the stratosphere. In our report we consider and rule out a number of reactions, but the reaction with O (^3P) triplet oxygen atoms remains a significant possibility.

We also need experimental confirmation of the existence of chlorine nitrate in the stratosphere. So far it is not clear how this might be done. The interaction with the NO_x cycle means that the concentrations of NO_x on NO_2 and HNO_3 in the stratosphere assume further significance. The existing measurements of these species in the stratosphere show some discrepancies, despite the attention given to them earlier in relation to the concern over the effects of NO_x emissions from aircraft flying in the stratosphere.

It is too soon to forecast the eventual impact of this development on the chlorofluorocarbon controversy. Even if their effect on the total ozone column turns out to be insignificant, there would still be some change in the vertical distribution of ozone, which could have climatic effects. Also, release of chlorofluorocarbons continued over many decades would raise the mean surface temperature of the Earth by 1 °C or so due to the "greenhouse" effect. It seems certain that we shall have to wait longer than previously expected before rational decisions can be reached on the need to control chlorfluorocarbons.

20 May, 1976

22

Monitoring halocarbons
in the atmosphere

JOHN GRIBBIN

For the first time, a global chain of monitoring stations has been established to keep tabs on the levels of halocarbons in the atmosphere. First results from this monitoring should emerge during 1978; but it will be five years before a good picture of the distribution of these compounds is established

The basis of the continuing debate about the possible harmful effects of fluorocarbons (FCs) from spray cans on the ozone layer of the atmosphere is the assumption that these compounds are not absorbed by natural processes – there are no "sinks" for them – so that they build up to provide a growing danger to ozone in the stratosphere. In addition, proponents of FC-induced doom also assume – often without explicitly saying so – that these compounds are the major source of chlorine, if not in the whole atmosphere then certainly in the stratosphere, where the element is the active ingredient in the chains of reactions that break down ozone. Both assumptions can be challenged; but until the end of 1978 neither side in the debate had any reliable global data on which to base an accurate assessment of just how much of the FCs produced by industry is remaining in the atmosphere, or of the extent to which this pollution compares with the natural level of halocarbons (for other halogens, as well as chlorine, can do the same job of destroying ozone).

This has now changed, with the establishment of four monitoring stations in a programme sponsored by the Manufacturing Chemists Association (MCA). Two of these stations, at Adrigole in southwest Ireland and in Barbados, are managed by Jim Lovelock and Peter Simmonds, of the University of Bristol; the other two, in Samoa and Tasmania, are being looked after by R. A. Rasmussen, of the Oregon Graduate Center. As data come in, a group at the Massachusetts Institute of Technology, headed by D. M. Cunnold, will look after the analysis and calculation of atmospheric lifetimes for the various compounds being studied. And, of course, the team will be cross-calibrating their observations with those made by other groups wherever possible.

With this global monitoring experiment only now being established, it is clear that the whole excited argument about the "threat to the ozone layer" has been rather putting the cart ahead of the horse for the past four or five years. The arguments, both pro and con, have been based almost entirely on hypothesis and theory, with no extensive underpinning of practical observations. The size of the possible hazard, of course, is the excuse for pressing action, including a ban on the use of FCs in spray cans, *before* the theories are checked out in the field. The theoretical arguments still rage, and no clear-cut model of just how real the hazard is has yet emerged. This debate, as it stands early in 1979, will be the subject of a second article; but, now that observations are being made, it seems appropriate to look first at the rather limited basis of atmospheric measurements from which the whole theoretical argument has sprung up.

Figure 22.1 *The outside of Jim Lovelock's automatic monitoring station in Barbados; recordings are made automatically with only occasional human intervention (Credit: Jim Lovelock)*

Experiments at sea

Jim Lovelock, a member of the present investigative team, was the first person to begin studying the concentration of FCs in the atmosphere back in 1968, when there was no thought of this very stable, biologically harmless compound posing a threat to mankind. Indeed, the stability of the material was seen as offering scope for meteorologists to trace the movement of air masses around the globe. In 1971, with this in mind, Lovelock made a voyage as a guest experimenter on board the *RRS Shackleton* from Wales to the southern hemisphere, taking measurements daily of FCs in the air and sea.

The observations showed a difference in the amount of fluorocarbon 11 (F11) between the hemispheres, with less present in the south, away from the sources in the industrialised world. This distribution was, and remains, consistent with the possibility that a natural "sink" removes F11 from the atmosphere at a rate of 10 to 11 per cent a year – but this explanation is not one that has been widely accepted in the heat of the recent debate. More recent measurements have shown a more even north–south distribution; Lovelock's own view is that too little emphasis is placed on the day-to-day variability of FC concentrations in different patches of air, depending on whether the wind is blowing from an industrialised region or not.

With such fluctuations from day-to-day one voyage or one aircraft flight, can give a very misleading picture of the global situation – hence the need for the new monitoring chain making regular daily observations at both high and low latitudes in each hemisphere.

But how do you know that the instruments in all four stations are making comparable measurements? It is one thing to take one detector around the world to measure the concentration of these trace gases, since you can be sure that whatever the "baseline" calibration it is meaningful to say that, for example, there is twice as much F11 in one place as in another. But now it is necessary to ensure that four widely separated sets of equipment are making measurements, over a period of years, that can be compared directly one with another. This is no trivial problem, as two recent international exercises have shown.

Almost all halocarbon analyses have been made using standard gas chromatography based on the electron capture technique. Free electrons produced by a beta-source ionise a carrier gas inside the detector; the ion current is held constant by a variable source of sampling pulses. When a trace of a compound that has an affinity for electrons is introduced, less electrons get through to the anode in the chamber, and the frequency of the sampling pulses rises. This provides a very sensitive way to measure the amount of trace gas present – for some gases.

The snag is that for FCs and other compounds that react very strongly with electrons, there is a "swamping" effect which changes the nature of the response from the straightforward linear dependence on concentration that applies for other gases. The detector still gives a seemingly precise measurement of something, but the non-linearity means that what is being measured is not always what the experimenters think. In a nutshell, for a few compounds, including FCs, this standard technique gives very precise numbers which may have very little relation to the actual amount of gas present. Two different instruments measuring identical samples can give "answers" that differ by well over 100 per cent.

In an attempt to evaluate the extent of this problem, the US National Bureau of Standards carried out a simple test. Two samples of air were each divided among a set of clean containers, and pairs of samples sent to 17 laboratories around the world for analysis. (This followed an earlier, similar survey made by Rasmussen but using only one sample.) The results of the different analyses were then compared using a "Youdon plot" in which the results for sample A are plotted against the results for sample B. In such a plot, if there are only random errors in the analyses then the plotted points all lie in a circle, and the smaller the circle the better, from the point of view of comparability of measurements. But if there are systematic differences between the analyses, the circle is distorted into an ellipse, with the ratio of the major and minor axes indicating the severity of the problem. The usual rule of thumb is that it is time to worry if the ratio exceeds 2; for F11 in the US NBS study, the ratio was 3.12, and for F12 it was 14.8. The report (*Evaluation of Methodology for Analysis of Halocarbons in the Upper Atmosphere: Phase 1*, NBSIR 78-1480, Department of Commerce, Washington DC, June 1978) concludes that "results reported from different laboratories can be expected to vary by as much as ±40 per cent" – not much help when the whole debate hinges around just how FC stays in the air.

One answer is to use alternative methods of analysis – less elegant than the constant-current electron capture method, and using equipment that can't be bought off the peg but has to be made in the laboratory, but that produces reliable and comparable results. This is one of Lovelock's contributions to the present study, a detector in which with the same ion current operating at the same temperature and carrier gas flow the response to a given quantity of halocarbon is always the same. Another step towards comparable measurements is provided by preparing "standard" samples containing a known proportion of FC which can then be used to calibrate the instruments – no mean trick when concentrations down in the parts per billion (10^{12}) are involved, but an approach being tackled by Lovelock with the aid of a large chamber in the remote Devon countryside, into which known quantities of FC can be introduced before samples are analysed.

Calibrated air

At present, the global study is using a primary standard sample of clean air kept by Rasmussen; secondary standards can be checked by measurements of both secondary and primary on the same instrument, then the secondary is taken to the observing site and used to calibrate the instruments there. Each station has six cylinders, each of 1000 litres of usable air, calibrated in this way. Four of these will be used each year, and the other two kept as "historic reference samples" against the day when measuring techniques become more precise still. With new calibration samples always compared with the previous year's, and with the primary standard, the team aims to ensure that relative and absolute values used throughout the study have a direct and checkable "lineage".

The siting of the four stations ensures that monitoring is occurring at representative locations in each of four roughly equal-mass regions of the atmosphere – temperate northern and southern latitudes, and equatorial zones either side of the equator. It would be foolish to anticipate just what the observations may reveal, but it makes sense to take stock of the possible natural sources of halocarbons that provide the background against which any potential damage to the environment from man-made halocarbons, including F11 and F12, must be assessed.

Most of the chlorine in the atmosphere, and probably most in the stratosphere, is not industrial in origin, although much of it may very well be the result of Man's activities. Among the natural "carriers" of chlorine in the atmosphere methyl chloride dominates – yet this was not discovered in the air until 1974, long after the first identifications of FCs in the atmosphere. No one doubts that methyl chloride has a short lifetime in the atmosphere, but such large quantities are present that some may well be surviving to enter the stratosphere. Typical concentrations measured by Lovelock over the past few years range from 0.6×10^{-9} parts by volume (pbv) to a peak of 3×10^{-8} pbv, a rather broad range but one that suggests a source of about 10 megatonnes per year. Industrial sources produce no more than a few kilotonnes – so where does the rest come from?

Front-runner among several candidates at present is combustion – natural forest fires and slash-and-burn agriculture. Whenever vegetable matter burns without a complete supply of oxygen, smouldering converts some of the chlorine present as chloride ions in the cell sap into methyl chloride. This phenomenon has been closely studied in tobacco burning, where each gram smoked produces 1 cm^3 of methyl chloride vapour. Other combustion, including the forest fires and agricultural burning, is less efficient at converting chlorine into methyl chloride; but with an estimated 40×10^{15} g of vegetable matter now being destroyed in this way each year (five per cent of the total biomass) there is still ample scope to account for almost all atmospheric methyl chloride in this way.

Andrew Watson, of Reading University, visited Kenya in the summer of 1976 to make measurements of atmospheric chloride, both as a background in the tropics and at locations near large fires. The background he found, confirmed by measurements a year later made by Rasmussen, was 2.2×10^{-9} pbv; the other part of the study was handicapped by the unusual weather of 1976, so dry that much of the grassland in Kenya had died off and little was left to burn. Ironically, though, the same bizarre global weather brought extensive heath and grassland fires in England that year, where Lovelock measured his peak observed levels of methyl chloride, above 2×10^{-8} pbv over a period of two days in Wiltshire, at a site 10 miles away from the nearest large fires.

Provided the methyl chloride is mixed into the stratosphere – which would be achieved very simply if the heat of burning stimulates development of a tropical storm with its powerful columns of convectively rising air – the resulting loss of ozone from this enormous influence could be four per cent a year. This is certainly a much greater influence, if real, than any claimed disturbance due to FCs, and if the processes that replenish ozone in the stratosphere can cope with such an impact then they can certainly cope with present levels of FC release. All this line of approach is supported by the few direct measurements of chlorine and chlorine monoxide in the stratosphere, such as those by J. G. Anderson and colleagues from the University of Michigan, using balloon-borne instruments, which showed surprising (to the theorists) concentrations of these gases in the stratosphere and imply "that chlorine compounds constitute an important part of the stratospheric ozone budget" (*Science*, vol. 198, p. 501).

Without good observational data, theorists are whistling in the dark. It is no use trying to fit the available data to the theories you prefer by claiming that all the results that disagree with theory are "anomalous"; theories have to be tailored to fit observations, not the other way around, but even this can only be done in a satisfactory way when there is a sufficient body of observation available. Meanwhile, the theorists will continue to argue – although, as I shall show later, there is no evidence from the present state of theorising on this problem to suggest that any great harm will come to Mankind or planet Earth if we wait for the appropriate five years or so to reap the benefit of the global monitoring programme before making decisions on whether or not to ban FCs. Meanwhile, anyone seriously concerned about the possible harmful effects on the biosphere of a decrease in stratospheric ozone might be better advised to kick up a fuss about the wasteful practice of slash-and-burn agriculture, and, come to that, widespread stubble burning in this part of the world.

18 January, 1979 © *John Gribbin, 1979; all rights reserved*

OZONE: CAUTIOUS INACTION NEEDED
Michael Kenward

A decade of scientific research has still not proved that chlorofluorocarbons used as propellants in aerosol cans and as coolants in refrigerators, will do irreparable damage to the Earth's stratospheric ozone layer. Caution should, therefore, prevail. This is the conclusion of the report *Chlorofluorocarbons and Their Effect on the Stratosphere* (second report), published by the Department of the Environment's Central Directorate on Environmental Pollution on Tuesday (Pollution Paper No 15, HMSO, £4.75).

The theory was put forward nearly a decade ago that chlorofluorocarbons (CFCs) can affect the ozone layer by interfering with the complex chemical reactions that take place in the stratosphere. The overall impact would be to reduce the amount of ozone in the air, and this would lower the atmosphere's effectiveness as a filter removing ultra-violet Solar radiation. Thus more UV light would reach ground level "with biological consequences potentially affecting human health and other forms of life and plant growth".

The Department of the Environment's report comments that since fears about the impact of CFCs on the ozone layer first arose, and since its first report on the subject in 1976, the consumer's dependence on these chemicals as aerosol propellants has diminished. "As a consequence it is expected that the amount of CFCs used in aerosols in the UK will decline to about 70 per cent of the 1976 volume over the next three years." The EEC is likely to experience similar trends. The report goes on to say that "in the light of the many uncertainties still prevailing such a reduction appears to be adequate, pending further research. Strict regulation is not warranted at present."

"A further review will be needed in two years' time" says the report "taking into account the extent to which the forecast reduction in emissions has come about." It will then be necessary to assess the evidence "to establish the case for further precautionary measures or even regulations".

The scientific evidence for the report was prepared by the Stratospheric Research Advisory Committee, which the Environment Department set up in 1976 to advise on environmental problems arising from stratospheric pollution, and its effects on the ozone layer in particular. This committee, whose report appears as part 2 of the pollution paper, says that current predictions suggest that the amount of ozone in the stratosphere could fall by 11 to 16 per cent if the release of CFCs continues at present levels. These calculations suggest that CFCs may already have reduced ozone levels by between 0.7 and 1.6 per cent. If we stop releasing CFCs into the air immediately the ozone concentration would suffer a maximum reduction, by about 2 per cent, in 5 to 15 years from now.

It is very difficult to measure such small variations in the ozone concentration because natural fluctuations are far greater. Thus it is difficult to determine whether CFCs really do have the environmental impact attributed to them. But because there is a possible deleterious effect most countries using appreciable quantities of CFCs have urged caution. The argument is over the degree of that caution. While the Department of Environment sticks by the policy advocated in 1976 in its earlier pollution paper on this subject – essentially that "strict regulation is not warranted at present" – other countries have been more dramatic in their responses. The US, for example, has banned the use of CFCs in all but essential applications; and earlier this year Sweden banned their import and manufacture except where the government grants special exemption. At the moment the argument is over the EEC's response to CFCs. The Common Market countries account for about a third of the world's CFC consumption.

The political fight is now on as to whether the EEC will follow the line of the US or the UK. CFCs are not a local pollutant – an aerosol spray squirted in Britain will have an impact on the environment over the whole world – so there is likely to be considerable political pressure from the US urging other nations to follow its line.

The DoE's report describes an inter-governmental meeting held in Munich at the end of last year. This concluded, says the report, that "because the ozone depletion hypothesis had been neither proven nor disproven precautionary measures to reduce the global releases of CFCs are needed". One consequence of this meeting was that in May 1979 the EEC recommended to its members that they should bring about a 30 per cent reduction in the use of CFCs in aerosols by 1981 compared with the 1976 level "whilst ensuring that the steps taken do not produce any barriers to trade" as the Environment Department report puts it.

25 October, 1979

23

Spray cans: the threat that never was

MICHAEL ALLABY AND JIM LOVELOCK

The United States acted with uncharacteristic speed to protect the environment when scientists suggested that aerosol cans might damage the Earth's ozone layer, allowing dangerous ultra-violet light to reach ground level. But aerosol propellants are less harmful than was feared

High above our heads a layer of ozone envelops the Earth, an invisible blanket that shields us from much of the Sun's ultra-violet radiation. The ozone layer protects us silently, rather mysteriously, and we are properly grateful. In no circumstances should we damage it.

Our concern for the health of the ozone layer is reasonable, but it seems to have generated such emotional fervour, especially in the United States, that governments are urged to enact "protective" legislation. Any criticism of such legislation brands the critic as anti-social. There is no doubt about the place the ozone layer now occupies in our culture. Some years ago a team of American scientists calculated the effects of a nuclear war. Amid the appalling mayhem such a war would unleash, the scientists saw fit to point out that a nuclear war would damage the ozone layer, as though this were as important as the rather more permanent destruction of human life, institutions and cultures. In fact, the team may have been wrong anyway, as nuclear warfare could enhance the ozone layer rather than deplete it.

One after another, threats to the layer have been postulated – jet airliners, space shuttles and the rest. Some have been discounted, others have been postponed to the fairly distant future; but in recent years chlorofluorocarbon (CFC) compounds have emerged as the single most realistic hazard to ozone and one of the principal uses of these chemicals, as propellants in aerosol cans, has allowed the "spray-can" to be cast in the role of arch-villain of the environment. It may prove to be a fairly harmless scape-goat, but so persistent is the myth of the ozone layer in America that popular magazines have published articles with headlines such as "The 'Death Spray' that menaces every American".

It was in 1974 that Sherry Rowland and Mario Molina published calculations to show that CFC compounds released into the air near ground level would travel upwards across the tropopause, where intense ultra-violet (UV) radiation would break up the molecules and release free atoms of chlorine. These atoms would catalyse the destruction of ozone, thus depleting the ozone layer. Rowland and Molina calculated that the manufacture of CFCs was growing at such a rate that the release of these chemicals into the atmosphere would deplete the ozone layer enough to increase substantially the amount of UV radiation reaching the surface. They argued that there would be a considerable biological impact, including an increased incidence of skin cancers in humans. A mere three and a half years later the US Environmental Protection Agency (EPA) announced a ban on most uses of CFCs as aerosol propellants. The "Death Spray" has been banned. Canada, Sweden and a few other countries imposed similar bans, but Britain's response was more cautious. The EPA was held not to have proved its case.

No one disputes that CFCs do dissociate in the stratosphere, that free chlorine can deplete ozone concentrations, that a reduction in the ozone layer will lead to increased UV penetration, or that UV radiation can damage living organisms. But a problem exists: the questions relate to the severity of the depletion. The EPA believes the threat requires urgent action and is exerting pressure on European governments to support it. We maintain that if the problem requires action at all, it should be deferred: no crisis is imminent and there are far too many uncertainties in the relationship between CFCs and ozone to warrant immediate action.

The American urgency seems to be due to a logical error in the EPA's argument, at least as this is rehearsed in the 1979 report of the National Academy of Sciences, *Protection against depletion of the stratospheric ozone by FC* (*New Scientist*, vol. 85, p. 223). If we assume that production and release of CFCs will continue according to the trend established during the 1960s and early 1970s, there would be very large amounts of these substances in the environment by the end of the century. Such large amounts

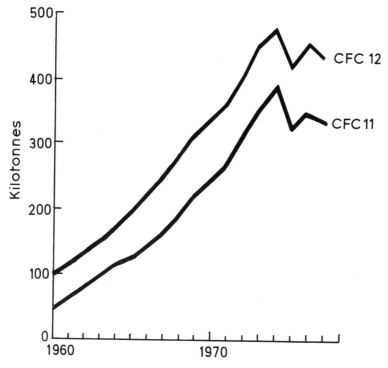

Figure 23.1   *Production of CFC aerosol propellants peaked in 1975. New figures from the US Chemical Manufacturers Association show that production decreased again last year. But the Chemical Specialties Manufacturers Association estimates that aerosol production increased using different propellants*

may produce damaging effects. So, the argument goes, to prevent the damage we must act immediately because if we do nothing now we will do nothing in the future. Neither assumption can be proved, but the first leads to a "worst-case" prediction that is justified by the second. In a word, the argument is circular.

In fact, as Figure 23.1 shows, production of CFC11 and CFC12 – the two CFCs used as propellants in aerosol cans (CFCl$_3$ and CF$_2$Cl$_2$) peaked in 1975, long before the ban, almost certainly because petrochemical feedstocks were becoming increasingly expensive.

Nor can the extent of ozone depletion be taken for granted. In the past few years studies of the stratosphere have revealed many

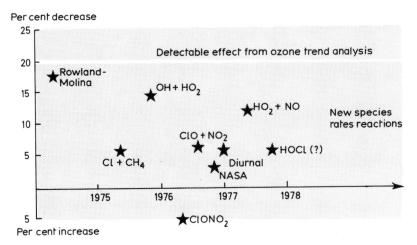

Per cent decrease

Detectable effect from ozone trend analysis

Rowland-Molina

OH + HO$_2$

HO$_2$ + NO

New species rates reactions

ClO + NO$_2$

Cl + CH$_4$

HOCl (?)

Diurnal
NASA

1975   1976   1977   1978

Per cent increase

ClONO$_2$

Figure 23.2   *Researchers have come up with different esti-mates of how chemical processes in the atmosphere could alter the ozone layer — none is as high as the estimate that first caused the scare*

reactions that affect ozone. Each discovery has modified the predictions: Figure 23.2 summarises them. No prediction is as high as Rowland and Molina's original figure.

The chemistry of the atmosphere is notoriously complicated. Even in the troposphere — whose gases are easily available for laboratory experiments and have been studied for centuries — there are many uncertainties. And the fate of methane, which is both produced and oxidised naturally, is not as simple as it might seem (Figure 23.3) and while the 50 or more — perhaps many more — reactions that occur in the stratosphere may be no more complex than what goes on in the troposphere, the stratosphere is relatively inaccessible and has been studied by chemists for only a short time. Figure 23.4 describes the route by which CFCs move between the troposphere and stratosphere and affect ozone, but it makes no comment on ways in which CFCs may be removed before they do harm. This is important; calculations of ozone depletion by CFCs depend crucially on how long they stay in the troposphere, their "residence time". Even a minor "sink", reducing the average residence time by a quite small amount, might have a major effect. It is the great stability of CFCs that makes them so attractive, of course, as aerosol propellants; they do not burn and

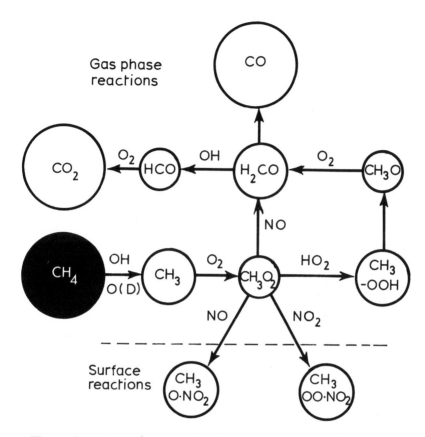

Figure 23.3 *Methane molecules endure a series of reactions in the atmosphere (the sizes of the circles denote the stability of the molecules)*

they are not toxic. It has been assumed that they survive indefinitely under tropospheric conditions and that we can estimate the rate at which they migrate across the tropopause. However, measurements of CFC11, which is less durable than CFC12, suggests that its total tropospheric lifetime may be anywhere between 15 years and infinity. If the true value is 50 years, the amount of ozone depletion it causes is halved; if its lifetime is 20 years, the depletion is reduced by 72 per cent.

It is clear, then, that we need to know much more about the fate of CFCs in the troposphere before we can make any sensible estimate of their effects on the stratosphere, but such information

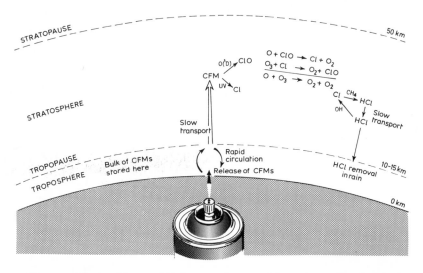

Figure 23.4　*How CFCs, such as chlorofluoromethanes, affect the ozone layer*

as we do have tends to undermine the EPA case. The fact that production CFC11 and CFC12 has peaked means that the "worst-case" supposition does not stand up.

Finally, we must consider the evidence of the ozone layer itself. As yet there are no signs of any depletion. Indeed, ozone concentration is increasing and the increase is most marked in the northern hemisphere (Figure 23.5). The EPA argues, of course, that ozone depletion may not be observable for some time and that by the time it is observed it may be too late to prevent a serious loss. At best the argument is not strong; at worst it is almost metaphysical as it requires us to act on a purely theoretical calculation, on evidence that cannot be produced. As the figures show, the amount of ozone varies from year to year. It also varies with latitude, and is generally much greater over the poles than over the equator. During the Arctic winter, when near-total darkness prevents the regeneration of ozone that is lost, the fluctuations are very large. Should there be any destruction of atmospheric ozone because of CFCs, therefore, the effect would be most pronounced in very high latitudes during winter. During summer we might expect the ozone to reform fairly quickly. By including the Arctic depletion in figures for the whole hemisphere the picture becomes distorted, both with regard to the amount of depletion at lower

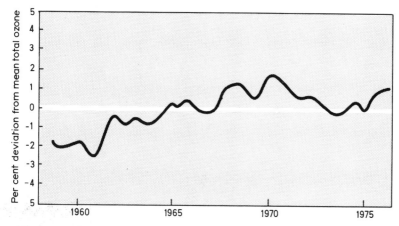

Figure 23.5 *Despite the predictions, ozone concentration is increasing*

latitudes and with regard to the resulting increase in the amount of UV radiation that would penetrate the atmosphere; very little UV radiation is received during the polar winter, of course.

The original estimates for ozone depletion were derived from one-dimensional models of the atmosphere, in which latitudinal and seasonal effects were averaged. The investigation of the latitudinal differences in ozone depletion rates was made by John Pyle and John Houghton of the Department of Atmospheric Physics at Oxford University, using a two-dimensional model that was much more sensitive to dynamic, as opposed to purely chemical, processes. In one series of calculations with the model, CFCs were found actually to enhance the ozone layer in the lower stratosphere over the equator by depleting it at higher levels: this let more UV radiation reach a lower altitude, and generate ozone.

If ozone depletion lets more UV radiation reach the ground this would be harmful – but how harmful? After all, UV radiation also has some beneficial effects: for one thing it stimulates production of vitamin D in humans. Another indication of the emotional intensity of the debate, and of another circular argument, is the change in terminology used to describe UV radiation. At one time the UV spectrum was divided simply, if arbitrarily, into bands A, B and C by wavelength. Now, though, part of the spectrum is known as "DUV" – damaging ultra-violet. No one has proved that a modest increase of UV is, on balance, malign, but the "D" suggests that proof exists.

We must distinguish carefully between effects produced by UV radiation and the significance of those effects. Some wavelengths of UV light can break DNA molecules. Of this there is not the slightest doubt. Unlike x-rays, however, UV does not penetrate far. It is easy to evade it, or for larger organisms to sacrifice or pigment surface tissues to shield themselves effectively. We should not under-rate the capacity of organisms to endure what they cannot cure; and to suppose that so ubiquitous an environmental factor is inimical to life does not conform at all well to what we know of evolution.

The idea that UV light is necessarily harmful derives from theories about the evolution of the Earth's atmosphere and about early life. The suggestion is that photosynthesising organisms evolved, that the oxygen they released led eventually to the formation of the ozone layer, and that it was only after the ozone layer had formed, and harmful UV radiation could not reach the surface, that organisms were able to colonise dry land and more advanced forms of life could appear.

Although apparently attractive, the scenario leads to difficulties. If the original photosynthesising organisms had to be protected from UV radiation they must have been confined to a layer of the oceans below the level to which UV light could penetrate but shallow enough for visible light to reach them. Could photosynthesis have evolved under such dim auspices? Perhaps it could, but could the activity in this layer have been sufficient to generate the oxygen needed to oxidise the reducing components of the atmosphere, surface materials, and then to accumulate free oxygen? The idea is plausible, but only just, and it ignores the stromatolites, those fossilised remains of great mats of blue–green algae that lived (and whose descendants still live) in shallow water, exposed to the air at low tide. We know the stromatolites are very ancient and we may speculate that they contributed much of the Earth's gaseous oxygen. Their protection against UV radiation was most probably an outer layer of dead cells – a kind of skin – so that to them UV light was no more than a minor inconvenience.

This idea of how life evolved on Earth depends critically on the rate at which ozone forms after oxygen is available. Calculations suggest that the first effect of a decrease in atmospheric oxygen concentrations is an increase in stratospheric ozone as the ozone layer moves down. They concluded that the atmosphere would have contained enough ozone to provide an effective UV shield when it had no more than about one per cent of its present amount of oxygen. The most recent estimates suggest yet another time sequence for ozone development. They all suggest that the ozone layer was present long before more advanced forms of life evolved. There is no telling evidence to associate the evolution of higher forms of life with the formation of ozone. Indeed, there are several mechanisms by which organisms are protected naturally from damage by UV light. These include the device used by algae, but a more interesting mechanism requires nothing more exotic than nitrogen salts – sodium nitrate and nitrite – which are good absorbers of UV radiation.

It seems, then, that by these and probably other mechanisms organisms endured the UV radiation to which they were exposed in an atmosphere with no ozone layer. Higher organisms will have

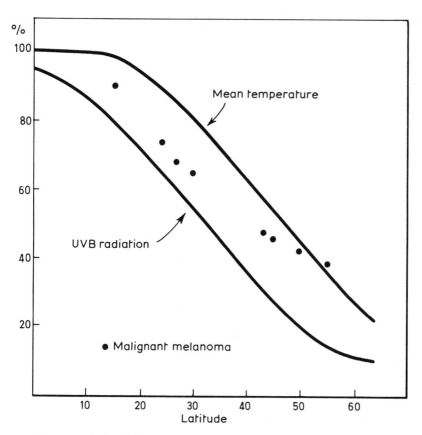

Figure 23.6 *Like ozone concentration, the intensity of ultra-violet radiation and the incidence of malignant melanoma varies with latitude, but so does temperature*

inherited at least some of these mechanisms. It is much more likely that evolutionary advances that led to the emergence of more complex organisms were related to improved cell division and, most important of all, to the development of hard parts to support larger bodies.

Exposure to UV radiation can cause skin cancers in humans. Even here, though, the defence mechanisms exist, and dark-skinned peoples, supplied with ample melanin, suffer no injury. The link between melanoma and UV is more tenuous. As Figure 23.6 shows, incidence of melanoma does vary with latitude, as does UV exposure, but average temperatures also vary with latitude, and the incidence of melanoma includes melanoma of the sole of the foot, which can hardly be caused by UV light.

We conclude, then, that the amount of damage CFCs may inflict on the ozone layer is far from certain, and that the biological effects of increased penetration by UV radiation may be less severe than has been supposed. We do not say there is no problem, or even that it may not be necessary to take some action in the future. All we say is that action taken now, such as the ban on CFC aerosol propellants, is precipitate. And while the use of CFCs as aerosol propellants is a convenient target for our atmospheric concern, if a ban on them is to be effective it must be extended to include all other uses of the chemicals, including use in refrigeration and air-conditioning, and in plastic foams. A ban on CFC aerosols may be inconvenient, and some of the substitutes for CFCs may be dangerous, but a ban on other uses of CFCs would incur a severe energy penalty as well as an economic one.

One of us first detected CFCs in the atmosphere and it is ironic to note that the original paper (J. E. Lovelock, *Nature*, vol. 241, p. 194) contains the sentence: "The presence of these compounds constitutes no conceivable hazard; indeed the interest lies in their potential usefulness as inert tracers for the study of mass transfer processes in the atmosphere and oceans." The risk of an emotional over-reaction was anticipated, but to no avail, and the anti-CFC campaign is in full hysterical flight.

While we squabble over the supposed harm spray cans may be doing to pale-skinned sunbathers – no one else would be injured – species are being driven to extinction, millions of our fellow humans are starving, and the world is teetering in the direction of war. Could it be that something is wrong with our sense of priorities?

17 July, 1980

OZONE: WINNING ON THE ROUNDABOUTS, LOSING ON THE SWINGS
Christopher Joyce

The latest research into the whims of the Earth's ozone layer, which protects humans from harmful levels of ultra-violet light, brings good and bad tidings. From a report the National Academy of Sciences published last week, the good news is that chlorofluorocarbons, which contribute to the destruction of the ozone in the upper atmosophere (stratosphere), are not as potent as researchers predicted in 1979, when the academy last published a study. Lest there be dancing in the streets, the academy also has some bad news: even small reductions in the ozone layer would significantly increase the rate of skin cancer and perhaps have previously unsuspected effects on human immune systems.

If production of chlorofluorocarbons continues at 1977 levels, by the end of the next century the stratosphere's ozone content could drop by only 5 to 9 per cent. That estimate is in sharp contrast to the estimate in the academy's 1979 report, which predicted reductions of between 15 and 18 per cent for the same period.

Atmospheric scientists attribute the revision to a better understanding of the atmosphere's hydrogen chemistry, in particular the quantity and behaviour of the hydroxyl radical.

The worry about chlorofluorocarbons arises from their habit of adding chlorine to the atmosphere, which breaks down the ozone and thus allows more ultra-violet light to reach the Earth. In combination with hydrogen, chlorine (as hydrogen chloride) is harmless to ozone, but when reacted with hydroxyl radicals, the chlorine is released to do its dirty work. Less hydroxyl radicals around, less chlorine, and a "healthier" atmosphere.

New measurements from ground stations, balloons and satellites show less hydroxyl radicals in the stratosphere than previously thought, according to Dr Robert Hudson who is in charge of NASA's research on ozone depletion. But while chlorofluorocarbons, which are banned as propellants in the US, are partly exonerated by the new findings, nitrogen oxides, by the same token, may prove a more insidious threat than expected. Nitrogen oxides also break down ozone, but are kept partially in check by the hydroxyl radical, which converts the nitrogen oxides to nitric acid. Thus, the fewer radicals, the more oxides of nitrogen. "We've tended to swop one problem for another" says Hudson.

Nitrogen oxides in the stratosphere come from the exhausts of supersonic aircraft and from nitrogen fertilisers.

As for biological effects, research shows clearly that a decrease in ozone concentrations will allow through more ultra-violet radiation in the wavelengths of 290 to 320 nm. Ultra-violet light in this range (called UV-B) causes 90 per cent of the skin cancer (other than melanoma, the most lethal type) in the US. The report concludes: "We estimate that there will be a 2 per cent to 5 per cent increase in basal cell skin cancer incidence per 1 per cent decrease in stratospheric ozone". The incidence of squamous cell skin cancer could be twice that rate.

Another, less well understood phenomenon is the effect of ultra-violet light on human immune systems. Research over the past two years on laboratory animals suggests that UV-B suppresses immune responses. In one study of humans, a mild sunburn damaged white blood cells.

8 April, 1982

24

Anybody want to save the ozone layer?

DEBORA MACKENZIE

Scientists and legal experts met in Geneva last month to try to decide how to safeguard the ozone layer. But as the complexities of atmospheric chemistry are better understood, it is becoming difficult to say whether the ozone layer needs to be saved – or if so, whether it can be.

What concerned the UN's Consultative Committee on the Ozone Layer (CCOL) was that, as it builds more and more models to try to explain what is happening, and the chemical industry tries to block any more regulations, hitherto unstudied trace gases are quietly building up in the atmosphere. They may be beyond our control already.

Concern for the ozone layer dates from the mid-1970s, when chemists realised that industrial processes were releasing gases into the air that had never been there before, that lasted a long time, and that interfered with ozone chemistry. Fingers were first pointed at chlorofluorocarbons, chiefly chlorinated hydrocarbons like freon, which are used as refrigerants and propellants for aerosol sprays. Early predictions warned of drops of five to ten per cent in stratospheric ozone if fluorocarbon releases continued unchecked.

This was cause for worry. Ozone strongly absorbs ultra-violet (UV) light from the Sun, removing virtually all of it before it reaches the Earth's surface. Enough UV still gets through to cause sun-tanning, and burning, and any more would play havoc with most biological systems. Among other things, it would affect crops, alter the oxygen cycle by damaging ocean phytoplankton, and cause malignant melanomas in humans.

But in addition to being a UV filter, ozone is an important

stabiliser of world climate. The lowest level of the atmosphere, the troposphere, is warmed by heat re-radiation at the Earth's surface. The rising, cooling and falling of this hot air is what causes winds and clouds.

But the stratosphere, the next layer up, is heated mostly at the top, where ozone absorbs UV and releases infra-red radiation. With no rising lower layer, it is resistant to the vertical mixing that perturbs the troposphere.

If there is less ozone in the stratosphere, more sunshine will

Figure 24.1   *Buffalo and paddy field: both produce methane and damage ozone (Credit: Keith Hill)*

reach and warm the Earth's surface, meaning a warmer lower troposphere, and cooler upper layers. This will destabilise the weather. Moreover, the effects will be different at different latitudes, leading to changes in lateral air movements.

On top of this, less ozone would change the stratosphere temperature profile and bulk stratospheric air movements. How this would affect the troposphere, and our weather, is a major gap in our current understanding of the atmosphere, scientists said in Geneva.

All this means that both the total amount and the vertical distribution of ozone are vital to the world's well-being.

Ozone is never present in the atmosphere at more than ten parts per million. If all of it were accumulated at the Earth's surface, the layer would be only 3 mm thick. This thin layer of ozone seems a delicate thing. But many atmospheric chemists believe it depends on so many different chemical processes that it would take a lot of changes to disturb it. Precisely how many changes, and which ones, is now the subject of debate.

Ordinarily, ozone is scattered throughout the atmosphere, with a peak at about 25 km up. It is produced when UV splits an oxygen molecule into atoms, and these come back together in threes:

$$O_2 + O_2 = O_3 + O.$$

The spare oxygen can either tag onto the more abundant O_2 and form another ozone molecule, or it can join ozone itself, turning O_3 back into two molecules of O_2. The amount of ozone in the air is largely set by how often this last reaction happens.

Some chemicals react with O and O_3 to speed up that reaction, thus effectively reducing ozone. For example, a chlorine atom from a chlorofluorocarbon combines with ozone to form ClO and O_2. ClO and a single oxygen then produce another O_2, and free chlorine again. The initial ozone is lost, and since chlorine is regenerated, it can go on to repeat the process – so not much is needed.

If a few parts per million of ozone is all that is needed to stabilise the stratosphere, parts per billion of chlorine are all that now seems to be needed to destabilise the ozone layer.

Chlorofluorocarbons are a problem because they are stable, and remain in the air long enough to rise slowly to the stratosphere and do their damage. It is this very stability that makes them useful in industry, and as the use of sprays and refrigeration spread, production volume multiplied eightfold between 1960 and 1974.

In 1974, controls started to limit production of CFC11 and CFC12, the major industrial compounds. They were banned from "non-essential" aerosol use in North America and Scandinavia. The EEC imposed a 30 per cent reduction; an upper production limit on all fluorocarbon production in the EEC may eventually prove more effective in limiting them than the US ban.

Despite the ban, chlorofluorocarbons are continuing to accumulate. As aerosol use dropped by half by 1983, non-aerosol use climbed almost as much. Release is now about constant, leading to an increase in the concentration of chlorofluorocarbons in the atmosphere of 7.5 per cent per year.

Other unregulated fluorocarbons, moreover, are becoming more popular, and could be adding a third as much again.

Gordon Diprose, an environment advisor at ICI, a major producer of chlorofluorocarbons, says the prospects for replacing them, especially for refrigeration, with a less dangerous molecule are slim. He says the industry has been looking hard for replacements since regulations first appeared a decade ago. But he has found there are very few molecules with the required properties that are not directly toxic themselves.

Besides, while chlorofluorocarbons may have constituted the earliest perceived threat to the ozone layer, scientists in Geneva all agreed that they are far from being the only one.

For instance, the El Chichón volanco in Mexico (*New Scientist*, 18 October, p. 28), combined with the El Niño climatic anomaly over the Pacific in 1983 to produce the lowest annual ozone measurement recorded in 60 years at the monitoring station in Arosa, Switzerland. This was probably because of a huge release of chloride.

Such natural variations make it hard to say for certain what trends in ozone concentrations are from year to year. It also provides ammunition for the chemical industry, which questions why it should pay with increasing regulation, when natural processes have a much more drastic effect on ozone.

Bob Watson, an atmospheric chemist at the US National Aeronautics and Space Administration (NASA), says the biggest change in scientists' understanding of the ozone layer in the past year has been the realisation of how strongly coupled all the trace gases in the air can be. All these interlocking reactions are now being fed into more and more complex computer models of the atmosphere.

But the complications are immense. Moreover, the early emphasis on chlorofluorocarbons means scientists know far more about them than they do about other important gases, such as carbon dioxide, nitrogen oxides and methane.

Methane is particularly disturbing. It seems to be building up in the atmosphere at a rate of one to two per cent per year, mostly in the upper troposphere. Scientists first guessed that the culprits were cows – every year there is more livestock in the world, hence more animal flatulence. But Watson says intensive cattle raising is accompanied by the development of more digestible fodder – hence fewer farts per cow. The overall balance of these conflicting processes awaits study.

A more probable cause is rice paddies. The production of methane, also called swamp gas, should increase as rice paddy area increases, which has been the case over much of Asia for the past two decades. Moreover, with new "green revolution" rice varieties, paddies are kept wet and producing far more crops per year.

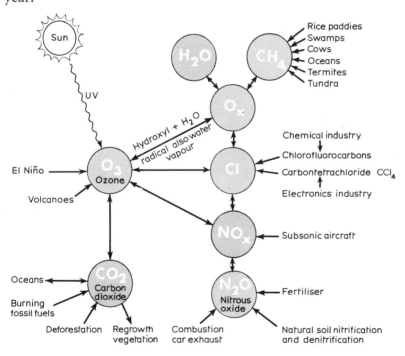

Figure 24.2 *How the world damages ozone, and ozone fights back*

At the same time, more swamps are being drained for agriculture and habitation, and on top of this the contributions of wet tundra, ocean carbon cycles and even termite mounds cannot now be assessed.

Much attention has been given to carbon dioxide's "greenhouse" effect in warming the Earth, but NASA's Watson says methane is as effective a greenhouse gas as carbon dioxide, and it is increasing three times as fast.

This brings us back to ozone, since all of the reactions affecting its concentrations are profoundly and differently affected by temperature. In addition, methane directly promotes ozone formation. Its slow oxidation converts ozone-depleting chlorine to hydrochloric acid, which is precipitated as acid rain. Hence, ozone is thought to be building up in the upper troposphere, even as it is depleted at higher altitudes.

All these considerations have changed the predictions scientists were making a few years ago. The good news in Geneva this year is that there has only been a three per cent depletion of ozone in the high stratosphere since 1970. The CCOL reported that "reasonable projections suggest less than one per cent change in total ozone over the next few decades" unless fluorocarbon production trebles.

But the bad news is that this small overall change represents a balance between a 14 per cent ozone decrease at an altitude of 40 km and an equivalent increase lower down.

If chlorofluorocarbons keep accumulating at their present rate, the total ozone column should be reduced by only 5 per cent by the year 2000, but with a 40 per cent decrease at 40 km.

But the model predictions vary enormously, depending on the scenario one picks for changes in trace gases. With constant chlorofluorocarbon release and methane, carbon dioxide and nitrous oxide increasing at present rates, the ozone concentration could increase dramatically by the year 2000. But this would be considerably slowed if the methane increase was not 1.5 per cent, but only one per cent per year.

On the other hand, if chlorofluorocarbon production increases, according to one predicted trend, by 3 per cent per year, nothing much will have happened by 2000, but there will be a precipitous drop in ozone by 2030.

This makes matters difficult for the legal minds in Geneva, who will keep meeting there until they have worked out a convention for the Protection of the Ozone Layer for the UN Environment

Programme. If one model is chosen, action should clearly be taken now to put a cap on chlorofluorocarbon production, as some environmentalists in Geneva recommend. If another is chosen it makes sense to postpone this until the science is better understood, as the chemical industry wants. It is all a matter of how fast things are changing, and how irreversible will be the effects of things we are doing now.

It is also a matter of how controllable the determinants of atmospheric ozone turn out to be. Alan Eggleton, the head of atmospheric pollution at the Atomic Energy Research Establishment in Britain, said in Geneva that it is one thing to limit aerosol sprays, but quite another to cut back on the use of refrigeration, which is vital to human health in much of the world.

One thing on which all of the debaters agreed is the urgent need for more research into atmospheric chemistry. The changes to be expected in the sources and sinks for such gases as methane, nitrous oxide and carbon monoxide are not clear. And there are not enough monitoring stations to get reliable world-wide estimates of their changing concentrations.

The various models in use do not take account of the effects on the chemistry of changes in temperature, resulting, say, from carbon dioxide build-up. Effects of temperature on bulk stratospheric and tropospheric air movements, which also feed back critically onto the chemistry, are also now unaccounted for by model predictions.

One problem is that there seem to be few funds for studying the matter. NASA's Watson estimates that the comparatively small sum of $50 million goes into basic research on ozone layer chemistry. Another $100 million is being spent on an upper-atmosphere satellite to be launched by NASA in 1989. Watson says governments should "critically review current funding policies with regard to their adequacy", given the importance of the situation.

One recent calculation shows how vital an increased research effort might be. It has just been predicted that the rate of ozone disappearance might increase very rapidly at critical concentrations of trace gases.

A series of recent calculations in several different laboratories predict that when stratospheric chloride exceeds nitrogen oxides, the rate of ozone depletion will shoot up, in an ever-increasing, non-linear way, with any further increases in chlorine. "If chlorofluorocarbons increase at three per cent per year" says Watson "things could enter a critical phase where chlorine exceeded nitrogen oxides, with significant decreases of ozone. But they will also be sensitive to methane and carbon dioxide concentrations."

Such predictions none the less have "significant implications for the interpretation of effects from increased fluorocarbon emission", the CCOL warned.

15 November, 1984

PART FIVE

The Human Impact: Acid Rain

The ozone layer is essential to all life on the surface of the Earth, and any threat to its continued presence is a global threat. Human activities that "only" affect the environment on a continental scale might seem less worrying, both for humankind and for the rest of the web of life that comprises Gaia. But while the debate about the "threat" to the ozone layer remains an abstract discussion among experts, with no proof yet that any harm is being done to our environment, the problem of acid rain is both real and immediate. Forests and lakes are dying across Europe and the North American continent. The reason, it seems clear, is acidity in the rainfall, produced by sulphur dioxide pollution. But who is to blame for the pollution?

The acid rain debate is as much a political one as a scientific one – and, like most political debates, by no means concluded yet.

25

Acid drops from fossil fuels

BRYAN SAGE

The ecological impact of acid rain is the focus of a major international conference being held in Norway next week. Scientists from a dozen countries will discuss recent research and try to suggest ways of dealing with what is proving to be a very complex problem

Much truth is there in the well worn saying that what goes up must come down. In some cases, though, what comes down is far worse than what went up. Certainly this applies forcibly to the phenomenon generally referred to as acid rain.

Acid precipitation is produced when atmospheric moisture combines with the oxides of sulphur and nitrogen emitted when fossil fuels are burnt in vehicles, factories and power stations. The acidification is at present caused primarily by emissions of sulphur dioxide and, to a lesser degree, of nitrogen oxides. Acid rain is a subtle form of pollution, it can damage aquatic and terrestrial ecosystems, man-made structures, and possibly human health – sometimes the damage is irreversible.

Sulphur compounds are removed from the atmosphere through two processes. First, there is dry deposition involving particulate matter and the absorption of sulphur dioxide on exposed surfaces. Dry deposition is a continuous process which depends mainly on the concentration of sulphur dioxide near the ground, and the amounts deposited generally decrease as the distance from the emission source increases. Secondly, there is wet deposition – in rainfall in which the sulphur compounds are frequently in the form of sulphuric acid. Wet deposition is obviously much more variable because it depends on such factors as the rainfall pattern and the quantity of sulphur compounds in the "mixing layer" of the atmosphere. In cold climates, atmospheric pollutants deposited during the winter generally accumulate in the snow pack, whence they are released in a concentrated form with the onset of thawing. This phenomenon can lead to sudden sharp increases in the acidity of adjacent water bodies and soils.

The problem of acid rain is growing, particularly in areas such as Scandinavia (southern Norway and south-west Sweden), and eastern North America. Factors such as topography, geology and prevailing winds that have passed over heavily industrialised areas all combine to produce a serious problem. Emission of sulphur dioxide in Europe from 1910 to 1950 was fairly constant with an annual emission rate of about 25 million tonnes. In the past decade or so there has been a substantial increase, and estimates suggest that the current emission rate is up to 70 million tonnes a year. Annual sulphur dioxide emissions in the United Kingdom are now about 5 million tonnes.

On 10 April 1974, Pitlochry in Scotland had a heavy rain-storm. There was nothing particularly remarkable about it, except that the rain was as acid as vinegar with a pH of 2.4 – the lowest pH for a single downpour ever recorded anywhere in the world. In the same month, a rain-storm with a pH of 2.7 was reported from the west coast of Norway. There can be no doubt that these events were related to increased sulphur pollution in the atmosphere.

A growing problem

The problem of acid rain is no better in North America. A report by the bilateral United States–Canada Research Consultation Group on the *Long-Range Transport of Air Pollutants*, published in October 1979, revealed the annual sulphur dioxide emissions to be nearly 5 million tonnes in Canada, and nearly 26 million in the US. Rainfall with high levels of acidity has been recorded in Los Angeles, San Francisco, Seattle and the Rocky Mountains. Rain in the Adirondacks, New York State, has a pH between 4.0 and 4.5, which is some ten times more acid than normal rain.

The problem of acid rain is almost entirely man-made. That it is increasing arises from the steady growth in the burning of fossil fuels. An ironic twist to the story, however, is that the great efforts made in recent years to reduce air pollution have actually made things worse. One widely adopted technique has been to build taller chimneys to ensure better dispersion of the emissions. The chimney of the copper–nickel smelter at Sudbury in Ontario, Canada, for example, rises to more than 400 metres. While tall chimneys certainly reduce pollution in their immediate vicinity, they set the stage for the aerial transportation of the pollutant to far-distant places. Acid rain, therefore, has become a hazard that recognises no national boundaries. For example, the acid haze that sometimes appears over Alaska is believed to originate in Japan. The joint US–Canadian report already mentioned concludes that the net flux of sulphur compounds is from south to north across the border. In Europe, the Swedes and Norwegians have long claimed that about 75–80 per cent of the airborne sulphur pollution is carried there by the westerly and southerly winds from the UK and the Continent. Even the tropical forests of Venezuela now suffer from acid rain-storms.

Local conditions aggravate the situation in southern Norway and south-west Sweden. It is an area where the moisture-laden polluted air is intercepted by high mountains, with resultant heavy precipitation. In some parts of Sweden the mean level of rainfall is such that every square metre receives an annual sulphur deposit of two grams. Equally unfortunate, southern Norway and Sweden constitute the only large area in Europe that has a low calcium and magnesium content in its bedrock. This means that the soils and water bodies in this area are weakly buffered and therefore sensitive to any change in the input of acid compounds.

Figure 25.1 *Power stations and cars contribute to acid rain. Tall stacks spread sulphur dioxide from coal-fired power stations (Credit: CEGB)*

The effects of sulphur pollution cannot be considered in isolation from each other. Acid deposits, for instance, affect soil chemistry, which in turn influences bacterial activity and plant growth. Soil-water influences the chemistry of surface waters, and this affects the survival of the freshwater fauna and flora. Natural ecosystems are extremely complex with numerous interactions at all levels of organisation, making it a difficult and expensive business to evaluate the effects of acid precipitation on these systems. Nevertheless, despite many gaps in our knowledge, the gross adverse ecological effects of airborne sulphur pollution are well known. Acid rain is said to have contributed to a decline in the annual productivity of coniferous forests in southern Norway and Sweden, and there is similar evidence from North America.

Figure 25.2   *Nitrogen oxides can be detected coming out of car exhausts (Credit: Bell Labs)*

While controversy rages over this aspect, so far as freshwater habitats are concerned the picture is much clearer.

A healthy lake has a pH of about 7.0 and sometimes a little higher. Where the pH drops to around 5.0 there is a marked decline in the variety of invertebrate animals, and some species of fish disappear. Water with a pH below 4.0 is lethal to fish of the salmon family. As the acidity of a lake increases, its waters become clearer and there is a shift in the aquatic flora from higher plants toward mosses and algae.

At the United Nations Conference on the Human Environment held in Stockholm in 1972, a Swedish delegate stated that if the pH of Swedish lakes continued to decline, then within 50 years around half of them would be acidified to a dangerously low, in ecological terms, pH (5.5–5.0). Recent data suggest that about 20 per cent of Sweden's lakes are now seriously affected by acidification. In southern Norway the acidification of thousands of freshwater lakes and rivers has adversely affected fish populations over some 33 000 km^2. The joint US–Canada report estimates that within 20 years 48 000 lakes in Canada will be seriously affected by acid rain. Such figures illustrate only too well the massive scale of the pollution.

Worse on the way

Acid rain is a problem that is likely to get worse before it gets better. In Canada it is anticipated that by the end of the century, despite remedial action, there will be modest increases in the level of sulphur dioxide emissions, and substantial increases in nitrogen oxide emissions. Part of the problem in North America still stems from the US's commitment to more coal-fired power stations emitting oxides of sulphur. When the Swedes and Norwegians, early in the 1970s, suggested that air pollutants could be transported for great distances in the atmosphere, nobody took them very seriously. In recent years, however, the gravity and international nature of the problem has been recognised.

There are no easy solutions – only acidic ones. Even if it were only an environmental problem there would still be difficulties in resolving it because our knowledge is riddled with holes. Even scientists disagree on the interpretation of existing data! A report entitled *Effects of Airborne Sulphur Compounds on Forests and Freshwaters* published in 1976 by the Central Unit on Environmental Pollution in Britain's Department of the Environment stated that "Even now, however, the effects of these sulphur compounds on the natural environment are not fully understood." Although we need more scientific data, enough is known for it to be obvious that remedial action must be taken. As Ray Robinson, Canada's assistant deputy for environmental protection, puts it, policy decisions will have to be taken "without the luxury of having all the scientific evidence".

As well as being a scientific problem, acid rain also has economic, political and social aspects, not to mention practical difficulties. For example, while existing control methods can reduce (at a cost) emissions of sulphur dioxide, no nitrogen oxide controls are known, yet nitrogen oxides will contribute increasingly to the acidity of rain over the next 20 years or so.

While those countries most affected by acid rain can alleviate the situation a little by reducing their own emissions, the problem can be cured only by concerted international action by the major industrial countries. The first tentative steps in this direction have already been taken. The UN Economic Commission for Europe (ECE), at a meeting in Geneva in November, adopted the first comprehensive convention to combat trans-national air pollution (*New Scientist*, vol. 84, p. 590). There were 35 signatories to the convention, including the United Kingdom, the Soviet bloc countries, Canada and the United States. The majority of ECE members accept that acid rain, originating mostly in England and Western Europe, is a serious problem in Scandinavia and one that warrants immediate attention. Only the UK and France think that more research is needed to prove the severity of the problem.

6 March, 1980

26

Warning cones hoisted as acid rain-clouds gather

FRED PEARCE

Scientists from Europe and North America met this week in Stockholm to plan an international strategy for fighting the global effects of acid rain on forests, lakes and crops. They will deliver a report on their deliberations to an international conference of government ministers in the same city next week. There, Britain will again be in the dock for failing to act to cut sulphur emissions from its power station's chimneys – the principle cause of acid rain hundreds of kilometres away in south Scandinavia.

Scientists investigating acid rain and its effects find themselves at the sharp end of a growing international political row. Anders Dahlgren, Swedish minister of agriculture, opened this week's conference by saying "We as politicians need you as scientists more and more . . . I ask you to work in pursuit of one major aim – to ascertain 'the truth' about acidification and the solutions to this severe and accelerating environmental problem".

Meanwhile, in London lobbying by acid rain investigators was already having one effect. Top-level meetings in the last two weeks appear to have persuaded ministers to reinstate the grant of £120 000 to the Institute of Terrestrial Ecology and others to investigate the damage to crops and forests in Britain from acid rain. The grant had earlier been axed by the Department of the Environment.

The Stockholm conferences take place exactly ten years after Sweden alerted the world to the death of fish in thousands of its lakes. A decade of research has largely justified the claim that acid – most of it imported on the wind and deposited by rain – is the root cause. Sometimes the acid kills. Sometimes it leaches toxic metals such as aluminium from soils and they kill.

But today the issue is no longer about a few Swedish lakes. It is much broader. This week scientists, including most of the big names in the acid rain debate, discussed the forests of Europe, the lakes of North America and Japan, and the farms and cities of Asia and Latin America. All are threatened by acid deposition in the form of gas, solid particles or rain.

The scientists are also looking for solutions. The technology of "scrubbing" power station emissions to remove sulphur is developing rapidly. Britain now appears to have dropped its claim that it would be impossibly expensive to use scrubbing on a large scale.

But speakers from Scandinavia and Canada, which is angry at President Reagan reneging on President Carter's commitment to control sulphur emissions in the US, are not satisfied. They want across-the-board reductions of 30–50 per cent in emissions of both sulphur dioxide and oxides of nitrogen from power stations.

Ellis Cowling, chairman of the US National Atmospheric Deposition Program, who published the first acid rain map of North America earlier this year, offered another approach. He suggested targets should be set for total acid deposition. A target of 10 or 20 kilograms of sulphur per hectare per year might prevent most ecological damage, he suggested (annual deposition rates in large parts of Europe exceed 50 kg/hectare).

Figure 26.1 *Acid rain from power station chimneys damages trees in the Black Forest and disfigures statues at Cologne Cathedral (Credit: above and opposite bottom, Pete Addis; opposite top Frank Darchinger)*

Delegates here agreed that research is urgently needed into acidification and terrestrial ecology. Cowling warned that, while the effects of acid rain on aquatic systems are well explored, "there is no compelling evidence that the effects on terrestrial systems are more damaging than beneficial. . . . But there is good reason to be suspicious" he added.

Spruce trees are dying at an increasing rate in New England in the US, in West Germany and probably elsewhere. The reasons are not clear. But Bernhard Ulrich, from Gottingen University, who dramatically warned last year that the Black Forest may be dying, suggested that toxic metals such as aluminium and cadmium are to blame. These metal ions are liberated in the soil after nutrients such as calcium and manganese are leached from the soil by acid rain. The calcium:aluminium ratio in soils may be an important indicator of danger, Ulrich said.

This emerging crisis in the forests is ironic because, initially, the nitrogen ions in acid rain are thought to increase tree growth by enriching the soil.

Despite the remaining uncertainties, the jScandinavians and Canadians want to see action. Norwegian government officials are considering an advertising campaign in British newspapers next winter. The Scandinavian pressure could lead to a British environment minister attending next week's ministerial conference, despite earlier reports that only civil servants would attend.

Government officials no longer accept reassurances from the Central Electricity Generating Board that there is no clear link between sulphur emissions and acid rain in mainland Europe. While ten years of political pressure are one cause of this change in attitude, the impact of scientific investigations has contributed – even though many questions remain unanswered.

Göran Persson of the Swedish Environmental Protection Board summed up his attitude to these uncertainties "Perhaps our role is like the weather forecaster" he said. "How would you feel if you turned on your television and the forecaster told you that the situation was rather complicated and he could not give a forecast for tomorrow until he had done more research. You would want him to do his best. He has the information and he should tell you what he thinks will happen even if he is not certain." That is what the delegates at Stockholm this week believe they are doing for governments in hoisting the warning cones as the acid rain-clouds gather.

24 June, 1982

27

Science and politics don't mix at acid rain debate

FRED PEARCE

British researchers and civil servants returned from a conference in Stockholm last week convinced that acid rain poses a real threat to forests and woodlands throughout Britain. In the next few weeks, they will tell ministers that it would be in Britain's interest to cut emissions of sulphur from fossil-fuelled power stations. And they will press for bigger grants to study the effects of airborne sulphur on soil and plant growth.

One senior civil servant at the conference of experts on acid rain told *New Scientist*, "Frankly, we thought the recent report of Central European forests dying from acid rain attack was a scare story got up by some pressure group."

But after some lengthy discussions with Professor Bernhard Ulrich, the West German biochemist who was a leading figure behind the "scare", British delegates believe that the diagnosis is correct. They will report that the woodlands of south-east England are just as likely a target of acid rain as are upland conifer plantations. The woodland trees could suffer a falling rate of growth and shorter lives.

The final report of the experts' conference says that one million hectares of forest in Central Europe have suffered damage by sulphur in the form of gases, acid rain and particles transferred to pine needles from mists and low cloud. Fred Last, chairman of the Natural Environment Research Council's committee on the effects of air pollution and assistant director of the Institute of Terrestrial Ecology, believes that the area of forest affected is nearer two million hectares.

Ulrich's work adds a novel dimension to the acid rain debate. His is the first strong evidence that acidic pollution affects terrestrial as well as aquatic life. Last says that Ulrich's investigations into the effects of acid rain, both in leaching nutrients from soil and in releasing toxic elements such as aluminium, are crucial. They suggest that attack on trees may be widespread even when there are no visible signs of damage. And attack probably occurs at levels of acidity that are common in both Britain and continental Europe.

Ulrich says that trees in West Germany may eventually have lives of only 30 to 50 years and that death may be sudden when acidity in the soil reaches a certain level. A drought could trigger thousands more deaths, he says.

Overall, Ulrich's revelations have pulled attention away from the Scandinavians, who tried to use the experts' conference to highlight damage from rising levels of acidity in Sweden's and southern Norway's thousands of lakes. Most delegates seemed more concerned about the damage caused by sulphur carried over short distances as gases and aerosols than with the effects of long-distance transport of acid rain. But, if industrial nations such as Britian and West Germany accept that sulphur from factories is causing damage in their own forests, they could help other nations' problems by acting to cut those emissions.

That is certainly the view of British civil servants who attended the conference. They believe that ministers will listen when they are told that the woodlands of Cambridgeshire and Essex, and the forests of the Lake District and Galloway are under attack, or that attempts by the Forestry Commission to plant new forests in the Pennines have failed because of the effects of sulphur pollution.

The Swedes said they were happy with the experts' report but they do not count the experts' conference a total success. They pressed scientists to recommend a target maximum for sulphur deposition rate throughout Europe of 0.5 gm^{-2} per year. But in one working party, Dr Gwyneth Howells, from the CEGB's scientific staff, could be heard strenuously opposing any such limit. It implied an impossible 80 per cent cut in sulphur emissions, she said, and she won the argument. The final experts' report merely noted that "lakes in sensitive areas . . . have in general not been acidified when the catchments received a sulphur load of 0.5 gm^{-2} per year or less". But that did not stop Swedish agriculture minister Anders Dahlgren telling the opening session of the ministers' conference that "the scientists agreed upon a limit value for sulphur deposition." They did not agree any such thing. The experts failed to meet their brief to establish "strategies and methods to control emissions of sulphur and nitrogen oxides". Their report reached "no firm conclusions" and merely noted that "clear goals have to be established". Nevertheless, the report was firm in its affirmation of the effects of sulphur emissions on lakes and forests.

But this week's ministerial conference took on a very different aspect. Giles Shaw, junior minister at the Department of Environment, wrote his speech before the experts' conference began and politics dominated the scene. For instance, the Swedes set up the conference as a political act and ministers like Shaw attended the conference only because it would have been damaging not to do so.

A fresh batch of civil servants arrived from Britain carrying the message, "We are here to see that nothing political emerges which we do not want." Americans arrived noisily, sat through the last day of the experts' conference, then handed out a line-by-line attack on a glossy report that the Swedes gave out before the conference. Much of their concern was that action to cut emissions of sulphur could not be justified economically. The hostile tone of the Washington-drafted attack so angered American scientists in Stockholm that it was swiftly withdrawn. ("Treat it as deep background, would you?" I was told, Watergate style.)

1 July, 1982

28

It's an acid wind that blows nobody any good

FRED PEARCE

Politicians from Britain and the United States walked away smiling from last week's international conference on acid rain in Stockholm. But delegates from Sweden, Norway and Canada, the countries most affected by acid rain, seemed bemused. Both sides thought they had won the scientific debate at the preparatory meeting of experts the week before the politicians met, but the countries suffering the effects of acid rain are now left with the uneasy feeling that the polluters have once again slipped away unscathed.

The leader of the US delegation, Kathleen Bennett from the Environmental Protection Agency, held a press conference to announce that she was "satisfied and pleased" with the outcome. The meeting of experts had, she said, "largely confirmed the US view". The US's view is that the current levelling off in the emissions of sulphur dioxide from power stations, the cause of much acid rain, is an important advance. It would be "scientifically insupportable" to go further because "the scientific community cannot tell us yet where and when to reduce emissions and by how much". Bennett's aides added that when scientists can demonstrate that a given cut in emissions will bring about a clear reduction in the acidification of lakes or soils, more action may be justified.

Canada, hundreds of whose lakes suffer because of the emissions of power stations in the US, is not so sanguine. "To procrastinate is indefensible," said Bud Olsen, its Minister for Economic and Regional Development. "I agree that all the facts are not in on acid rain, nor will they ever be. In science it is always possible to gather more information . . . Here we have a clear case where the need for action is urgent and scientific knowledge points to appropriate actions."

Matters in Europe are much the same. Britain, which provides more of the sulphur that is killing thousands of Norwegian lakes than does Norway, has reduced its sulphur emissions in the past few years, largely as a result of reduced industrial output. "How" asked Giles Shaw, Under-Secretary of State at the Department of the Environment, "can we justify the additional costs of fitting equipment to remove sulphur from the emissions of existing power stations? We cannot be sure that they will be effective in curing the environmental problems."

Both the polluting and the polluted countries ransacked the report of the experts' meeting to justify their stances. The Scandinavians pointed to the consensus among scientists that sulphur emissions are definitely killing lakes and forests and that any reduction in sulphur emissions would help. The US and Britain stressed the remaining uncertainties.

Bennett felt it crucial that the experts had said that "if a general decrease in emissions were to take place within a large industrial region, specific areas – presumably the sensitive regions – might experience significantly smaller or larger decreases in deposition". Shaw said "A large reduction in emissions in one country may have only a marginal effect on another country".

However, the official report of the ministers' conference noted that "even if deposition remains stable, deterioration of soils will continue and may increase unless additional control measures are implemented . . . further concrete action is urgently needed".

The only joker in the pack was West Germany. The Britons and Americans had expected support from the industrial heartland of Europe. Instead, the West Germans, impressed by the newly discovered threat to their forests from acid rain, promised to reduce their sulphur emissions by 50 per cent by 1985 and warned that "action not taken today will cost us a lot more in a few years' time".

The great victory for the British and US governments was that no specific goals for reductions in either sulphur emission or deposition emerged from the conference. Their only commitment remains the nostrum that emerged from the 1979 convention on acid rain: to use economically viable means to cut emissions.

Anders Dahlgren, Sweden's agriculture minister, had thoroughly alarmed the US government when he recently flew to Washington and told officials that he would demand a 50 per cent cut in emissions. The Canadians still want a 50 per cent cut. But at Stockholm, the Swedes switched to advocating a policy of flexible emission standards based on limits on the total deposition of acid rain in sensitive areas. The threshold for damage in southern Scandinavia appears to be about 0.5 grams of sulphur/square metre/year. But the scientists' meeting refused to adopt this or any other figure because local environments vary so much.

The US delegates at the ministers' conference latched onto this. They suggested that scientists should establish thresholds for every threatened area so that emission standards could be adjusted to reduce depositions.

But what of Eastern Europe? East Germany, with its smokey lignite coal, is a bigger polluter of Swedish and Danish lakes than the better-known villain, Britain. The Soviet Union is the leading polluter of Finland and devastating evidence is emerging about the damage that Eastern European countries are inflicting on each other.

The Soviet Union initiated the 1979 Environment Convention (under which the Stockholm conference was held) partly, the British say, to counter bad publicity about violations of human rights in the USSR. But the Soviet Union is still the world's biggest sulphur polluter. Faced with the prospect of a hiding to nothing in Stockholm, the Soviets took the easy way out. They did not turn up.

8 July, 1982

29

The menace of acid rain

FRED PEARCE

Sulphur dioxide from power stations and oxides of nitrogen from power stations and motor cars are dissolving in rain and showering Europe in dilute acid. The forests and the lakes are dying. Already the damage may be irreversible

Trees cover almost half of West Germany. Giant primeval woodlands like the Black Forest are the traditional playgrounds for Germans. So it came as a shock when Professor Bernhard Ulrich, a quiet-spoken biochemist, last year told his countrymen through the pages of *Der Spiegel* that their forests are dying. The cause, he told them, is sulphur dioxide from power stations and heavy industry in the great industrial heartlands on the Ruhr and the Rhine. His claim struck a raw German nerve and, with the Green Party growing all the time, he struck a raw political nerve, too. Inside a year the German federal government is committed to halve sulphur emissions by 1990.

Now the word of Ulrich is spreading further. His theories on the effect of acid deposition on soils and forests are fast becoming the cornerstone of scientific thinking. They suggest, according to scientists who gathered recently in Stockholm to review research into acid rain, "that tree growth may be decreased . . . at concentrations that prevail over large parts of Europe". In the coming months Ulrich's findings will cause many countries to rethink their assumptions that the costs of cutting sulphur emissions outweigh the benefits. Not least among the rethinkers will be Britain.

Across Bavaria some 1500 hectares of forests have died in the past five years, according to government estimates. Another 80 000 hectares of forests in Bavaria and Baden-Wurttemberg are seriously damaged. Some German forests have taken from industry doses of sulphur amounting to 100 kg or more per hectare every year for more than a century. After several years of observing forest soils deteriorating at his research station in Solling, Ulrich believes they can stand no more.

He told the Stockholm conference that "after the next warm dry year, the forest damage will drastically increase. Dead forests, till now restricted to the most centrally situated countries (Czechoslovakia, Poland, East Germany) will become apparent also in West Germany. In less exposed areas the existing forests will gradually be damaged by the die-back of trees. This die-back starts at forest edges, at suppressed trees and at trees extending beyond the canopy. Especially endangered are dense pure coniferous stands of age 20 to 40 years. In the long run trees will not get older than 30 to 40 or 50 years even under optimal soil conditions."

Ulrich says that acid deposition is causing far-reaching, probably irreversible, changes in the soil of wide areas of central Europe. The destruction goes through three phases, he says. In the first, the nitrogen content in the acid rain is dominant: it acts as an additional source of nutrients to the soil, and trees may grow more rapidly – in the past century tree growth in central Europe actually increased. That process has now stopped in Germany, but continues in Scandinavia, where the trees thrive as the lakes die.

Today, phase two of Ulrich's cycle is taking hold in West Germany. Most soils have a natural ability to neutralise acid, and are able to replace lost nutrients such as calcium from the underlying bedrock. But this ability is becoming exhausted. Acid is accumulating first in the surface layers and then farther down. At the same time sulphate from the acid rain combines with nutrients such as calcium and magnesium and leaches them from the soil. An early sign of this phase is the yellowing of pine needles, indicating magnesium deficiency.

The loss of nutrients slows the growth of trees and damages the wood, but much worse soon follows. As the nutrients are removed so the sulphate begins to combine with metals in the soil. The most important is aluminium, which is present in huge quantities in most soils. Normally, aluminium is harmlessly bound up with organic materials. But when these links are severed and the metal goes into solution with sulphate it becomes very toxic. Today, aluminium is emerging as the main toxic agent in acid soils and lakes. The release of toxic aluminium into solution in soils marks the third and fatal phase in the saga of acid rain, according to Ulrich's thesis.

The acid reaches a critical level at a pH of 4.2. Below that figure aluminium is released from its "polymerisation" with organic matter and becomes toxic. Ulrich says aluminium toxicity becomes a problem as the amount of aluminium in the soil approaches the amount of calcium. It worsens when the aluminium is dominant and stops growth completely when the ratio of calcium to aluminium reaches 1:7: one atom of calcium to seven of aluminium. At Ulrich's forest research station at Solling this ratio has fallen from 1:1 in 1972 to around 1:5 today. Dead tree tops mark this calcium deficiency. But this is only a prelude to the acute poisoning that occurs as the aluminium starts to inhibit the division of cells in the roots of the trees, and destroy its defences against disease organisms. First to be attacked are the fine root ends through which trees extract moisture from the soil. Any aluminium in the moisture will damage the root endodermis, the innermost layer of the cortex of the root which controls the movement of liquid into the plant. Ulrich says, "if the endodermis is damaged the plant has lost the ability to control the ionic composition of the sulphur entering the vessels . . . the plant has lost its integrity in the soil".

The toxins invade, damaging cells as they go. The tree cannot seal the damaged root system and the spores of bacteria, fungi, viruses and other pathogens invade and work their way in. In this way secondary diseases begin. The tree is doomed. Death will come slowly by a mixture of starvation, disease and poisoning.

Other processes may reinforce the cycle of death described by Ulrich. Aluminium also damages the soil bacteria which decompose vegetation and recycle plant nutrients. As a result the soil system may start to generate its own acid which, according to Ulrich, may contribute as much to the continued acidification of the soil as acid rain.

In addition, parts of West Germany are regularly shrouded in low cloud which is often highly acidic. Aerosols of tiny sulphur particles are held in the cloud's moisture and may be absorbed by pine needles, with which they come into contact. Professor Fred Last of the Institute of Terrestrial Ecology in Edinburgh believes that these aerosols may have an especially severe effect on trees on high exposed hillsides in Germany. Spruce, the tree that has suffered more than any other in Germany, traps three times as much solid sulphur as the beech.

Ulrich believes that today some two million hectares of forests in Germany may be close to the threshold where toxic aluminium will begin to damage tree roots. "The leaching of base cations from the rooting zone is completed in many acid forest soils" he says. "The ecosystem has a very low resilience. The next warm, dry year will give rise to a new acidification push in the rooting zone . . . and at the same time reduce the dissolved organic matter."

Aluminium will go into solution and the trees will die. Ulrich concludes, in his slightly disjointed English, "a strong increase of forest damages in central Europe is forecasted during the next decade".

The Lakes of Scandinavia

Salmon started to disappear from the lakes of southern Norway shortly after the First World War. Inland stocks of brown trout became scarce after 1920. They have disappeared from nearly 2000 lakes and today many other species of fish are virtually extinct across 13 000 km^2 of the country. In the four southern most counties more than half of the fish population has been lost in the past 40 years.

In Sweden they noticed the disappearance of crayfish first. Today the Swedes retain their love of crayfish but rely on imports from Turkey. Nine thousand Swedish lakes, including a large proportion in the south of the country, show heavy fish losses. Four thousand lakes are effectively dead. In both countries the cause is clear: acidification.

A tell-tale mucus clogging the gills shows that the fish are under attack – not from the acidity of the water itself but from the aluminium washed by acid rain from soils into the lakes and rivers. As in German forests, so in Scandinavian lakes: aluminium is the killer.

The fish die because the system for regulating salt in their bodies cannot cope with the toxic aluminium. The gill, a most sensitive organ, takes both oxygen and salt into the fish. Aluminium deposited on the gills inhibits this process. The fish pants for breath and, as the salt level in its body falls, proteins are destroyed and the fish eventually dies.

The toxicity of lakes develops in a way remarkably similar to processes in soils. The solubility of aluminium increases as the pH of the water falls. It is most soluble at a pH of 5, when aluminium hydroxide is precipitated in large amounts onto the gills of fish. The calcium/aluminium ratio is as important to toxicity of lakes as it is to soils. Norwegian biologists have found that lakes with a low calcium content die most quickly. The critical pH level for fish life to continue in a lake may vary by one unit of pH or more depending on the calcium level. Without calcium, toxic inorganic forms of aluminium hydroxide dominate over harmless forms in which aluminium is chemically linked to organic material. The toxic forms are lethal to fish at concentrations as low as 70 μg l^{-1}.

It is not just fish that die. Acidification changes the whole aquatic ecosystem. An acid lake is crystal clear. On the bottom a thick mat of white moss covers the sediments. A green carpet of algae covers boulders and on the shoreline leaves collect, with grass, twigs and other organic debris. The debris decomposes much more slowly and this mass of vegetation traps valuable nutrients.

The disappearance of fish allows a few invertebrate carnivores to thrive, despite the decline in plankton, insects, crustaceans, snails and mussels. Some sensitive species, such as the mayfly and freshwater shrimps and snails, die as the pH of the lakes drops below 6. But for most the levels of toxic aluminium secure their fate.

The discovery that aluminium is the toxic element in aquatic as well as terrestrial acidification has helped forge the scientific links between the effects of acid rain on terrestrial ecosystems and on aquatic ones. Soil chemistry is crucial to what happens in lakes. It helps explain why southern Scandinavia, where the rate of acid deposition is only a fraction of that found in central Europe, suffers such exceptional damage to lakes, and why Scandinavian forests thrive as the lakes die.

A crucial factor here appears to be the period in spring when the winter's snow melts. During this time the soils become saturated and the "snow-melt" which contains several months' accumulation of sulphur acids, washes straight through the thin soils and into streams and lakes. The normal ion-exchange processes, during which the soil is acidified and the water is neutralised, will not have time to take place.

Scientists estimate that acidification begins in most Scandinavian lakes when sulphur is deposited at around 0.5 g m^{-2} per year. Some Swedish scientists put the "safe load" for their most sensitive lakes even lower, at 0.3 g. The current rate of deposition is around 2–3 g m^{-2}/year. For 10 years now the rates of deposition in Scandinavia have remained stable as emission rates have stabilised in recession-hit Britain and elsewhere. But the Norwegian scientist

Ivar Muniz told the Stockholm conference there were "no signs of levelling off in the progressive acidification of lakes". The reason for this is likely to be that the environment is becoming steadily more sensitive to acid. More than half the brown trout of Norway are lost and Muniz says "if this trend persists more than 80 per cent . . . will vanish during this decade". Trout losses in the north of the country are now "strikingly similar to the situation we experienced in the south".

The Swedish Environmental Protection Board warns that "the acid load in southern Scandinavia has to be reduced to at least one-third of today's load, if all the former good fishing waters are to be saved".

Europe and the CEGB

The rates for sulphur deposits are highest in Czechoslovakia and East Germany, which also emit the most. The East Germans burn sulphurous lignite coal and, like other East European countries, are reluctant to spend money on pollution controls. Damage to crops, forests and rivers is widespread in these countries. East Germany has recently overtaken Britain as the leading source of sulphur pollution in Sweden.

Britain is freer than any other country in Europe from other people's emissions. Yugoslavia is the principal source of sulphur imports to five neighbouring countries. The power stations and factories of northern Italy may be starting to kill fish and forests in Switzerland and Austria. Thirty per cent of all Europe's emissions land up in the Soviet Union. Britain sends 6 per cent of all its emissions to Russia.

There is a remarkably low level of deposition in Scandinavia, where highly sensitive soils cause some of the worst acid rain effects found anywhere.

It is, perhaps, no wonder that Britain cannot see eye to eye with Norway and Sweden over acid rain. Looked at from Britain the fuss may look absurd. Norway and Sweden between them receive only four per cent of the sulphur emitted from Britain's power stations. The chimneys that send that acid to Scandinavia also deposit up to a quarter of Britain's emissions harmlessly into the North Sea. Sulphur is deposited in Scandinavia at only one-tenth of the rate that it is in East Germany and Czechoslovakia. Is it Britain's fault, civil servants wonder, that Scandinavian lakes and rivers are so sensitive?

Look at the problem from the other side of the North Sea and it looks different. Lakes cover 10 per cent of Sweden and they are dying as a result of inaction by a foreign country. Now the forests, a major economic resource, could be threatened. Norway receives more than five times as much sulphur as it produces; Sweden more than twice as much. Only 17 per cent of the sulphur poisoning their lakes arises within the two countries. Britain, Europe's biggest emitter of sulphur outside the Soviet Union, is the main culprit. Britain emits 43 per cent more sulphur per head of population than Sweden and 200 per cent more than Norway. But less than half as much sulphur is deposited in British soil as is emitted from British chimneys. By contrast, twice as much British sulphur lands on Norwegian soils as does Norwegian sulphur.

The controlling body of Britain's power stations is the Central Electricity Generating Board. The CEGB is rightly proud of its post-war policy of erecting stacks 200 m or more high to reduce pollution from sulphur dioxide at ground level in Britain's urban areas. This policy played a significant part in ending the notorious London smogs, which once killed thousands of people each winter. However, the CEGB contests the frequent claim that tall stacks simply "export" pollution. CEGB member Gill Blackman points out that international models of long-distance pollution suggest that "long-range transport is a function of total emissions and that height of emission is of minor importance". This bears out another CEGB observation (often intended to imply that acid rain does no harm) that animals were dying in Scandinavian lakes at the start of this century, long before tall stacks were built. Low chimneys cause acid rain, too. But the board rests its defence on the absence of proof that acid rain is the main cause of acidified soils and lakes. "It is premature to conclude that the long range transport of sulphur dioxide has been proved responsible" Blackman told the National Society for Clean Air recently. The CEGB says that most of the links in the acidification chain are not proven. Blackman points out that rain in Europe did not appear to become more acid between 1965 and 1975, when European emissions rose by 35 per cent.

But this may be because a moving parcel of air can hold only a limited amount of sulphuric and nitric acid. Importantly, this implies that a similar reduction in emissions might have only a marginal effect on the acidity of rainfall, though it might have a far greater effect in reducing "dry" deposition in the host country of the power station. However, the board is certainly right to highlight the complexities and uncertainties that remain in the scientific debate. Current research by the CEGB, financed by the

California-based Electrical Power Research Institute, employs an old Hercules aircraft to plot the progress of sulphur dioxide plumes from the Egborough power station in Yorkshire, and may clarify some of these issues. But the board's insistence that "only if it can be proved that pollutants transported over long distances play an important part in the decline of fish stocks in Scandinavia will it be necessary to consider reduction of pollution at source" irritates many scientists. The international community – and even British government officials – now accept that, whatever the finer points, the evidence against emissions from power stations is overwhelming. The Stockholm meeting of experts in June, at which CEGB scientists presented their arguments, agreed that "if a general decrease of emissions were to take place within a large industrialised region (Europe, for example) specified areas within this region might experience significantly smaller or larger decreases in deposition. However, the total deposition over the whole industrialised region would decrease approximately in proportion to the reduction in emission." And they concluded that reductions in emissions would reduce acidification.

12 August, 1982

30

Acid rain erodes our credibility

TAM DALYELL

Declare war on acid rain! If Britain were to make such a gesture we would be doing an international service. And even over a period as long as 15 years we would be paying a lot less (£184 millions) than the £684 millions that will go next year to safeguard the Falkland Islands from the Argentinians – a matter that many ecologists see as a fight between two bald men over the possession of a comb.

I write with some conviction on acid rain having recently attended a well organised meeting on the subject in the Upper House. Credit for its success is due to Lord Craigton, chairman of the All-Party Conservation Committee that meets about once a month in the House of Lords. Craigton invited Dr M. H. Unsworth of the Institute of Terrestrial Ecology (ITE), at the Bush Estate, Penicuik, Midlothian; and Dr Gwynneth Howells of the CEGB, to speak on "acid inputs to the natural environment". Plenty of people turned up, including Mark Lennox Boyd, one of the influential and able new generation of Conservatives, and MP for ITE Merlewood, the Father of the House, John Parker, who has been campaigning on the environment and forestry since 1935, and a Green troika of David Clark, Opposition spokesman on environment, Peter Hardy, author of a book on badgers, and chairman of the Council of Europe Agricultural Committee, and me.

How many, two years ago, would have supposed that "acid rain" would become a topic of importance? You would have been forgiven for a knowing smile then, but now acid rain is no laughing matter. What those little droplets have absorbed after the burning of fossil fuels is of grave concern, not only to the anglers of Scandinavia, but to most Europeans. The potential sources of acid rain are not only in Britain and the Ruhr, but also in Czechoslovakia and Poland. The monster does not recognise national boundaries, nor even the divisions between East and West. Twenty per cent of all lakes in Sweden are highly acidic. Six per cent of all lakes in wild Ontario are affected and downwind from Sudbury Smelter 19 lakes have no fish. Nova Scotia has lost much of its salmon spawning. Half of the more acid lakes in southern Norway have no fish at all.

We need to be monitoring for more data. We do not know enough about how often acidic reservoirs occur. Of course, vegetation and the nature of the soil can make a difference. For example, if acid rain falls on a spruce forest, the rain can become even more acid. Moreover, acid rain can alter the ecology by dissolving aluminium in the soil. Acidifying droplets can reduce the growth of trees and crops, at concentrations far lower than had been suspected up to now. Circumstantial evidence suggests that many trees have died in areas of Germany where acid rain is most prevalent. Rain falling through canopies of spruce forests becomes more acid probably because dry deposits on leaves are washed off and because of chemical reaction with the leaves. It appears that deciduous trees do not acidify in this way. Whereas agricultural soils are usually maintained close to neutral by adding lime the problem is altogether more serious with forest and moorland soils: extra acid inputs may release aluminium in various chemical forms to the ground water. The modifications of the quality of acid rain as it passes through soils depends on the soil properties, organic matter, microbial activity and underlying rock. Most of the rain that reaches rivers and lakes has first passed over vegetation and through soils, so the land use and soil type can influence the acidity of water courses. At present, I am told, the subject is not well understood. Like study of the forest, it may take a generation to quantify the effect on fish stock. A direct causal relationship may not be easy to establish. Changes in land use might have to be taken into account. The relationship between rain acidity and surface water acidity will vary from area to area. Conditions will determine the different degrees of neutralisation: even lakes next to each other can have different acidities. Ever since the 1920s, the Norwegians have used lime, in some lakes, to produce better fish stocks. Again, conditions in which calcium is leached from the soil may be beneficial for brown trout.

Persistent acid conditions may inhibit the reproduction of fish. Deaths of trout and salmon have been connected with acid input to streams in spring and autumn. In spring melting snow releases pollutants; in autumn rain probably removes the acid accumulated during the summer. For the most part, the damage is done by soluble aluminium released from soil by acid water. Professor Fred Last and his colleagues in Edinburgh have also observed effects on other aquatic animal and plant life.

What to do? Britain has signed the European Convention on the Environment, promising our best efforts to limit and reduce emissions, and to exchange information in collaborative work. But, in practice, there should be a long term programme of washing coal, extracting the sulphur from carbon, extracting flue gases, and building fluidised beds. The technology is available, and should certainly be used in any new coal-burning power station. The acute question is – do we try to introduce such ideas into existing power stations?

Dr Howells and Dr Unsworth said when asked the inevitable MPs' question about the price, that for £500 million spent between now and the end of the century we could reduce toxic emissions, by half, at the cost of increasing the price of electricity by 15 per cent. One of the attractions of this work is that it would employ a lot of labour. If we say we cannot afford it, the reply is that we pay out more and more millions of pounds in unemployment benefit.

24 February, 1983

ACID COMMENTS

There is a tradition among criminals known as laundering. Money gained by robbing banks isn't spent just on wine, women and song, or on setting up the next job: some of it is put into legitimate businesses. In this way, the Mafia is rumoured to have become one of the largest corporate concerns in the United States. No one – or not many people – would think of describing the Central Electricity Generating Board in the same terms as the Mafia, although Sir Walter Marshall, its chairman, certainly carries something of the "godfather" image. But the board has learned something from the laundering business.

On Monday, the CEGB revealed that, together with the National Coal Board, it plans to spend £5 million over the next five years to investigate acid rain. The money is to be laundered through the Royal Society, which prefers to talk of "acidification of surface waters in Norway and Sweden". Therein lies the clue to "the Royal's" involvement. The CEGB admits that it would be kicked out were it to send a team of researchers into Scandinavia to investigate acid rain – the board is already infamous as a polluter in Sweden and Norway – but the Royal Society has persuaded its Norwegian and Swedish counterparts to join in the study. Thus independence is guaranteed.

There is nothing wrong with the Royal Society taking the money and operating independently of the NCB and CEGB. Indeed, the Royal Society has praised similar arrangements in its evidence to the House of Lords Select Committee on Science and Technology. And there is no denying that there are still many unknowns in the acid-rain saga. But science and politics aren't the same thing.

Political agreements have already been devised demanding "significant reductions" in the emissions of sulphur dioxide into the atmosphere. Walter Marshall said on Monday that it is unrealistic to expect the CEGB to make substantial reductions in its emissions. To do so would cost a fortune – a capital investment over £4000 million and annual costs over £700 m.

So what will happen if, after five years, the Royal Society's study shows that acid rain really is wrecking Scandinavian lakes? Sir Walter agrees that the CEGB will be forced to act: but what will it do? One answer may not be to add "scrubbers" to the power stations, but to dump chemicals into the lakes to neutralise the effects of the SO_2. At least, some will argue that, leaving the way open for another round of debate and research.

Who knows? Perhaps the polluters can keep this one running and running, then by the time the CEGB is forced to act, either nuclear power will be acceptable and commonplace or there will be new and cleaner coal-burning technology such as the pressurised fluidised-bed boiler that was once the apple of the NCB's eye but that the CEGB tried to ignore.

If this does happen, the environment will survive. The problem of acid rain has grown up over centuries. It makes no sense to try to eliminate it in years, especially if the standard of living has to fall throughout Europe in return for marginal improvements in Scandinavian lakes and in the life style of German trees.

It seems obvious that any new power stations built in the UK must deal with the problem of SO_2 emissions. After 50 years, perhaps even less, the problem would have gone away as new power stations replaced the old polluters. That probably isn't what the environmentalists have in mind as they press for the clean up of the world's power stations.

There's no denying that there are some in the power industry who would be delighted to be told that they cannot keep on burning that mucky black stuff. Indeed, it could even be that by the time the scientific evidence is there to prove that acid rain is wrecking the Scandinavian environment, that coal-fired power stations are a major source of that acid, and that the best way to save Scandinavia is to clean up the CEGB's act, fast reactors are a commercial reality. That would add to the coincidence that led the Secretary of State for Energy to release a statement on Britain's fast reactor programme just minutes before the Royal Society unveiled the acid-rain project.

Peter Walker's statement on fast reactors says little: you have to read between the lines to get the true picture. "The government has decided" said Mr Walker on Monday, "to open formal nego-tiations to seek agreement on joint development of fast reactors with France, Germany, Italy, Belgium and the Netherlands." You can be pretty sure that such a statement would not have been made had there been any chance of those negotiations failing. Thus the Department of Energy has already been tipped the wink by France, the only country in the world let alone Europe with an aggressive programme on fast reactors.

Not long ago France was confidently ploughing ahead with its fast-reactor programme. Super-Phenix was far ahead of anything under construction elsewhere. It would be the model for a whole series of "commercial" fast reactors. Super-Phenix turned out to be expensive. The French realised that they didn't have all the answers. So they cut the price of joining their club. At one time France wanted the UK to pay a sizable sum to join the European fast-reactor effort. There was some argument over this in the British nuclear establishment. That price has now come down to a price the country can afford − nothing. So the way is open for further negotiations, negotiations so promising that the govern-ment can admit that they exist.

We can expect that soon after those government-to-government talks are over − perhaps some time this autumn − the CEGB and the UKAEA will begin to talk to their counterparts in Europe. Then that £5 million set aside for the acid-rain work will vanish into insignificance as the talk turns to billions. But there is no denying the connection. Render coal unburnable and nuclear power becomes even more attractive to the electricity utilities. Up goes the price of uranium, and with it the attraction of the fast reactor.

"COMMENT", 8 September, 1983

ONE-THIRD OF GERMAN TREES HIT BY ACID RAIN

More than a third of West Germany's trees have now been damaged by acid rain, according to a national survey completed this summer and just published. The proportion has leapt from 7.7 per cent to 34 per cent in one year – partly because more thorough investigation has found damage missed last year.

The deterioration was discussed by a committee of the West German parliament on Monday. Damage is worst in the most heavily forested areas. In Bavaria, 46 per cent of trees are damaged; in Baden-Württemberg, which includes the Black Forest, 49 per cent are damaged.

For the first time the methods of data collection in each area have been standardised. Light damage means less than 20 per cent of needles have been lost; medium damage 20–60 per cent; severe damage more than 60 per cent lost. A similar gradation is applied to deciduous trees.

The survey reveals a dramatic increase in the number of trees with medium or severe damage. It has increased by five times to 700 000 hectares – or one tree in 10 – since last year.

Professor Hans-Ullrich Moosmayer, the director of the Baden-Württemberg forestry commission, said "We are very much concerned about that five-times increase, as the 60 per cent stage of damage seems to be a point of no return for species like fir and spruce."

The survey has identified fir and spruce as the trees most affected. The spruce, the country's most widespread tree and planted on nearly three million hectares, is badly hit. A total of 41 per cent of spruce trees are damaged with 11 per cent showing medium or severe damage. But worse still is the fir with three out of four trees damaged and 7 per cent of them dying. Moosmayer warned that the devastation of the fir meant that there was a real risk of whole forests being destroyed.

Deciduous trees such as the oak and the beech are also under threat. Twenty-six per cent of beech trees and 15 per cent of oaks have been damaged.

Moosmayer said "The figures clearly indicate the necessity to intensify the efforts to cut down pollutant emissions as well as to intensify the efforts to come to unleaded fuel regulations for new automobiles."

"THIS WEEK", *27 October, 1983*

31

MPs back curbs on acid rain

FRED PEARCE

A committee of MPs will today throw its weight behind calls for Britain to act now to cut its contribution to acid rain in Europe. The environment committee of the House of Commons adds its voice to a similar report from the House of Lords' European Communities committee. A month ago, the lords called for "immediate action" to cut the amount of sulphur dioxide and oxides of nitrogen that disappear up power station chimneys.

The MPs are expected to go further than the lords by calling for more action faster. They will certainly want Britain to join the growing band of nations in the "30-per-cent club" which are committed to an immediate reduction of 30 per cent in sulphur dioxide emissions.

But they will also want Britain to back the proposals in an EEC draft directive which will, if adopted, require a 60-per-cent cut in emissions by 1995. This sweeping proposal, which the Central Electricity Generating Board (CEGB) estimates would cost it £2 billion, did not win the support of the lords.

The MPs believe that the main burden in attacking acid rain should fall on the CEGB, whose power stations are responsible for more than half the sulphur dioxide pollution produced in Britain. But they are expected to make a number of proposals to bring in new controls on both sulphur dioxide and oxides of nitrogen at other industrial plants and on oxides of nitrogen in the exhausts of new and existing motor vehicles.

Both the lords and MPs criticise the British government's central claim that too little is known about the extent of the effects of acid rain for expensive remedial measures to be justified. They believe that there is now a consensus among scientists in Britain, as well as elsewhere, that action is required against the causes of acid rain now, despite the remaining uncertainties.

MPs have been impressed by forthright evidence from scientists from the Natural Environment Research Council who see action as imperative. By contrast, the role of Sir Walter Marshall, chairman of the CEGB, in advising the government about the poor quality of much research to date is met with scorn.

Britain is once again in danger of becoming politically isolated on an issue that raises temperatures on the mainland of Europe more than at home.

Those who have seen the Commons' report say that it includes a much more wide-ranging assessment of the science of acid rain than that attempted by the Lords. Evidence ranges from the declining snail population in Norwegian lakes to an investigation of the damage to venerated British buildings such as Westminster Abbey and York Minster.

MPs have been told that the damage to forests in West Germany is continuing apace. This time last year scientists there reported that 34 per cent of trees showed signs of acid-rain damage. A new survey this summer finds that the damage exceeds 50 per cent.

The committee has also heard about damage to fisheries in the south of Scotland, the Lake District and parts of Wales, as rivers become acidified.

In defence of its role, the CEGB points out that its sulphur dioxide emissions have fallen by more than a third since 1970. So if the 30-per-cent club had set its baseline date at 1970 rather than 1980 Britain would already have met the target. But, as others pointed out to the MPs, Britain remains the largest emitter of sulphur dioxide in Western Europe.

8 September, 1984

32

Ministers reject clean-up of acid rain

CATHERINE CAUFIELD AND FRED PEARCE

The British government this week snubbed two parliamentary select committees, the Royal Commission on Environmental Pollution, and its own environment department in rejecting their calls for action on acid rain.

A white paper rejects the recommendations of all four bodies. In September the House of Commons select committee on the environment called for Britain to cut its emissions of sulphur dioxide (SO_2) and nitrous oxides by 60 per cent by the year 2000, in accordance with an EEC draft directive. The previous month, the House of Lords select committee on the European Communities recommended the immediate fitting of flue-gas desulphurisation equipment on at least two power stations. Last February the Royal Commission called for a pilot scheme to cut SO_2 emissions from coal-fired power stations.

Environment ministers and expert advisors had lobbied privately for Britain to join the "30-per-cent club" of countries committed to reducing their emissions of SO_2 to 30 per cent of their 1980 levels by 1995. But they were over-ruled by the Treasury and the Department of Energy.

The white paper gives two reasons for the government's decision not to join the club. First, it is not necessary, because Britain's emissions have already declined by nearly 40 per cent since 1970. Secondly, "stronger growth in electricity demand could reverse these trends" and could necessitate the expenditure of several hundred million pounds if Britain was to meet the requirements of the club.

The government has decided to accept the calls of the Commons select committee and the Royal Commission for a more extensive network of air pollution monitoring stations. A network of about 20 nitrous oxide and 10 ozone monitors "is currently being considered".

The white paper rejects the Commons select committee's call for research on the health effects of air pollution. The Clean Air Act, it says, has eliminated the "clear-cut acute effects of air pollution on health", and other pollutants are not present in concentrations high enough to "suggest the likelihood of significant effects".

Ministers are certain to face an angry reaction to their decision when the Commons debates acid rain next week. And they will have to defend their position again when the first summit of environment ministers meets in London the following week.

Behind the politics the scientific debate over acid rain is still in full flow. The claim from the British electricity industry that nitrous oxides from car exhausts are an important source of acid rain is now accepted by environmentalists.

Friends of the Earth this week said that 30 per cent of rain acidity in Britain now comes from nitrous oxides rather than SO_2. And it agreed that ozone (again caused by car exhausts) was a main cause of forest damage.

But the group stood firmly by another assertion: that any fall in acid emissions should cause a proportional reduction in acid deposition.

6 December, 1984

PART SIX

The Human Impact: the Carbon Dioxide Greenhouse Effect

Carbon dioxide is a colourless, tasteless, transparent gas that is present in very small quantities in the air that we breathe in, and rather larger quantities in the air that we breathe out, since it is a waste product of the processes by which we maintain life. As such, it is a fundamental component of Lovelock's Gaia. It also has the interesting property that while it allows the electromagnetic energy of the Sun's rays to pass through it unhindered to the surface of the Earth (just as do the other gases of the atmosphere of our planet), when the warm surface of the ground or ocean radiates heat upward at infra-red frequencies this heat is absorbed, very effectively, by carbon dioxide. This process by which heat is trapped near the surface of the Earth is called, for obvious reasons, a "greenhouse effect". It operates for other gases in the air, as well as carbon dioxide. But, unlike those other gases, the proportion of carbon dioxide in the air is steadily increasing as a result of human activities.

The most simple-minded conclusion to jump to in view of the fact that (i) carbon dioxide traps heat and makes the Earth warmer and (ii) the amount of carbon dioxide in the air is increasing, is that the world is going to warm up, perhaps to a disastrous extent. This is just the simple-minded conclusion that some researchers presented to an astonished world in the middle of the 1970s. This led to a spate of activity among climate researchers – and others – which produced a series of sometimes contradictory and confusing reports on this greenhouse effect. The articles from *New Scientist* presented here give a flavour of the swings and roundabouts nature of this debate. By the middle of the 1980s, it seems that some sort of consensus is emerging from the climatologists, and that the important, but not dominant, role of the greenhouse effect in the climate of the twenty-first century is beginning to be understood.

33

Fossil fuel: future shock?

JOHN GRIBBIN

Every time we burn coal, gas or oil we pump yet more carbon dioxide into the atmosphere. Now that the initial scare stories about the impact of high levels of atmospheric carbon dioxide have subsided, climatologists are able more accurately to predict the likely outcome

The impact of carbon dioxide from burning fossil fuel on the climate of the Earth has become a major focus of scientific attention, with the publication of a US National Academy of Sciences report *Energy and Climate* (see *New Scientist*, vol. 75, p. 211) last year and papers appearing almost weekly in the specialist journals. Put at its simplest, the argument holds that burning fossil fuels (oil, coal and gas) releases carbon dioxide into the atmosphere; carbon dioxide, through the "greenhouse effect", warms the surface of the Earth by retaining heat that would otherwise escape from the lower atmosphere. If the argument is valid, we must ask how much fossil fuel we can burn before a long-lasting and damaging climate shift becomes established.

With the unstated assumption that warming of this kind must be a "bad thing", the argument is used in its most extreme form by proponents of a nuclear-based energy strategy to argue the case against coal. This is perhaps going a little too far as at present there is a great deal of uncertainty about the links between carbon dioxide and climate, about the ability of the oceans and biomass (particularly plants) to absorb more carbon dioxide, and even about whether or not a warmer Earth is necessarily a bad thing. But it is clear that these are possibilities that must now be considered by planners and policy makers, especially as we start to look beyond the year 2000. The first priority is to establish the real nature of the links between carbon dioxide and climate, and between carbon dioxide produced from burning fossil fuel and the amount that stays in the atmosphere.

Since the late nineteenth century, the concentration of carbon dioxide in the air has increased from about 290 parts per million (ppm) to about 330 ppm, a trend that is certainly significant and that coincides with the growth of industry worldwide. But this increase corresponds to about half of all the carbon dioxide released from burnt fossil fuel and destruction of forests over the same period. So there must be "reservoirs" that have so far been capable of absorbing about 50 per cent of the carbon dioxide released. Are these reservoirs full, so that in future carbon dioxide concentration in the atmosphere will increase more nearly in line with what is produced from burning? Or, on the contrary, might they be so empty that we could find ways of using them to absorb almost all the excess carbon dioxide now being produced by human activities?

Perhaps the best guide initially is provided by the figures for total carbon stored in different reservoirs. In the atmosphere itself, the total is some 700 Gt (1 Gt = 10^9 tonnes), while the biomass on land contains about 1800 Gt, similar to the amount stored in oceanic surface waters; the deep oceans contain about 32 000 Gt.

On this evidence, once we start talking about human activities doubling the carbon dioxide concentration in the atmosphere (which is the sort of figure people are starting to worry about), then there must be some problems in hoping that the biomass can be built up to relieve the situation. The problem is made even worse, however, by the fact that the world's forests (the chief terrestrial growing biomass reservoir) are almost certainly shrinking at the hands of developers. And, not only does this reduce the biomass reservoir, it also puts carbon dioxide back into the atmosphere when the trees are burned.

Input from fossil fuels

Professor Minze Stuiver, of the University of Washington, for example, calculates that from 1850 to 1950 a total of 120 Gt of carbon was pumped into the atmosphere from deforestation and burning dead organic material, while over the same period the increase from burning fossil fuels was only 60 Gt (*Science*, vol. 199, p. 253). Some people contend that this biospheric trend is now levelling off, and even Stuiver agrees that in the immediate future the dominant input of carbon dioxide to the atmosphere will come from fossil fuel. There are a great many uncertainties in this area, however, and the links between carbon dioxide and the biomass certainly merit more attention than is usually provided by energy lobbyists, whatever their flavour.

For long-term and massive storing of carbon dioxide, though, the oceans do seem to offer interesting possibilities and now contain more than ten times as much carbon as the biomass and atmosphere put together. This, almost certainly, is where the "extra" 50 per cent of carbon dioxide production is going each year, and optimists such as Dr Cesare Marchetti, of the International Institute for Applied Systems Analysis (IIASA) in Austria, speculate about the possibility of injecting 10^{10} tonnes of carbon dioxide a year into the Mediterranean water that flows out through the Strait of Gibraltar at a rate of 10^{14} tonnes a year and sinks slowly into the deep ocean where it mixes on a timescale of thousands of years (*Climate Change*, vol. 1, p. 59). Conversely, some authorities suggest that sea-water is nearing saturation with carbon dioxide and that as the global temperature rises the problem is made worse because this causes a fall in solubility of the gas.

Other optimists point out that there are no obvious technical problems to scrubbing carbon dioxide from the gases produced by burning fuels, and storing it in solution or solid compounds – this would certainly be less dangerous than stored nuclear wastes. No real efforts have been made in this direction yet because carbon dioxide has not been classed as a pollutant. But a little legislation could work wonders. That said, however, the incentive for any such legislation must come from an understanding of the likely consequences of leaving the carbon dioxide in the atmosphere to do its worst.

Taking fossil fuel alone, how much carbon dioxide is likely to be produced over the next 50 to 100 years, and what would that mean in climatic terms if no precautions to remove excess carbon dioxide were taken? Up until the end of the 1940s, the dramatic warming that set in at the end of the nineteenth century could have been taken as an indication of the effects of the carbon dioxide then being added to the atmosphere. But the subsequent cooling, equally dramatic in the short term, shows that as yet anthropogenic carbon dioxide emissions by no means dominate the changing climate. Climate is always changing, on a variety of timescales, and there seems little point in worrying about anthropogenic influences that are of the same magnitude and duration as these natural short-term fluctuations. That's probably just as well, as climate modelling today is inadequate for providing any worthwhile information about such flickers. What we need is information about longer-lasting and larger effects than the natural changes of, say, the past millenium, and that is something the models can tell us about, if only approximately.

Painting with this broad brush, the smallest change we can reasonably ask the modellers to tell us about is a doubling of atmospheric carbon dioxide. Over the past 15 years or so, estimates of the consequences of such an increase have ranged from about 10 K increase in mean surface temperatures to about 0.7 K increase; the best rule of thumb at present (although not yet a consensus view) is that a rise of average temperatures by about 2 K, with more pronounced effects at high latitudes, is likely.

Limitations of models

Apart from such interesting consequences as melting of polar sea-ice, such a shift would, by decreasing the temperature gradient between poles and equator, certainly shift climate and rainfall belts; but these models must still be taken with a large pinch of salt, as they do not include such important effects as changes in cloud cover. A warmer Earth, with increased evaporation from the oceans, ought to be a more cloudy place (with increased rainfall), and clouds tend to reflect heat from the Sun away before it reaches the ground, perhaps cancelling out part of the carbon-dioxide-induced warming. We simply do not know, from the models at least, what a warmer Earth would be like to live in. We can, however, get some feel for the timescales involved by looking at a study carried out at the IIASA for the United Nations Environment Programme.

The figures are derived from a 30 TW fossil-fuel energy "strategy" ($T \equiv 10^{12}$), in which world demands for energy levels off at this figure early in the twenty-first century and there is no significant use of any energy sources except coal, oil and gas. (Coal is the only long-term fossil fuel, with reserves that could last centuries, compared with just decades for oil and gas.) In such a scenario, the temperature change starts to dominate over any natural trends in about 50 years time, when it reaches a magnitude of 2 K. But it would be far too late then to attempt to restore the natural balance, as it takes decades to change the pattern of primary energy use, or indeed to achieve widespread use of "pollution" controls on carbon dioxide, let alone such grand schemes as dumping the carbon dioxide in the deep ocean, or restoring the biomass to something of its former glory.

In some ways, these IIASA projections are a "worst-possible" case. With any significant use of Solar, wave or nuclear power, or any effective controls on the amount of carbon dioxide released, or any effective means of disposing of the gas other than release to the atmosphere, the figures for carbon dioxide in the atmosphere and the resulting change in global temperature will be less. What the projections tell us is that one or more of these options must be taken up soon – unless there is some good reason to accept that the consequence of a rise in global temperatures of 6 K or more is something that our grandchildren will be happy to live with.

It would be mischievous to suggest, given the present state-of-the-art in climate studies, that a significantly warmer Earth might be a better place to live in, and that we therefore should not worry about the likely carbon-dioxide-induced warming of the twenty-first century. But it is just as mischievous to assume, as so many people do, that a warmer Earth must be a worse place to live and that therefore panic measures are necessary to preserve the *status quo*. In particular, there is some reason to believe that a slight warming might be welcome, given the perspective of the past thousand years or so, and on this basis we have a breathing space in which to plan a considered reaction to this situation.

Professor Will Kellogg, of the US National Center for Atmospheric Research, has recently looked at all currently recognised anthropogenic influences of climate, and concludes that, indeed, these "will probably begin to dominate over natural processes of climatic change before the turn of the century, and will result in a decided warming trend that will accelerate in the decades after that". Because of the deficiencies of present models, Kellogg has tried to sketch out what this might mean for agriculture and human society by comparison with the previous warm epoch, the so-called Climatic Optimum of 4000 to 8000 years ago. Various pieces of proxy data – pollen changes in sediments, changing water levels in lakes, tree rings, ice cores and others – have been combined to give a broad picture of this period, after the most recent ice age, which saw the rise of human civilisation. Of course, the reason for a warm Earth then was not increased carbon dioxide in the atmosphere; but, again in Kellogg's words, "using the real Earth for a model is at least as good as, and probably better than, the theoretical numerical models".

This "real-Earth" model shows us a warm Earth with conditions more favourable for agriculture in North Africa, Europe wetter, Scandinavia dryer, and a belt of grasslands across North America. Such a warm Earth would be by no means a less desirable place in which to live, and the rainfall patterns in particular seem to be more favourable to agricultural production globally than those of today. At the same time, the increased growing season produced by a warmer climate would also help agriculture.

A few places would suffer in the changed climate, not least central North America. But the possibility of having a climate more suitable for feeding a large population should also be taken into account when the "danger" of an imminent carbon-dioxide-induced global warming is being discussed. The argument in favour of the *status quo*, however, is that we do manage (just) to cope with the vagaries of the present climate, and any change is going to require a painful period of adjustment in farming practices and food trade. In the very long term, beyond the next 100 years, it is almost certain that our descendants will want to avoid a runaway global warming sufficient to melt polar ice and raise sea-level dramatically, so the potential to meet all projected energy demands for the next 200 years from coal alone is certainly unrealistic.

The key argument, as with debate about harmful effects of fluorocarbon-propelled aerosol sprays on the ozone layer and similar issues, is that we should not commit ourselves to a course of action without being sure that it is safe; the legal maxim "innocent until proven guilty" has to be reversed when considering the prospects of possibly permanent damage to the environment. We do know we can stand a warming of a degree or two, but now is precisely the time to be worrying about the possible harmful effects of larger increases in global temperature, and to be finding ways of controlling the impact of carbon dioxide.

This is the right time to study the issues with the priority they deserve, to set up national and international institutions as called for by the NAS report I mentioned earlier, to consider legislation that would class carbon dioxide as a pollutant, to look at ways of removing carbon dioxide from exhaust emissions and either storing it on land or in the oceans, and, not least, to improve our understanding of climate to the point where we can be sure what a given increase in carbon dioxide will mean, and have a proper basis to decide whether that is a "good" or a "bad" thing to happen. But this is not the time for a panic reaction against fossil fuels, least of all if it pushes us along the nuclear path. While all the theories and issues are being resolved, we need a good mixture of energy sources – a flexible system – so that when the time comes to make a decision for or against coal, or fission, or fusion, or whatever, there are alternatives available to provide the right "best mix", in the light of all the relevant evidence.

24 August, 1978 © John Gribbin, 1978; all rights reserved

34

Woodman, spare that tree

JOHN GRIBBIN

There is no doubt that burning fossil fuels – coal, oil and natural gas – releases carbon dioxide into the atmosphere. According to a large body of scientific opinion, the steady build-up of atmospheric carbon dioxide is a serious threat to our climate through the so-called greenhouse effect: the gas traps infra-red radiation that would otherwise escape, thus pushing up the global temperature. Although not all scientists are worried by a warmer world (see *New Scientist*, vol. 79, p. 541), the change in atmospheric composition is undeniable. What comes as a surprise to many people studying this problem, however, is that the lungs of the world – its forests – appear to be producing more carbon dioxide than they are breathing in. The reason is simple: every year more trees are

Figure 34.1 *Destruction of the tropical forests in Malaysia (Credit: Tony Whitten)*

destroyed than are planted – the annual deficit is roughly 11 million hectares.

The importance of plants as a modulator of the carbon dioxide content of the atmosphere is clear from Figure 34.2, where the annual rhythm of northern hemisphere photosynthesis is superimposed on the rising trend of carbon dioxide concentration generally attributed to the result of burning fossil fuels. Until recently, the conventional wisdom was that increased carbon dioxide concentration encouraged photosynthesis, stimulating plant growth both on land and in the sea and removing much of the "extra" carbon dioxide from the atmosphere. But the latest analyses suggest that the net effect of man's activities is, and has been for a century or more, destruction of the world's plants, particularly forests, so that as much carbon dioxide is being added to the atmosphere each year from burning wood, slash-and-burn agriculture and oxidising humus as from burning fossil fuel. This raises some interesting questions – not least, where is all the carbon dioxide going? – but the greatest importance of the new work is the implication that even with our profligate use of fossil fuels the forests of the Earth are still controlling the carbon dioxide concentration. If we stopped destroying the biomass on such a large scale, it might well be able to cope with the extra carbon dioxide from fossil fuel, removing once and for all the threat of the global greenhouse.

Confusion has arisen because of the difficulties of estimating how much living material there is on the Earth, and how much is being created or destroyed each year. But a clear picture began to emerge from the confusion in 1977, when John Adams and colleagues at the University of Sao Paulo carried out an examination of the available forestry data (*Science*, vol. 196, p. 54). They pointed out that in the US the carbon produced by the net annual wood loss is only two per cent of the amount being released as carbon dioxide from fossil fuels; by contrast, in Brazil the ratio of net wood loss to net fossil fuel loss is at least 5:1 – five times as much carbon released from forestry and agriculture as from fossil fuel each year.

This huge loss of biomass from Brazil alone sets a lower limit on global release of carbon dioxide from non-fossil sources of about one-tenth of the total from fossil fuels each year; adding in estimates for other regions of the globe, it seems that the fossil and non-fossil sources must now be running neck and neck as providers of carbon dioxide, and that in the past destruction of the biomass overwhelmed the production of carbon dioxide from burning fossil fuels. As Adams' team put it, "without concurrent deforestation in this century, the build-up of atmospheric carbon dioxide . . . would have been very minor at best".

A. T. Wilson, of the University of Waikoto, New Zealand, went one step further in 1978, suggesting that the single most important shift in the carbon dioxide content of the atmosphere in the past 100 years was the pioneer agriculture explosion in the second half of the nineteenth century across North America, eastern Europe, Australia, New Zealand and South Africa (*Nature*, vol. 273, p. 40). The effect can be monitored in principle, because burning wood releases from storage in the living material a different mix of carbon isotopes from that in the surrounding air, making up a new isotope mix which then gets laid down in new trees and can be studied today. The model suggests that the "pioneer agriculture effect" increased carbon dioxide concentration in the atmosphere by ten per cent within a few decades, and Wilson goes on to speculate that this may have been a major factor in the roughly 0.5 °C rise in mean global temperatures in the late nineteenth century which pulled us out of the "Little Ice Age" and into the more comfortable weather of the twentieth century.

How much carbon?

This extreme swing of the pendulum towards seeing deforestation as the *major* cause of climatic change in the past century by no means represents the mainstream view, but shows how much we are shifting away from the old ideas of the biomass as a sink for carbon dioxide. Probably the best current "middle-of-the-road" estimates are those from Professor George Woodwell, of the Marine Biological Laboratory, Woods Hole, Massachusetts, and his colleagues, again published last year (*Science*, vol. 199, p. 141).

There are about 700×10^{15} g of carbon, as carbon dioxide, in the atmosphere, slightly more in the living biomass, and something around 2000×10^{15} g estimated in the organic material of soil, humus and peat. At least ten times as much is dissolved in the world's oceans, which must modulate the equilibrium concentration of the atmosphere on a very long timescale (thousands of years), but of which only the surface layers (containing about 600×10^{15} g of inorganic carbon) can interact rapidly with the atmospheric carbon dioxide reservoir. The dissolved organic material in

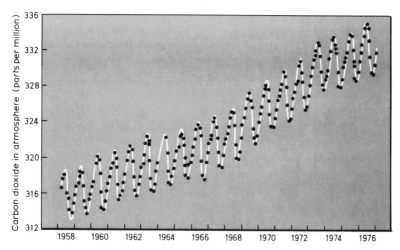

Figure 34.2 *The upward trend of atmospheric carbon dioxide concentration is shown in observations at Mauna Loa, Hawaii*

the oceans probably totals about the same as the organic matter in soil on land.

Against this background, we know about 5×10^{15} g of carbon are released as carbon dioxide from fossil fuel each year, and that of this 2.3×10^{15} g, less than half, seems to be staying to build up in the atmosphere (Figure 34.2). Either the "extra" carbon dioxide is being absorbed by the oceans, or it is being taken up in plants in photosynthesis, or both. According to present models of the chemistry of the oceans, it is difficult to find a home for 2.7×10^{15} g of carbon a year, so chemical oceanographers were happy to accept that part of the production from fossil fuels, at least, was going into biological reservoirs. But now this view has been completely overturned.

Like Adams' team, Woodwell and his colleagues calculate that in round terms as much carbon is getting into the air from Man's forestry and agricultural activities each year as from burning fossil fuels. One of the key elements responsible for this shift of opinion has been the realisation of the part played by all that humus, containing several times as much carbon as is actually present in the trees themselves, which is opened up to the air and oxidised when forests are cleared. So, according to present evidence, at least 10×10^{15} g of carbon is entering the overall world system each year as a result of Man's activities, and the measured increase in atmospheric concentration is less than one-quarter of the total released. Clearly, the chemical oceanographers' models are hopelessly incorrect, since they state unequivocally that the oceans cannot absorb 7.5×10^{15} g of carbon each year, and yet there is nowhere else the carbon can possibly be going!

So the most clear-cut immediate conclusion is that although there is now intense interest in the possibility of a carbon-dioxide-induced greenhouse effect, the world carbon budget simply is not understood, and is not likely to be understood in detail in the immediate future. The contribution of burning fossil fuels to such a greenhouse effect, however, must now be viewed in a different perspective, even before those details of how carbon moves around the world become clear.

Since over 7.5×10^{15} g of carbon, from all sources, are being absorbed in those global systems each year, and since only 5×10^{15} are being released by fossil fuels each year, it seems very likely that if deforestation stopped tomorrow then there would no longer be any net increase in the carbon dioxide concentration of the atmosphere. Tropical rain forests alone hold 42 per cent of all carbon that is now held by terrestrial vegetation, and all forests of the world put together account for 90 per cent of vegetable carbon. So the relatively minor ups and downs of agriculture can be ignored; as long as the forest is left intact, the natural carbon dioxide balance of past decades and centuries could be maintained for the immediate future however much coal, oil and gas we burn.

The fact that a lot of carbon is going somewhere (presumably into the oceans) and that we don't know where, or how, means that even if we did stop chopping down trees and burning them tomorrow it would still be urgently necessary to study the global carbon budget and find out if any other natural equilibrium might be being disturbed by Man's activities. Clearly, though, with the pressures of an increasing population on agricultural land, there is no prospect of halting deforestation immediately, so it becomes equally urgent to find out how far we can go before doing irreparable damage to this remarkable system which has such a capacity for keeping the carbon budget in balance. Nevertheless, in a situation where it seems that we don't actually have to do anything constructive to save the situation – we don't need to turn agricultural land over to forest – but simply have to stop doing something destructive (stop burning forests, all too often for a short-lived agricultural benefit followed by rapid deterioration of the soil and creation of new dust bowls) while still being allowed a degree of latitude in flinging carbon dioxide into the air from just about every industrial orifice, we have only ourselves to blame if we don't cry "Halt!" in time to stop a massive and irreversible alteration in our delicately balanced atmosphere.

29 March, 1979 © *John Gribbin 1979; all rights reserved*

35

The politics of carbon dioxide

JOHN GRIBBIN

Climatologists now seem to be agreed that increases in atmospheric carbon dioxide will raise the temperature of the globe enough to change the world's pattern of agriculture; enough, indeed, to produce some interesting shifts in the balance of power between North and South

If the world continues at the present rate to increase its demand for energy, and for fossil fuels in particular, then the "natural" concentration of carbon dioxide in the atmosphere will double by about AD 2025. Many climatologists agree that such a change will, by enhancing the "greenhouse effect" that keeps the surface of the Earth warmer than if there were no atmosphere, increase mean temperatures over the globe by 2–3 °C. The increases would be greatest at high latitudes and there would be associated shifts in rainfall patterns. It is impossible to predict exactly how the climate will change, but several analyses of the differences between warm and cold years of the recent past suggest that regions that would be both warmer and drier include the grainlands of the US, Europe and the USSR, while the changes in some parts of the Third World could benefit agriculture. This realisation has added a new dimension to the debate about the carbon dioxide "threat", emphasising its global nature and highlighting the differences between the "rich North" and the "poor South".

The only certainty in the whole debate is that the concentration of carbon dioxide in the atmosphere has increased significantly over the past 100 years and is increasing rapidly today. Carbon dioxide is released to the atmosphere when forests are destroyed, both when the wood itself is burnt and because the carbon-rich organic humus layer is exposed to the air and soon oxidises. Until about 1950, the clearance of forests was probably the dominant factor in the carbon dioxide build-up (*New Scientist*, vol. 81, p. 1016) although some doubts have been expressed recently about the accuracy of the techniques by which this is measured (*New Scientist*, 2 April, p. 20). For the past two decades, however, and certainly today, burning fossil fuel, especially coal, is the main reason for the rapid build-up of carbon dioxide in the atmosphere.

Carbon dioxide concentrations have been monitored accurately at the Mauna Loa Observatory in Hawaii – far from any sources of industrial pollution – since 1957. Then, the concentration was just over 310 parts per million by volume (ppmv, or just ppm). In 1980, the same recording site reported a mean concentration of 335 ppm, a rise of eight per cent in 23 years. Estimates of the "pre-industrial" concentration of carbon dioxide vary, but there is some agreement that the concentration in 1860 must have been about 275 ppm, perhaps even a little less and quite possibly as high as 285 ppm, but certainly no more than 295 ppm. At present, the average concentration (leaving aside seasonal fluctuations) is increasing by 2–4 ppm each year.

This increase corresponds to about half of the carbon dioxide being produced by burning fossil fuel each year. Most of the excess is being dissolved in the oceans, but as chemists believe that this "sink" is not efficient enough to account for all the "missing" carbon dioxide, a lively debate continues about the details of the global carbon cycle. It is not clear yet whether the clearance of forests still represents an input of carbon dioxide to the atmosphere each year, or whether trees and other vegetation – stimulated by the increased concentration of the carbon dioxide they need for photosynthesis – provide another sink for carbon dioxide today. But these details are not important for general forecasts of the implications for the climate of a "business as usual" approach to the use of fossil fuel.

In round terms some five gigatonnes of carbon are burnt as fuel each year (1 Gt = 10^9 tonnes). This is equivalent to an input of 20 Gt of carbon dioxide, as each carbon atom captures two oxygen atoms during combustion. (There is no threat to our life-giving oxygen supply from burning fossil fuel however; 21 per cent of the atmosphere is oxygen, and burning all the carbon on Earth would still leave far more oxygen than we need to be able to breathe.) The uncertainty about forest clearance means that the best estimate of anthropogenic input of carbon into the atmosphere each

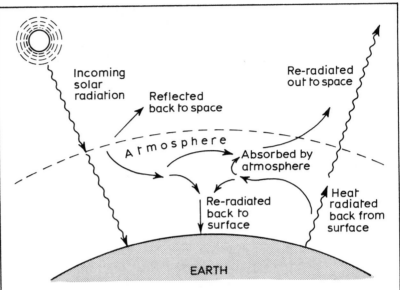

The "greenhouse effect" certainly works in the atmospheres of planets, although it is now thought that it may not be the dominant warming effect in greenhouses. The Sun emits radiation in a band of wavelengths centred around those of visible light and this radiation passes through the atmosphere of the Earth with very little absorption, warming the ground or sea at the surface. The warm surface of the Earth re-radiates energy outwards, but at the much longer infra-red wavelengths. Infra-red radiation is absorbed by both water vapour and carbon dioxide in the atmosphere, warming the lower layers of the atmosphere which in turn radiate some heat back down to the ground and some out into space. Up to a point, increasing the concentration of carbon dioxide in the atmosphere increases the amount of outgoing infra-red radiation absorbed, and increases the warming influence of the greenhouse effect. But at some concentration the carbon dioxide captures all of the radiation at the right wavelengths for absorption, and any further increase in concentration cannot lead to a further rise in temperature. So, no matter how much coal is burnt, there is no possibility of a "runaway" greenhouse effect which might lead to desert conditions all over the Earth, resembling those on Venus today. (Real greenhouses trap heat mainly because the glass roof lets sunlight in but inhibits convection, stopping warm air from rising and escaping; the glass does reflect back some infra-red, but this is a secondary effect.)

Figure 35.1 *The greenhouse effect*

year should be stated as 5 ± 1 Gt, but the burning of fossil fuel definitely dominates. Even at present levels of consumption, however, fossil fuel poses no hazard in terms of a dramatic "greenhouse effect" (see box). Growth is the key factor – the increased use of fossil fuel by Third World countries to provide the energy they need for development programmes that enable them to catch up with the developed world.

The world's total recoverable reserves of fossil fuel, 90 per cent in the form of coal, are thought to be around 300 000 quads, where one quad is 10^{15} BTU, and one quad per year is roughly equivalent to 20 one-gigawatt power stations. One quad per year represents the energy consumption of 10 million inhabitants of the US today. At present, the world uses 250 quads per year, and at this rate known recoverable reserves of coal, oil and gas would last for 1200 years, and the build-up of carbon dioxide would be slow enough for adjustments to be relatively painless.

But at present the global consumption of fossil fuel is increasing by slightly more than four per cent a year – doubling every 16 years. Available reserves of fossil fuel could easily support continued growth at this rate for about another century, but would then be depleted rapidly. It is this combination of rapid growth and available fuel that makes carbon dioxide a real problem.

One example of the "business as usual" approach to forecasting global energy demands in the next few decades comes from Ralph M. Rotty, of the Institute for Energy Analysis, Oak Ridge Associated Universities. He has divided the world into six sectors, and projected the growth of fossil fuel use in each for the period 1974–2025, using data from the late 1970s to set the pattern. Thus:

(1) zero energy growth in the US, consumption steady at 125 quads, 15 per cent of this non-fossil;
(2) 2 per cent growth in Western Europe, 15 per cent non-fossil;
(3) 4 per cent growth in Eastern Europe, including the USSR, with 15 per cent non-fossil;
(4) $4\frac{1}{2}$ per cent growth in Communist Asia (mainly China), with very little non-fossil;
(5) *population* growth in the developing world of 1.5 per cent, with energy growth sufficient to reach the *per capita* average of the developed world in 1970 – that is, 5 per cent energy growth per year.

This "business as usual" approach would change the pattern of carbon dioxide production, while bringing a doubling of the preindustrial concentration. The total energy demand for 2025 is 1090 quads, compared with 250 quads in 1980; the figure is typical of all "business as usual" scenarios. It implies that by 2025, annual burning of carbon dioxide will reach almost 25 gigatonnes, increasing the atmospheric concentration of carbon dioxide by 11 ppm in a single year, assuming that roughly half the carbon dioxide is being taken up by the oceans and other sinks.

This *caveat* highlights the main problem facing the climatic forecasters. As we do not know today just where all the missing carbon dioxide is going, we cannot be sure that when the concentration has doubled half the carbon dioxide produced each year will stay in the atmosphere. Perhaps the "sinks" will become saturated, so the build-up will be even quicker; perhaps increasing concentration will stimulate some "sinks" into increased activity, slowing the build-up. In the absence of any better guide, the "guesstimate" that half the carbon dioxide produced each year will continue to stay in the atmosphere is the only rule of thumb we have. So what would be doubling of the carbon dioxide concentration involve?

The best computer models – general circulation models, or GCMs – predict a mean warning of 2–3 °C. The average disguises a very modest increase in the tropics and increases of three or more times the mean at high latitudes. Some scientists think that all these models are making the same mistake, and that any warming due to the greenhouse effect will be much more modest. But strictly in terms of taking out insurance against the worst, the GCM forecasts have to be taken seriously. It will be too late to wait and see if the world warms up before taking action, as by then the warming will be irreversible. And now it is possible to assess the regional implications of this kind of warning, using the Earth itself as the model.

One such approach to the problem, by a team at the University of East Anglia, Norwich, was reported in *New Scientist* last year (vol. 85, p. 15). Since then, other groups around the world, using similar analyses, have come up with similar scenarios. The basis of the approach is that we have good records of temperature and rainfall from around the northern hemisphere, going back to 1925. By picking out data from warm years and then data from cold years, we can build up two composite images of typical patterns of rainfall and temperature – one for each extreme – and these provide a scenario (not, the climatologists stress, a prediction) of the way the world's weather could change.

Taking the figures of the University of East Anglia's team, based on extremes of warm and cold in the 50 years from 1925 to 1974, the two composites represent years with average temperatures differing from one another by 0.6 °C – only a quarter of the warming expected to result from a doubling of carbon dioxide concentration in the atmosphere. But, like the GCMs, the composites show a greater increase in temperature at high latitudes (1.6 °C above 65 °N) and only a small change in the tropics. This "real Earth" model, however, goes beyond the GCMs in giving an indication of regional, not just latitudinal, changes. They show, for example, that while a region from Finland, across Russia, to 90° longitude East in Siberia, warms by up to 3 °C, and much of North America warms by 1–2 °C, some regions – Japan, India, Turkey, Spain – show a small *decrease* in temperature.

The warm composite also shows a one to two per cent increase in rainfall over land, compared with the cold composite, but again the regional changes are much more important. The increase over India and the Middle East is bigger than average, while the US, Europe, Russia and Japan show a decrease in rainfall, coupled with the changes in temperature. Although this is "only a scenario" the information looks particularly interesting as the climatologists can explain the changes in regional temperature and rainfall from the way the pattern of atmospheric circulation changes from the cold composite to the warm one. There is an intensified westerly air flow, with deeper depressions (low pressure systems) between 50 and 70 °N, and a westward displacement in winter of a feature known as the Siberian High. So the meteorological changes can be explained in terms of the known workings of the atmosphere, and the composites agree with and go beyond the forecasts of the GCMs. There is certainly a convincing enough picture here to justify serious consideration of the implications of such changes for global politics.

There is very little doubt that a combination of warmer and drier conditions would be bad for the main regions of grain growing in the world; it suggests a return of the dust bowls to North America and elsewhere. In the corn (maize) belt in the US, *any* change in temperature (up or down), and a decline in rainfall in August in particular, could together prove disastrous. Each change of 1 °C in the mean would reduce yield by 11 per cent, quite apart from the losses due to drier conditions. Different crops in different regions of the globe will be affected in different ways. But W. Bach, of the Centre for Applied Climatology in Munster,

Germany, spelt out some implications in his contribution to the book *Carbon Dioxide, Climate and Society* (edited by Jill Williams, Pergamon, 1978). For instance, a reduction in the yield of wheat in Kazakhstan of 20 per cent for a 1 °C rise in temperature emphasises that the USSR – already a major purchaser of grain on the world markets – would suffer in line with the US, at present just about the only source of grain for those markets. But for a global warming of 1 °C or more, rice yields would be increased even if rainfall decreased, while in regions where a slight warming plus increased rainfall are forecast, rice yields could go up by ten per cent or more.

Figures like this emphasise the political explosiveness of the carbon dioxide issue. As yet, Third World countries have scarcely been aware of the "problem", having more pressing issues to occupy their time and resources. But now it seems, on this naive picture, that although the Third World countries will produce the greenhouse problem by the early twenty-first century (because of their economic growth), they will suffer few adverse consequences themselves, and may even benefit as a result. Meanwhile, their traditional enemies in the rich North will suffer the worst consequences of the developing world's carbon dioxide "pollution". This is, to say the least, an interesting reversal of the historic pattern whereby the poor South has had to suffer the consequences of the developed world's exploitation of the resources of our planet. But the picture is not so simple, even if this simple interpretation is correct.

If agriculture were run effectively to feed the greatest possible number of people, present resources could feed twice the present world population in reasonable comfort. But in the real world, through a combination of political and economic factors (which means that the poor, both individuals and nations, starve because they have no money to buy food, not because there is insufficient food in the world) the North American grain harvest is vital. Virtually all of the world trade in food is North America's grain surplus; a ten per cent reduction in North American grain yields would cut off this surplus at a stroke, affecting the poor and hungry people of the Third World immediately but hardly being noticed by the average citizen of the US or Canada. It would also, of course, leave the USSR with no grain to buy at any price. Famine might occur on a wide scale before the hungry had chance to take advantage of improved opportunities for growing rice.

On top of this sobering possibility, some climatologists now suggest that whatever the new long-term climatic balance, the transition from a natural "cool Earth" state to an unnatural "greenhouse Earth" would be a time of chronic and severe variations in the weather. These erratic fluctuations in temperature and precipitation from year to year would become noticeable before the rise in mean temperatures was detected, and could even explain – at least partially – the unusual weather variability of the 1970s. In 1972, for example, the Sahel drought reached a peak, the region around Moscow experienced the worst drought for 300 years, Soviet food production fell 8 per cent, there were droughts in Australia and South America, the anchovy crop off Peru failed, and a failure of the Indian monsoon brought an eight per cent drop in rice production. At the time, this looked like a freak year. Since then, Europe has experienced record-breaking drought in 1976 while parts of the USSR had floods; the US has experienced the worst winters as well as some of the worst droughts for a hundred years; and other regions of the world have continued to be afflicted by "unseasonable" frosts, or heat, or floods, or drought. Some climatologists believe that the variability of the weather of the 1970s was the first response of the "weather

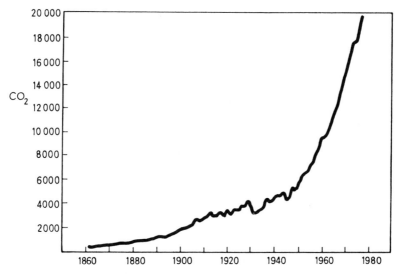

Figure 35.2 *Man's annual production of carbon dioxide, chiefly from burning fossil fuels, rose steadily from the middle of the nineteenth century, but rapidly increased after the 1940s*

machine" to disturbances brought on by the greenhouse effect, and, therefore, bad years like 1972 may be repeated through the 1980s and beyond.

But the problems of development – of the Third World catching up with the rich North – remain more urgent and pressing than any of the speculations about detrimental climatic changes resulting from burning fossil fuel. The nuclear lobby, of course, can produce figures showing that fission power could solve all our energy problems without using any coal at all – but it is growth in the developing world that is the problem. No government in the rich North, as yet, is willing to embrace a policy of supplying nuclear reactors to the Third World to fuel development and ensure that the coal stays in the ground! And this, perhaps, highlights the real point about the energy debate, the point usually ignored by protagonists in the US and Europe. What we in the West do about energy scarcely matters, in global terms, now that our population growth and energy growth have essentially stopped. We are in the hands of the developing countries, who need rapid growth and who can most easily achieve it using coal as their main source of energy. Of course, 90 per cent of known coal reserves are in the US, USSR and China, and it is possible to imagine a world in which those three powers conspire to keep coal off the world market, so as to keep the poor regions under their collective thumb. But this is hardly a plausible scenario, and given the timescale for making decisions and the lifetime of power stations once constructed, there seems very little real prospect of avoiding a build up of carbon dioxide in the atmosphere sufficient to produce noticeable changes in climate and agriculture. Most probably, it *will* be business as usual and we'll just have to live with the consequences – not in the remote future, but in only 20 years or so from now.

36

Carbon dioxide – an alternative view

SHERWOOD B. IDSO

Carbon dioxide is only a trace constituent of Earth's atmosphere – with a concentration of about 0.03 per cent by volume. Yet CO_2 stands in the centre of a raging controversy about climate. The gas is fairly transparent to Solar radiation, but rather opaque to some wavelengths of thermal radiation, and so acts as a classic "greenhouse gas": it allows the rays of the Sun to pass through the atmosphere and heat the Earth, but it absorbs a significant proportion of the heat radiated by the land and sea, and radiates some of this energy back to the Earth's surface. Thus the Earth is warmer than it would be if there were no CO_2 in the atmosphere. But how much warmer? That is the question that now divides the world's meteorologists.

At the end of last century two Swedish physicists, S. Arrhenius and T. C. Chamberlin, estimated that if the concentration of CO_2 were doubled, the Earth would be warmer by 8 °C. Later, scientists came to agree on a figure of 2–3 °C. This latter figure is also predicted by the most sophisticated general circulation models (GCMs) of the atmosphere but it is an order of magnitude greater than several recent experiments imply. Consequently, the views of scientists have become polarised. At one extreme many physicists look to the computer models and view the steadily rising concentration of atmospheric CO_2 as a prelude to climatological catastrophe, while, at the other extreme, a group is beginning to emerge that concentrates on more empirical data. This group suggests that increase in atmospheric CO_2, far from being detrimental, is actually beneficial. These scientists feel that any change in the climate caused by the rising levels of CO_2 will be indistinguishable from those natural climatic fluctuations. But more significantly they foresee that higher concentrations of CO_2 will tend to stimulate photosynthesis, and so increase the productivity of crops and

Figure 36.1   *Dust clouds roll across the state of Colorado. Dust in the atmosphere can blanket the Earth in the same way that CO_2 does, thus providing a "natural experiment" on the effects of increasing CO_2*

the efficiency with which they use water, thus helping to feed the world's population.

The divergence of opinion is becoming more acute because the burning of fossil fuels, such as coal and oil, is causing the concentration of CO_2 in the atmosphere to increase at such a rate that experts estimate that by AD 2025 it may be twice as high as it was before the Industrial Revolution. This date is close enough to prompt the scientists who belong to the "CO_2 catastrophe camp" to urge the world's governments to curtail the use of fossil fuels. But if the emerging group of more empirically minded scientists is correct, such pressures can only be counter-productive to our future well-being. Given the seriousness of the problem (or nonproblem, depending on how one views it), along with its many political ramifications (*New Scientist*, vol. 90, p. 82), we must endeavour to break the impasse.

As an advocate of what is currently the minority viewpoint — that increasing CO_2 in the atmosphere will not lead to imminent catastrophe – I would like to set forth the alternative to the long-unchallenged majority position, to help those in power to reach a decision in an open-minded manner. To this end I will present the case against CO_2 as a significant modulator of the Earth's climate.

First, I should make a philosophical distinction between the two approaches. Those who work with general circulation models calculate on theoretical grounds the effect of a twofold increase of CO_2 on the radiation passing both to and from the Earth. They then feed that information into a computer, which calculates the resulting change in global temperatures.

The empirical approach on the other hand, depends on finding some natural event – such as the passage of a dust cloud through a particular locality – which temporarily disturbs the heat balance of the atmosphere. By monitoring the temperature changes and the flow of radiative heat during such natural events, it is possible to *measure* the response of the real world to the perturbation. I call this response the Earth's "surface air temperature response function"; we observe the change in temperature of the lower atmosphere in the face of a measured change in heat flow and extrapolate from this the expected global effect of a doubling of CO_2.

The first investigators to publish an empirically derived value for this response function within this context were R. E. Newell of Massachusetts Institute of Technology and T. G. Dopplick of Scott Air Force Base in Illinois. Writing in the June 1979 issue of the *Journal of Applied Meteorology*, they concluded from studies of the temperature of tropical sea surfaces, and the way energy is transferred between the oceans and the atmosphere, that for every extra watt applied to the surface of the Earth the mean surface temperature would increase by 0.1 °C; that is, that the mean global value of the Earth's surface temperature sensitivity was about 0.1 °C per watt/sq. m. I applied these values to calculations of the radiative perturbation – changes in the passage of energy radiating to and from the Earth – caused by doubling the amount of atmospheric CO_2. From this I was able to conclude independently that the resulting increase in the mean global surface air temperature if CO_2 were doubled would be only about 0.25 °C.

In coming to this conclusion, I had drawn upon more than a dozen years of field experience related to three independent "natural experiments". The first of these concerns the way in which dust in the atmosphere above Phoenix, Arizona, redistributes itself in altitude between summer and winter. In a series of papers in *Science, Nature* and elsewhere, I wrote that dust low in the atmosphere exerts a significant thermal blanketing effect on the Earth, much like a greenhouse gas, but that dust at higher levels has a much smaller effect. Thus, from measurements of radiation and temperature, I could evaluate the radiative perturbation that the vertical redistribution of dust produced, and the effect it had on surface air temperature. By dividing the change in temperature by the radiative perturbation, I produced a local value for the surface air temperature response function – that is, the amount the temperature changed for a given change in local radiation. It was 0.173 °C per watt/sq.m.

The effects of moisture

The second natural experiment I used was the annual arrival of the summer monsoon season at Phoenix. From equations I had developed that relate atmospheric thermal radiation with surface air temperature and vapour pressure. I could calculate the changes

Figure 36.2   *Rain-clouds over Arizona. The arrival of the monsoons in Phoenix provides a second "natural experiment"*

caused by the influx of moisture over the city. Checking long-term weather records, I found that in going from a surface vapour pressure of 4 to 20 millibars, the surface air temperature just before dawn increased by approximately 11.4 °C. Dividing this change in temperature by the change in energy that caused it yielded a second value, 0.196 °C per watt/sq.m, for the local surface air temperature response function. This was very similar to the figure calculated from the data on dust storms.

The third natural experiment dealt with the change in surface air temperature caused by the annual variation in Solar radiation received at the Earth's surface. I made this evaluation at 105 stations scattered across the United States – and for all interior locations the mean result for the surface air temperature response function was 0.185 °C per watt/sq.m, the same as the average of the two "local" results from Phoenix. For 15 stations on the West Coast, however, where the Pacific Ocean greatly influences the climate, the result was only half as great. I took this number to represent an upper limit for the world's seas, and therefore calculated an approximate upper limit for the whole globe, taking account of the area covered by land and by sea, of 0.113 °C per watt/sq.m.

The good agreement among the separate evaluations of the surface air temperature response function gave me considerable confidence, as they involve three different perturbing mechanisms (variation in altitude of dust, a temporal variation in water vapour, and the movement of the Earth in its orbit around the Sun), two different wavelengths of radiation (Solar and thermal), and two different timescales (days to months). All that was lacking was a demonstration that this common result also applied to timescales of the order of decades to centuries, and that it incorporated effects due to the thermal inertia of the oceans – that is, the fact that the temperature of the oceans responds only sluggishly to changes in energy input.

I approached this task by considering the Earth without an atmosphere. A simple calculation gives the mean equilibrium temperature of an airless globe as −18.6 °C. The current mean temperature of the globe is about 15 °C, so the total greenhouse effect of the entire atmosphere is to raise the surface air temperature by about 33.6 °C.

The heat the atmosphere radiates back to the Earth's surface is 348 watts/sq.m. Dividing the temperature change of 33.6 °C (the difference between an airless Earth and the present state) by this radiative energy yields a mean global surface air temperature response function of approximately $0.1 \,°C/watt/sq.m$; and this result must have included within it the effects of all significant feedback processes between the Earth, the oceans and atmosphere that operate over large timescales.

This number is just slightly less than the value of $0.113 \,°C/watt/sq.m$, which I had acknowledged must be an upper limit. It is identical to the value that Newell and Dopplick determined, so it seems to be the value of the Earth's surface air temperature response function that should be used in evaluating the climatic effects of CO_2. And this value gives a temperature increase of $0.25 \,°C$ for a doubling of CO_2 concentrations in the atmosphere.

The computer modelling and empirical approaches both make the same assumptions about the radiative changes that would be caused by an increase in atmospheric CO_2, so I find no recourse but to reject as erroneous the great temperature increases predicted by the GCMs, as generally run. However, when these models are run with the constraints on sea surface temperature that Newell and Dopplick have noted, they too give an increase in temperature of $0.3 \,°C$ for a doubling in the CO_2 concentration, as has recently been demonstrated at Oregon State University.

So where do we go from here? The case for the empirical evaluation of the surface air temperature response function seems complete; and it cannot be significantly in error. Let me use it to make further extrapolation concerning the climate.

At present the atmosphere reflects about 90 per cent of the energy from the Earth back to the ground: that is, its emissivity is 90 per cent. Suppose the atmosphere were to send even more radiation back. I have shown that in going from a value of zero (assuming the Earth had no atmosphere) to the current value of about 90 per cent the surface air temperature response function has averaged the same as its current value – that is about $0.1 \,°C/watt/sq.m$. Thus, there is good reason to believe that it would not change significantly if the atmosphere's emissivity were to increase by ten per cent, to unity – that is, if the atmosphere reflected *all* radiation from the Earth back to the ground. This being the case, it is easy to show that the maximum temperature increase that this change would cause is just slightly over $4 \,°C$. With a response function an order of magnitude greater however, the GCMs predict a temperature increase on the order of $40 \,°C$. Which estimate is more realistic?

One way to approach this question is to look at past climates.

We do not know for sure how the composition of the atmosphere has changed in the distant past, but there is reason to believe that the proportions of certain greenhouse gases may have varied considerably; and it is possible that at some time over the past several million years the atmospheric emissivity may have been significantly greater (or smaller) than it is now.

But how has the temperature varied? At the meeting on past climates at the "Carbon dioxide and climate research program conference" held in Washington DC in April 1980, W. Broecker noted that over the past few million years the Earth may never have been more than a couple of degrees warmer than at present; and this seemed to be the consensus of most of those at the meeting. Also R. K. Matthews and R. Z. Poore, writing in *Geology* (vol. 8, p. 501), have suggested from data on changes in concentration of one isotope of oxygen, O^{18}, that ocean surface temperatures have over that entire period remained relatively constant at about 28 °C. Thus, whereas the GCMs lead one possibly to expect significant temperature excursions from the present mean global value, the available empirical evidence indicates that this is not the case for at least the past 50 million years, and possibly the past 200 million years (*Geological Society of America Bulletin*, vol. 88, p. 390). Consequently, the GCM predictions that temperature would increase by 2–3 °C due to a mere doubling of the atmospheric concentration of CO_2 seem highly suspect.

But let us consider again the temperature rise that could be caused by an increase in the atmosphere's emissivity. How big is the effect on emissivity of doubling CO_2 in the atmosphere? In reality, very little. If the atmospheric CO_2 were to increase by a factor of 10, it would still fill in only about 20 per cent of the atmosphere's "window" to electromagnetic radiation. Thus, even an order-of-magnitude increase in the concentration of atmospheric CO_2 would increase the mean global air temperature by only about 0.8 °C; and such an increase in concentration is considerably greater than any current predictions.

There is one more point we can learn from past climates. Recent studies of air trapped in ice cores show that the amount of CO_2 in the atmosphere 18 000 years ago was about half what it is now (*Nature*, vol. 284, p. 155). And other work has shown that incoming Solar radiation at that time was not much different from now (*Meteorological Monographs*, No 34, American Meteorological Society). The GCMs predict a drop in temperature for that time of more than 2 °C (*Nature*, vol. 290, p. 9), but data obtained from three cores in the subtropical gyre – a current of the Atlantic at 20 °N – show essentially no temperature difference at all between then and now (*Geological Society of America Memoranda*, No 145, p. 43). This again indicates that the results of the models are at odds with reality.

Considering all the available *evidence*, then, there seems no reason to suppose that carbon dioxide gas, present in the atmosphere only as a "trace", has any more than a "trace effect" on Earth's surface air temperature. Thus, we should not regard potential increases in concentration due to the continued utilisation of fossil fuels as bad. Quite to the contrary, such an enrichment of CO_2 in the atmosphere is desirable – because of its helpful effects on the growth of plants.

12 November, 1981

37

Carbon dioxide, climate and the sea

ANDREW CRANE AND PETER LISS

Only half of the carbon dioxide produced by burning fossil fuel stays in the atmosphere. The oceans absorb the rest. If we want to understand our climate, we must understand how the atmosphere, ocean and biosphere interact

For more than a century, people have known and understood that increasing concentrations of carbon dioxide in the atmosphere could cause significant changes in the world's climate. As early as the 1860s, John Tyndall, in Britain, suggested a link between changes in the composition of the atmosphere and variations in the climate. At the turn of the century, the Swede Svante Arrhenius predicted that if the concentration of carbon dioxide in the atmosphere doubled, then the global climate would warm by 4–6 °C. The figure is remarkably close to present-day estimates.

Since 1900, the concentration of carbon dioxide in the atmosphere has risen dramatically. So why has no one identified a clear-cut carbon-dioxide "signal" in the records of global temperature? Various explanations have been put forward, some with a sound scientific base, while others are more speculative. The absence of the signal does not imply that the predictions are wrong. Atmospheric concentrations of carbon dioxide are on the increase and have been so since precise measurements were started in the late 1950s at Mauna Loa in Hawaii. Indeed, there is considerable evidence that the increase began early in the nineteenth century but, of course, the reliability of the measurements that far back is much less certain. A key factor in understanding how the build-up is likely to affect our climate is the role of the oceans in absorbing carbon dioxide.

There is a considerable seasonal variation in levels of carbon dioxide, which is generally attributed to biological processes, and this variation is greater than the net annual increase. Secondly, the size of the yearly increase is only about half of what we would expect if all the carbon dioxide produced by burning fossil fuel remained in the atmosphere. Scientists think the oceans take up most of the rest.

Increasing concentrations of carbon dioxide affect our climate because the carbon dioxide molecule transmits short-wavelength radiation from the sun but absorbs a portion of the longer-wavelength radiation emitted by the Earth. This is called the "greenhouse effect". The amount of carbon dioxide in the atmosphere has increased by 20–30 per cent since the beginning of the Industrial Revolution. This rise may well have already produced some warming of the atmosphere, but most researchers think the increase is too small to detect against the natural variations that are always present. Sometime next century, it is almost certain that human activity will have doubled the carbon dioxide in the atmosphere. By then, the warming will be 2–3 °C on average throughout the globe, but substantially higher in polar regions.

People are not the only agents circulating carbon dioxide between the various environmental reservoirs. There are even bigger natural flows, due to plants and animals, or arising from seasonal changes in the surface temperatures of the oceans. But these flows balance out on average over the whole globe and throughout the year. For example, in temperate zones, the biosphere extracts carbon dioxide from the atmosphere in spring and summer, when photosynthesis is dominant, and returns an equivalent amount to the atmosphere during the rest of the year, when respiration and decomposition of plants dominate.

Although most people attribute the observed increase in atmospheric carbon dioxide to the burning of fossil fuel, there is another possible man-made source – the cutting of virgin forest, and the conversion of well-balanced ecosystems either to agricultural land or to urban and industrial developments. This flux could be as large as the input into the atmosphere from combustion of fossil fuels.

Three properties determine the ocean's ability to remove man-made carbon dioxide from the atmosphere: the capacity of seawater to dissolve and react with the gas, which is determined by the chemistry of the water; the rate at which carbon dioxide transfers from air to sea; and the rate of downward mixing of water that has absorbed carbon dioxide at the surface.

Seawater can take up approximately eight times more carbon

dioxide than distilled water; because seawater contains carbonate ions (CO_3^{2-}), which react with dissolved carbon dioxide to form bicarbonate (HCO_3^-). Such a chemical reaction is not possible in distilled water, which can take up carbon dioxide only by dissolving.

In its passage from the atmosphere into the ocean, the first kinetic hurdle a carbon dioxide molecule must overcome is the boundary layer at the sea's surface. Using wind-tunnels, researchers have studied the rate at which the sea absorbs carbon dioxide under different conditions (such as different wind speeds), but these results disagree substantially with those obtained at sea. This discrepancy makes it difficult to calculate the rate at which the oceans take up carbon dioxide from the atmosphere in areas such as polar seas that scientists believe are important in the carbon dioxide cycle. We do, however, know the global rate of exchange rather better, since we can monitor it by studying the movement of radioactive carbon-14 (both natural and that produced by the testing of nuclear weapons) in the atmosphere–ocean system. Best estimates indicate that it takes the top 75 metres of the oceans (the surface-mixed layer) about 120 days to respond to a change in the concentration of atmospheric carbon dioxide. This time is short compared with the time it takes excess carbon dioxide in the atmosphere to double (more than 20 years) and also with the rate at which the carbon dioxide mixes down into the ocean deeps (tens to hundreds of years). So exchange between air and sea is the main barrier to ocean uptake of carbon dioxide.

The chemistry of the ocean's well-mixed surface layer, and its small depth, mean that the surface layer itself can accommodate only about 10 per cent of the carbon dioxide that flows in to the atmosphere each year. But nearly half of the carbon dioxide from burning fossil fuel "disappears", so significant amounts of water below the surface layer must be absorbing carbon dioxide if the oceans really are the major sink for the non-airborne carbon dioxide.

By measuring concentrations in the ocean of natural carbon-14, which decays at a rate of 1 per cent every 83 years, we can get an idea of the turnover of the deep water. Minze Stuiver, of the University of Washington, and Gote Ostlund, from the University of Miami, have shown that an average parcel of water in the Deep Atlantic comes to the surface only once in about 275 years. Pacific deep water has a much longer residence time – almost 600 years.

The circulation is so sluggish because the ocean, which the sun heats from the top, has a stable temperature structure, which suppresses deep convective mixing. There are only two regions of the ocean where deep instability occurs: in the Greenland and Norwegian Seas of the North Atlantic, and in the waters around Antarctica. There, winter cooling and increased salinity due to ice formation increases the density of the surface water which, carrying the gases it absorbed from the atmosphere, sinks to great depths. This water flows slowly through the deep Atlantic and around the Antarctic, eventually penetrating the deep Indian and Pacific Oceans. The return flow to the surface takes several hundred years, as the waters mix slowly upwards over a large area.

In 1972, the Geosecs experiment monitored the distribution of tritium (a radioactive isotope of hydrogen) in the oceans and provided a graphic illustration of the way in which surface water in the North Atlantic sinks. In the early 1960s, tests of nuclear bombs injected significant amounts of tritium into the atmosphere. Gote Ostlund traced how the tritium penetrated into the Atlantic during the first ten years after the bomb tests. A second set of measurements, made during the Transient Tracers in the Ocean (TTO) experiment in 1981, traced further movements of tritium downward and towards the equator.

Although the regions where this deep convection occurs take up tracers very rapidly, their surface area is small and they are unlikely to be the major sinks for the carbon dioxide produced by burning fossil fuel. Less than a third of the tritium that entered the North Atlantic by 1972 had sunk below 1000 m. Because the ocean layers are stable for much of the year, mixing in the region separating the surface and deep ocean layers (the thermocline) is generally lateral, along surfaces of constant density which are almost horizontal. These "isopycnals" closely follow surfaces of constant temperature. Those that lie deep beneath warmer waters in low latitudes rise to the surface nearer the poles, so surface water in high latitudes can mix into deeper layers at lower latitudes.

Jorge Sarmiento at Princeton University has modelled these exchanges of surface and thermocline water in the North Atlantic using the tritium data. His results suggest that the water in the thermocline stays there for only 10 to 40 years, so clearly the termocline, and its counterpart in the other oceans, should be quite active in taking up carbon dioxide from fossil fuel.

Although such studies have advanced our ideas on thermocline mixing, a great deal of the accepted thinking on how the oceans take up carbon dioxide derives from the simple box model. Such models suggest that the oceans as a whole could take up about 35 per cent of the carbon dioxide from burning fossil fuel. If half of this carbon dioxide has remained airborne, a small fraction must have been absorbed elsewhere. Photosynthesis may increase if the atmosphere is enriched in carbon dioxide and this could remove some carbon dioxide. But problems arise in accounting for that released by deforestation if, as some believe, this has been significant in recent decades. So perhaps the oceans take up even more carbon dioxide than the simple models suggest.

This possibility has encouraged researchers to develop more realistic models that explicitly include the spatial variations in the oceans. Ideally, we would like to construct a three-dimensional model for the general circulation of carbon dioxide – the oceanic equivalent of a global model for predicting the weather. But much remains to be done. At present, Bert Bolin's group at Stockholm University, in collaboration with Berrien Moore at the University of New Hampshire are pioneering multi-box, multi-tracer models that seem to offer the best hope for improved predictions of carbon dioxide. The approach used in these models is to deduce the mixing rates, oceanic flows and rates of biological production and decay, that simultaneously best fit the measured distributions in the oceans of a range of tracers, such as the Geosecs and TTO campaigns have obtained. Once calibrated, the model can be tested to see if it reproduces observed distributions of other tracers not used in its construction. We have been developing a detailed 84-box model of the Atlantic Ocean comprising 12 geographical regions and up to eight layers of density. The model involves solving some 696 simultaneous conservation equations.

While we await the results of these more sophisticated models, what other possible marine sinks are there for carbon dioxide? Carbon dioxide dissolved in the water can interact with living organisms, which take up carbon from carbon dioxide as they photosynthesise, or with carbonate minerals, either suspended in the water or in sediments on the bottom. In the past, scientists have argued that carbon dioxide is unlikely to react with these minerals in the water since surface and mid-depth seawater appears to be supersaturated with the dominant forms, calcite and aragonite. However, other researchers have suggested recently that carbon dioxide can also interact with carbonate minerals containing magnesium as well as calcium, especially in coastal

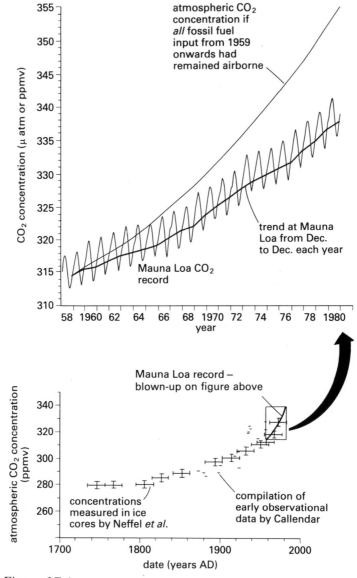

Figure 37.1

sediments. In addition, observations made in the North Pacific, and reported in the past year, suggest that dissolved carbon dioxide can attack the shells of aragonitic pteropods (small mulluscs) at depths of only a few hundred metres.

Marine plankton take up carbon dioxide during photosynthesis, but the supply of nutrient elements (such as phosphorus and nitrogen) in surface waters limits the uptake. Although much of this carbon dioxide is returned to the water when the plankton die and decompose, some of it reaches the sea bed where it becomes buried. In order for this cycle to be a net absorber of carbon dioxide, we would have to assume that the surface oceans receive more plant nutrients, at the same time as the carbon dioxide levels in the atmosphere rise. Although the idea is appealing, since human activities produce both carbon dioxide and nutrients, it has proved extremely difficult to obtain positive evidence for the effect, let alone a reliable estimate of its magnitude. It remains a tantalizing but unproven possibility.

Even if this particular biological mechanism turns out to be insignificant, some scientists have argued that natural changes in ocean biology may still be important in controlling levels of carbon dioxide in the atmosphere.

A group at Berne University has measured the concentration of carbon dioxide in air trapped in ice. The results suggest that large swings in atmospheric carbon dioxide levels have occurred that correspond with known climatic changes. During the most recent ice age, concentrations of carbon dioxide in the atmosphere were around two-thirds of their values during the nineteenth century. This difference, of 90 parts per million, would have contributed substantially, if present climatic models are correct, to the estimated rise in temperature of the ocean's surface, of about 2 °C, at the end of the ice age. The temperature rise itself would not have been enough to release such a large amount of carbon dioxide from the ocean, even though colder water can absorb more carbon dioxide, so what additional mechanism might have been operating?

We know that the concentration of carbon dioxide in the surface water of the ocean is lower than the average for the ocean as a whole due to biological consumption. The carbon is eventually returned to solution at greater depths where biological decay occurs. Since the concentration of carbon dioxide in the atmosphere is on average in equilibrium with the carbon dioxide dissolved in the upper ocean, any mechanism for altering biological productivity would affect the amount of carbon in surface water and thereby the concentration of carbon dioxide in the atmosphere. Wallace Broecker and colleagues at Columbia University first suggested that when the ice age ended, the rising waters would have deposited nutrient residues on coastal shelves. This increase in nutrients could have reduced productivity and so increased the concentration of carbon dioxide in the air. But in a recent article in *Nature* they argue that this hypothesis will have to be abandoned. New data from Greenland ice cores suggest that brief oscillations by as much as 60 parts per million in concentration of carbon dioxide occurred *within* the ice age and over periods as short as 100 years. These data are not yet confirmed, but to account for these changes, one would need to invoke mechanisms involving redistribution of carbon and nutrients brought about by substantial changes in ocean circulation and biological cycling. What little evidence there is suggests that the production of deep water in the North Atlantic was less during the peak of the most recent ice age. However, the link between changes in rates of formation of deep water and changes in biological productivity has yet to be established. Furthermore changes in the circulation patterns of the oceans would themselves directly influence the climate.

There are gaps in the new theories of climatic change provoked by these findings. But it is becoming increasingly clear that understanding climate is not just, or even primarily, an atmospheric problem, but involves unravelling the complicated interactions that exist between atmosphere, ocean and biosphere.

21 November, 1985

The box model of carbon transfer

The simple box models of the ocean envisage three ways of transferring carbon into the sea water. Between well-mixed reservoirs – the atmosphere and surface ocean – the model assumes that the flux is proportional to the carbon content of whichever reservoir contains more carbon. Within the deep ocean, vertical mixing is often modelled as a diffusion process. In addition, the model can include a simple circulation with direct input to the ocean bottom from the surface ocean, balanced by upward motion throughout the deep ocean to represent convective processes.

From experiments on tracers such as carbon-14, we can calculate the coefficients for the exchange between atmosphere and surface ocean, diffusion into the deep ocean and the flow rate for the vertical circulation.

Rate of change in carbon-14 content (zero for steady-state) = (sum of fluxes from surface ocean reservoirs) − (sum of fluxes to surface ocean) + (carbon-14 production in atmosphere) − (carbon-14 decay in atmosphere).

For the deep ocean, the conservation equation is a partial differential advection–diffusion equation. The diffusion coefficient is chosen to best fit the observed mean vertical profile of carbon-14 in the oceans.

Using the model, we can estimate the uptake of carbon dioxide from fossil fuel by integrating forward in time from an assumed pre-industrial steady value, while inputting to the model's atmosphere the estimated year-by-year release of carbon dioxide from fossil fuel. At each time-step, we calculate the fluxes of carbon between the various reservoirs and change the carbon contents and concentration profiles accordingly.

21 November, 1985

38

Another hot year in the greenhouse

JOHN GRIBBIN

New evidence of the growing influence of the "greenhouse effect" on the world's weather has been produced by the Climatic Research Unit at the University of East Anglia. The unit's world temperature watch has revealed that last year was the fourth warmest on record, following hot on the heels of 1981, which was the warmest year ever recorded. This reinforces the evidence of a trend to warmer weather affecting the northern hemisphere.

Philip Jones and Mick Kelly from the unit have been investigating, as part of a project funded by the US Department of Energy, the likely impact of the atmospheric build-up of carbon dioxide. Jones says that the warming trend fits the hypothesis of a "greenhouse effect" from the carbon dioxide, although it is too early to claim that the hypothesis has been proved correct.

Carbon dioxide has been steadily accumulating in the atmosphere since the start of the industrial revolution, as fossil fuel has been burned and trees cut down. Carbon dioxide molecules trap infra-red radiation, that is heat, which would otherwise escape

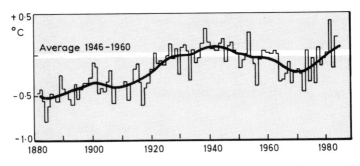

Figure 38.1 *A hundred years of warming in the northern hemisphere*

into space from the warm surface of the Earth. What has been unclear is how soon this might have an effect on the world's climate – and how big an effect it might become.

Jones says that a slight cooling trend in the northern hemisphere before 1970 seems to have reversed, since when the world has experienced both a marked warming and an increased variability of weather from year to year. The past ten years have seen more erratic fluctuations in temperatures than any decade on record. Many climatologists see this variability as further evidence that human activities are altering the natural climatic balance.

The heat of 1983, although not as great as 1981, is even more impressive if account is taken of the major volcanic eruptions which, most climatologists believe, cause the atmosphere to cool. After the eruption of the Mexican volcano El Chichón in 1982, many experts predicted a fall in world temperatures in 1983. Either the volcano theory is wrong, or some other factor has upset the calculations. The extent of the warming, if it is due to the greenhouse effect, also implies that the more extreme forecasts of the climate modellers are likely to be proved correct, implying an average warming round the globe of 2 °C by the year 2050.

Last year the US Environmental Protection Agency warned that a noticeable warming due to the greenhouse effect could start in the 1990s (*New Scientist*, 27 October 1983, p. 247).

15 March, 1984 © John Gribbin, 1984; all rights reserved

39

Hot summers and cold winters ahead

JOHN GRIBBIN

It now seems very likely that the build-up of carbon dioxide in the atmosphere will make the world warmer in the near future (*New Scientist*, 6 September, p. 17). What effect will this have on details of the weather? Will all seasons warm by the same amount? And how might rainfall patterns be altered? These important questions have been addressed by J. P. Palutikof, T. M. L. Wigley and J. M. Lough, of the Climatic Research Unit (CRU) at the University of East Anglia, in a report, No TRO12, to the US Department of Energy. Their most surprising conclusion is that very cold winters may be *more* common when the world warms up.

There are two ways to model the weather patterns of a warmer world. One is to feed the warming parameters into a computer model, and calculate the effects on rainfall and so on. The other is to look at the different patterns of seasonal temperature, rainfall and wind in the real world, comparing cold years with warm ones. The second approach is the one favoured by the Norwich team, both because it provides more detail than any computer model yet available and because it does indeed deal with the real world.

Members of the CRU pioneered one version of this technique a few years ago. They took data for the five warmest years of the twentieth century to date, and averaged them to make a warm-year composite. Similarly, the five coldest years of the century gave them a cold-year model. Comparing the two gave an indication of how the weather patterns of the world might change when it goes from a cool to a warm state. But now they have improved upon this.

The obvious flaw in the previous model was that it just happens that the five coldest years are 1955, 1964, 1966, 1968 and 1972, while the warmest are 1937, 1938, 1943, 1944 and 1953. So, broadly speaking, the resulting comparison is based on a *cooling*

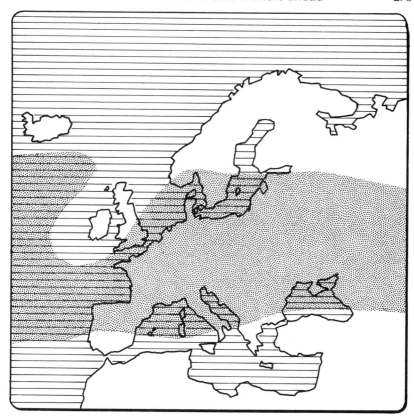

Figure 39.1 *The stippled area shows the region of Europe that will experience colder winters when the world warms, according to the CRU team's "best" scenario*

trend, from the 1930s and 1940s down to the 1960s. It would be better to make the comparison over a genuine warming trend.

One way of doing this is to choose the coldest set of 20 consecutive years in the climatic record of the northern hemisphere, and compare this with the warmest set of 20 consecutive years. It happens that these are 1901–1920 and 1934–1953 respectively. So, using this approach, the warm years do follow the cold years. And as a bonus, there is at least a possibility that the warming in the first half of the century really was due, in part, to the carbon dioxide greenhouse effect. Because this approach uses long runs of consecutive years, the climatologists are also able to compare the year-to-year variability of weather within each 20-year sample.

This approach is the most favoured of four different lines of attack discussed in the US DoE report. Picking out the European data (the team also looks at North America), it suggests that although spring, summer and autumn are all warmer when the world is warmer, there is a greater likelihood of cold winters over the whole of central Europe, 10° either side of latitude 50 °N. This is because changes in the circulation of the atmosphere make "blocking" conditions, with persistent high-pressure systems, more common, and stop warm westerlies from the Atlantic penetrating in to Europe. (The same blocking conditions in summer produce fine weather and drought, as we have just experienced in Britain.)

Overall, Europe is drier in spring and summer, but in autumn everywhere north of 47 °N is wetter in the warmer world.

The discovery that winters may be more extreme when the greenhouse effect gets to work is particularly important in planning energy consumption, and is unexpected. The changes in rainfall patterns are equally important for agriculture. Although all such forecasts are to some extent tentative and uncertain, the latest CRU study begins to provide the kind of data that ought now to be taken into account in political decision making – it would provide invaluable input into the EEC's Common Agricultural Policy, for example.

13 September, 1984 © John Gribbin 1984; all rights reserved

40

Meteorology blows hot and cold

JOHN GRIBBIN

There are now clear signs that the world's climate is changing. But, as the experts will discuss at the British Association meeting in Norwich next week, in which direction is the weather going?

Whenever we experience a period of extreme weather, a drought or a flood, a very hot summer or an unusually severe winter, someone is sure to claim that this is a sign of climatic change. The fashion a few years ago was for the headline writers to see each flurry of snow as the harbinger of a new ice age; the trend today is to link summer droughts, like those of 1976 and 1984 in England, with the onset of a global warming due to the "greenhouse effect" of carbon dioxide in the atmosphere. The recent extreme variations in the weather may very well be an indication that the weather machine is changing gear, but nobody can yet say with certainty which way.

The simplest definition of climate is the "average weather", but just what you regard as normal climate, or weather, depends on the period of time over which you take the averages, because climate, like weather, is always changing. In general, the pattern for the past million years or so has been one in which a full ice age, some 100 000 years long, is succeeded by a 10 000-year-long interglacial period, then by another 100 000-year-long ice age, and so on. The relatively mild and pleasant conditions of the past 10 000 years, the millenia during which all of human civilisation has developed, actually represent a short-lived aberration, an interglacial period with higher global temperatures and considerably reduced ice cover. The simple fact that the present interglacial set in roughly 10 000 years ago is enough to suggest that the best is over and that, in geological terms, the next ice age is due – although it may hold off for another millenium or two.

From the geophysical traces such as the marks left by the advance and retreat of blaciers and by the changing of sea levels, from biological indicators such as the kinds of pollen deposited in old lake beds, and from direct historical records going back nearly 5000 years in China, we can read the climatic history of the past 10 000 years, and get a feel for how much conditions can change, even within the comparatively short interglacial periods. Hubert Lamb, the founder and first director of the Climatic Research Unit at the University of East Anglia, has identified four distinct climatic periods within the interglacial. According to his book *Climate: Present Past and Future* (Methuen, 1977), the first was a warm epoch that followed the latest ice age, causing its end. It peaked between 5000 and 7000 years ago. From 5000 BC to 3000 BC, sea-level rose rapidly as the ice sheets melted, the climate of the Sahara was wetter than it is today, and average temperatures in Europe and North America were about 2–3 °C warmer than today. This climatic optimum, as it is sometimes called (on the assumption that warmer conditions than those of today would be more pleasant), was followed by a colder epoch, which corresponds very closely to the Iron Age, and which was at its worst between about 2300 and 2900 years ago. This brought not just a cooling, but a great increase in wetness across northern Europe from Ireland to Scandinavia and Russia, where the great, gloomy forests spread southwards as the summer temperatures fell.

Figure 40.1 *Extreme weather conditions in the US where heavy snow brings life to a halt (Credit: AP Laserphoto)*

After the cold period of the Iron Age came a warm interval, less pronounced than the post-glacial optimum and therefore known as the "little" climatic optimum. This reached a peak in the early Middle Ages about 800 to 1000 years ago. By this time – AD 1000 to 1200 – we have good historical records, as well as relatively easily interpreted archaeological and geological evidence. All the evidence shows that summer temperatures were about 1 °C

Figure 40.2 *Dried-up reservoirs typify recent weather extremes in the UK (Credit: Fred Wilson)*

warmer than the present average in Europe and North America. It was possible to cultivate vines 3° to 5° latitude further north than now, and 100 to 200 m higher above sea-level. The last of the four main climatic periods of the present interglacial, however, marked a return to colder conditions, which, because it was worse than anything since the last ice age proper, has been dubbed the "Little Ice Age". It was at its most extreme between 550 and 125 years ago. From the fifteenth century to the nineteenth, with the worst conditions in Europe in the seventeenth, the Little Ice Age brought an extension of the Arctic pack ice far beyond its boundaries during the little optimum, a general shift of climate belts towards the equator, and a variety of troubles for humanity.

For example: the heyday of the Norse voyagers, who pioneered the northern route from Europe to America and who founded colonies in Iceland, Greenland and perhaps even in North America, occurred during the little optimum. When conditions changed and sea-ice made the established routes impassable, the Greenland colony died out; America was forgotten except in the sagas; and the colony on Iceland survived the ravages of the Little Ice Age only because of its importance as a base for whalers, who kept the island supplied. In Europe, the Little Ice Age was not a time of unrelieved cold, and many summers in the second half of the seventeenth century were hot and dry, with drought a problem. Both the plague and the Great Fire of London are associated historically with Little Ice Age droughts.

The closer we come to the present day, the more are details visible in the record, so more subtle and more rapid changes become apparent. Since about 1880, the world has warmed slightly once again. Lamb has pointed out that, as a result, the interval from about 1910 to 1960 was the mildest 50-year period of all comparable intervals throughout the past millenium. Ironically, this was just the time when twentieth-century meteorologists were establishing the averages that define "normal" weather and climate: our standards of normality are based on the most abnormal conditions of the past 1000 years.

Was this little warm interval a passing phase within the Little Ice Age, or does it mark the onset of another little optimum, a last fling of the present interglacial before the ice returns? By the middle of the 1970s, it had become clear that a global cooling had set in from about 1950 to 1970, suggesting that a return to the Little Ice Age might be on the cards. But the latest twist in the story is that the anthropogenic greenhouse effect may be beginning to

Figure 40.3 *A weather station at the University of East Anglia (Credit: John Gribbin)*

make itself felt, altering the natural course of events. Since 1980, or a little before, the Earth has, it seems, begun to warm up.

The truth is that we have no clear idea why the climate has changed within the interglacial period. But over the past few years a group of researchers in the United States has come up with a very good explanation of the way global mean temperatures have changed over the past few hundred years.

The most solidly established leg of the tripod on which this model is based is the link between volcanic eruptions and global – or at least hemispheric – cooling. Hubert Lamb has developed a dust veil index (DVI) for historical eruptions, setting Krakatoa as 1000 units – the standard against which other eruptions are compared. Now refined and improved, this index provides a guide to how much the atmosphere has been obscured by eruptions for any decade over the past few hundred years (*New Scientist*, 21 January 1982, p. 150). Krakatoa is far from being the biggest of these eruptions, in terms of the DVI. The 1815 eruption of Tambora, in Indonesia, produced a pall estimated at 3000 DVI units. It and other, lesser, eruptions combined to give a total DVI of 4400 during the period from 1811 to 1818. The second decade of the nineteenth century was indeed a time when temperatures in the northern hemisphere dipped sharply, contributing to the success of "General Winter" in the rout of Napoleon's troops before Moscow, and making 1816 notorious as "the year without a summer". More recently, the El Chichón eruption in Mexico in April 1982 contributed a DVI of about 600, and had only a marginal influence on northern hemisphere temperatures (*New Scientist*, 14 April 1983, p. 88). For the past hundred years or so, volcanic eruptions have been monitored carefully enough for climatologists to have an accurate idea of the changing dust veil. In reality, the veil is not just dust but also a sulphuric acid haze. The absence of major eruptions contributed to the warmth of the middle of the twentieth century, but this is clearly not the only factor at work.

The second leg of the tripod has been provided by the astronomers. In the late 1970s, Jack Eddy, of the High Altitude Observatory in Boulder, Colorado, suggested that changes in both the size and heat output of the Sun might account for the extreme cold of the seventeenth century peak of the Little Ice Age. After a great deal of work by many different astronomers, it emerged that although the effect is smaller than Eddy initially supposed, it is indeed real. The size of the Sun does vary, and Ronald Gilliland, of the same observatory, found evidence of a 76-year-long pulsation (associated with variations over a range of just 0.28 per cent in Solar luminosity) and longer-term, but comparably small, changes in both the size and brightness of the Sun. When he combined these changes with the volcano data, he ended up with very good agreement between the calculated temperature changes since 1880

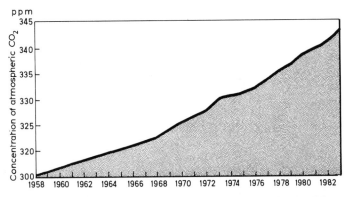

Figure 40.4   *Measurements in Hawaii show the build-up of carbon dioxide in the air*

and the actual meteorological record (*New Scientist*, 3 March 1983, p. 592). Now, both the theoretical calculations and the available historical data have been improved, providing a still closer agreement when the contribution of the carbon dioxide greenhouse effect is also included.

This is the third leg of the tripod, and the least secure. Direct measurements of the build-up of carbon dioxide in the atmosphere show an increase from 315 parts per million (ppm) by volume in 1957 to 340 ppm today, and it is estimated that at the beginning of the last quarter of the nineteenth century the concentration was between 280 and 290 ppm. There is no doubt that the amount of carbon dioxide in the air is increasing, and that this is because we are burning fossil fuel (oil and coal) and destroying the tropical forests that breathe in carbon dioxide. Nor is there any doubt that carbon dioxide is very efficient at absorbing and holding in infra-red radiation, the wavelengths that the warm surface of the Earth radiates into space.

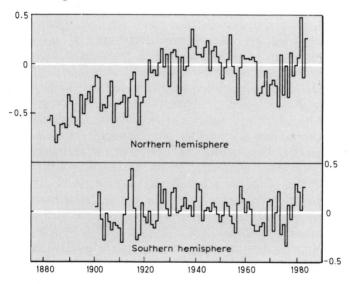

Figure 40.5 *Changes in surface air temperature over the northern (top) and southern (bottom) hemispheres have been determined by a team at the Climatic Research Unit, East Anglia. These plots show deviations from the 1946–1960 average, including the recent sharp warming. Actual changes can only be explained by theory if the greenhouse effect is included*

How much warmer will the world become, and how quickly? The best computer simulations indicate that doubling the nineteenth-century concentration of carbon dioxide (something that could conceivably happen by the end of the twenty-first century) would increase global mean temperatures by 2–4 °C. This global mean would disguise a range of changes: from a modest increase in the tropics, to perhaps three times the average increase at high latitudes. Such a change may or may not be a bad thing, but it is certainly something we need to know about as soon as possible, so that appropriate plans can be made.

Gilliland, in collaboration with Stephen Schneider at the US National Center for Atmospheric Research, in Boulder, has now taken the data on Solar variations, on the volcanic dust veil, and, with an allowance for the greenhouse effect, fed them into a computer model simulating how temperatures ought to have changed since the 1880s. The model takes account of the balance between land and sea, and can provide estimates for each hemisphere separately, as well as for the globe as a whole. There is only a modest amount of leeway allowed by the DVI and Solar pulsation data, which are based on well determined observations. But the contribution of the greenhouse effect is more of a guesstimate, which can be adjusted to "fit" the model to reality.

The real changes in global temperature since 1880 have been painstakingly compiled by Tom Wigley, Peter Jones and Mick Kelly, of the Climatic Research Unit at the University of East Anglia. Gilliland and Schneider find that they get the best agreement between their model and the real world by including a greenhouse effect rise in mean temperatures of only 1.6 ± 0.3 °C for a doubling of the carbon dioxide concentration. This is on the low end of the standard forecasts. But they do require this *soupçon* of greenhouse effect to get the fit between model and reality just right (*Nature*, vol. 310, p. 38).

This suggests that the three legs of the tripod may well be the only base we need to understand recent fluctuations of climate (apart from the inherent randomness in the system). The computer models are not subtle enough to say anything about the effect of any change in carbon dioxide concentration short of a crude doubling. But, according to Gilliland and Schneider, "barring some dramatic new counter-evidence, the advent of a significant greenhouse warming in future decades should not come as a surprise". A continued, or increased, high level of volcanic activity, with more eruptions like El Chichón or bigger, could delay this, but would not prevent the warming unless we stop burning fossil fuels.

Is there any other evidence that the climate is changing? It may well be that the bizarre juxtaposition of extremes experienced in the past ten years does indicate that something is going on. Britain has suffered droughts and floods, wet summers and severe winters in that time; the north-eastern US experienced the "worst winter for a hundred years" in 1977, and then one even worse in 1978. Other regions have suffered similarly. For the northern hemisphere as a whole, 1981 was the warmest year on record and 1983, in spite of El Chichón, the third warmest ever recorded. Lamb says that similar periods of erratic fluctuations of weather from one extreme to the other can be identified in the historical record just before major shifts in climate, including the period just before the onset of the worst decades of the Little Ice Age.

Extending the weather machine analogy, these hiccups really can be taken as a rather jerky attempt to change gear. But which way? Until recently, Lamb suggested that, since the past millenium has been cold and the past 50 years slightly warmer, the evidence of a change in the weather might best be read as an indicator of a return to the Little Ice Age. Now he is not so sure. With the greenhouse effect seemingly a proven reality, and those two very warm years of 1981 and 1983 just behind us, the possibility of a major warming in our lifetimes has to be taken seriously. Lamb still says that, although it is not a proven connection, "periods of very erratic weather such as we have been having for the past few years are a symptom of instability and it could go either way", but the smart money is beginning to go down on the prospect of an imminent warming. Only an inveterate gambler on the outside chance would go for a return of early nineteenth-century weather in our lifetimes. But on the longer timescale, once this minor geological hiccup of human interference with the carbon stored in fossil fuel has been sorted out, the return of the ice age within a very few thousand years seems inevitable.

6 September, 1984 © John Gribbin, 1984; all rights reserved

PART SEVEN

Economics, Politics and Climate

The study of climatic change is different from many other scientific disciplines. It concerns the real world of everyday life, and forecasts of which way the weather is likely to jump next have an immediate practical value. So the experts are forced out of their ivory towers and encouraged to apply their understanding of the weather to making the best predictions they can. Sometimes, as in the case of the ozone debate of the 1970s, and perhaps in the case of the present discussion of how the build-up of carbon dioxide in the air is going to affect our weather, the need to "go public" with ideas that are important to all of us encourages researchers to present ideas that are still only half-formed, not fully thought out, tried and tested. If the first calculations of the likely impact of CFCs on the ozone layer had been correct, there would have been no time to spend ten years refining and improving the calculations. By then, the harm would have been done. As it happens, ten years' refinement and improvement of the chemistry showed the threat to be much less than originally feared. Should the researchers always go public when they first discover a possible threat to Gaia? Or should they keep quiet while refining the calculations and testing their theories? These are political issues, and the answers to the questions raised must be influenced both by politics and our ability to predict climatic changes accurately.

In this short concluding section, I give you some reminders of the economic impact one severe winter can have, and of the difficulties we still have in making detailed climatic forecasts. I provide as an example a case study of how one major engineering project might affect the weather of a continent or a hemisphere; and I conclude with the most chilling, and political, of all climate models, the calculations of the "nuclear winter" that might follow an all-out war between the superpowers. That, surely, is the ultimate human threat to Gaia.

A postscript from Lord Ashby provides a framework in which to assess all of the work reported in this book.

41

Cold winters and the economy

WILLIAM BURROUGHS

In Britain we all too frequently forget how finely tuned our society is to the normal climate and how extreme conditions soon expose many weaknesses. Moreover, only when the atmosphere settles into some abnormal circulation pattern that brings certain types of extreme weather do we recall the lessons of the past which are so easily ignored in more normal times.

The severe cold of last winter in the United States provided a timely reminder of the problems that face an industrial country in the northern mid-latitudes. Why does such persistent weather arise; and how may we better prepare for such winters in the future? These are not idle questions for, although last winter was billed as the "worst of the century", other years – notably 1918, 1940 and 1963 – have featured prolonged periods of cold only marginally less severe. So such weather cannot be dismissed as being beyond the bounds of probability. What made 1976/77 noticeably different was the combination of a precarious state of the nation's energy supplies and the fact that people's expectations of mobility and comfort have risen. The net result is that both the scale of the disruption and the public reaction to it were greatly magnified.

The fact that here in Britain we escaped a severe winter last year does not mean we can ignore the American lesson. Twice in the past 30 years – 1947 and 1963 – we have experienced extreme winters and the type of disruption seen in the United States. Both winters are of special interest; 1963 for its prolonged severity in Britain and the global scale of the weather anomalies; and 1947 for the cold and snowfall which led to such a massive disruption of the country. The experience of 1947 more closely parallels the 1976/77 American winter in terms of human suffering. I will consider certain features of each winter starting first with a description of 1947.

The winter of 1947

The winter of 1947 did not start in earnest until late January, but it made up for lost time! The last week of January combined heavy snowfall and intense cold – a negative temperature anomaly of −6 °C. The first week of February started slightly milder but a predicted thaw turned to heavy snow. By 8 February the then Minister of Power, Emanuel Shinwell, announced to the House of Commons that, owing to general fuel shortages and weather-induced disruption in coal supplies carried by both train and coastal shipping, electricity would not be available to many industries. The restrictions would apply to London, the South-East, Midlands, and the North-West excluding Yorkshire. Domestic supplies were cut off for five hours a day (9 to 12 a.m. and 2 to 4 p.m.). Television ceased for a month and radio services were cut to a skeleton schedule. The electricity restrictions applied until the 24 February and were progressively relaxed over the following three weeks. The consequence of these restrictions was that by the middle of February the number of unemployed and temporarily laid-off workers rose to over two million.

Figure 41.1 *Newspapers headline extensive power cuts (Credit: John Frost)*

The cold continued unabated throughout February reaching its greatest intensity around 25 February. At Woburn, Beds, the temperature fell to −20 °C; at Oxford the temperature fell below freezing on the evening of the 10th and did not rise above this level until the morning of the 26th. The mean temperature for the month over much of Britain was below −1 °C. The most disruptive effect was not, however, the low minimum temperatures but the continuous frost by day with frequent snow showers and strong easterly winds. At Kew no sunshine was recorded during 20 consecutive days. On 22 February the Dover–Ostend ferry service was suspended because of pack-ice off the Belgian coast.

Early March saw some slackening of the cold in the southernmost part of the country but no let-up in the north. On 5 and 6 March an intense snowstorm swept central England with up to 50 cm of snow around Bedford causing massive disruption. Another snow-storm struck northern England on 12 March bringing the worst conditions of the winter. Heavy rain in the south, and melting snow, brought some of the worst floods on record. Kew recorded the wettest March in 250 years. Despite the return to more normal weather the huge accumulation of snow in upland areas was such that in the Cotswolds and Pennines snow-banks could still be seen in July during the glorious summer of 1947.

The impact of the power crisis and the cold weather on the economy can be seen in diagrams of economic activity and the annual agricultural returns. The impact on manufacturing industries of the cold in February reduced the index of production by 25 per cent but the effect was short-lived, output returning to normal in April. In the case of agriculture, both the winter and the wet March had a more lasting effect with many crops showing a significant decline in output for the year. But the most striking decline is that of sheep numbers. Around 20 per cent of the country's sheep died (some four million) with mortalities as high as 80 and 90 per cent being recorded in the hardest-hit hill-farming areas. The sheep population did not fully recover for five years.

The winter of 1963

The impact of the more prolonged and severe winter of 1963 was less dramatic in Britain. That was because the economy, and in particular energy supplies, were more robust, and the snowfall over the country was less frequent and disruptive. Even so, certain areas were cruelly exposed. The gas and electricity industries made valiant efforts to meet demand but limited generation capacity, and weaknesses in the distribution network, caused many difficulties. Economic activity dropped by about 7 per cent in January 1963, while electricity and gas consumption rose by between 15 and 20 per cent above normal.

The important feature of the winters of 1947 and 1963, and also 1977 in the United States, was the fact that the global atmospheric circulation became fixed in a persistent pattern. An essential component of this process is the establishment of "blocking" anticyclones at high latitudes. The blocking "highs" tend to obstruct the normal westerly zonal flow high in the atmosphere and the corresponding movement of surface weather systems around the hemisphere. A noticeable feature is that such blocks cause a splitting of the upper westerly airstream into two branches, one passing north and the other south of the quasi-stationary high. In between, there is a zone of easterly winds, light aloft, but often strong at the surface. The position of these highs appears to be related to the topography of the land masses in the northern hemisphere, in particular to the Rocky Mountains.

The winter of 1963 provided a classic example of such blocking conditions. Data on the mean average height of the 700-millibar surface in January 1963 give a good impression of the air currents aloft that steer the surface weather systems. In January 1963 the remarkably well defined anticyclones off the coast of Oregon (40 °N, 125 °W) and just south of Iceland (60 °N, 15 °W) set the stage for the extreme weather. Cold Arctic air was drawn down into the central United States, and into Europe, round the two blocking anticyclones. Conversely, warm tropical air was drawn up into Alaska and western Greenland. The net effect was that while an extreme negative temperature anomaly of −10 °C for the month was observed in Poland an equal positive departure occurred over western Greenland.

The counterbalance of extremes results from the meridional transport of weather systems around the blocking highs. The overall effect in 1963 was that the mean temperature of the atmosphere in the northern hemisphere did not deviate appreciably from the climatic normal. A similar pattern of extreme warmth and cold over adjacent regions – notably Alaska and the eastern United States – was observed in last year's winter.

Although we can identify the outward symptoms of such extreme winters we cannot yet adequately explain why they occur. A great number of propositions have been put forward. A leading contender in explaining why the atmosphere settles into a particular pattern is the existence of large-scale sea surface temperature anomalies. This is a subject that has received considerable attention from meteorologists during the past 20 years. Notably they have cited the winter of 1963 as a good example of how winter weather over the United States is influenced by the temperature of the mid-Pacific, high temperatures being correlated with cold winters in the eastern half of the continent. The circulation in January 1977 again provided support for this theory.

The British Meteorological Office has recently focused attention on the possibility that high sea surface temperatures in the Atlantic off West Africa were implicated in the effects of the winter of 1963 on the British Isles. A number of other interesting studies show how the importance of sea surface temperature anomalies effect global atmospheric circulation. Clearly this is a subject in need of much greater analysis if our efforts to understand the causes of prolonged bouts of abnormal weather are to bear fruit.

How can we reduce the impact?

The impact of cold winters on both Britain and other industrial countries can be so great that there is a pressing need to seek to reduce these effects. I think we must adopt a two-fold approach. Since we cannot predict accurately the occurrence of such winters we should plan on the basis that they come in a quasi-random manner every 10 to 20 years. This is reasonable as many of our economic investments are made to meet such an eventuality. We must not fall into the trap of a series of mild winters lulling us into a false sense of security so that we do not maintain our defences in readiness. Furthermore, if there is any truth in the fear of some climatologists that our climate is becoming more variable then this warning becomes even more important.

At the same time, we should continue to seek to unravel the mysteries of which geophysical parameters are important in causing prolonged anomalous weather patterns. This understanding should eventually provide us with a greater chance of predicting severe winters accurately. The economic consequences of improved forecasting, and also obtaining a better appreciation of how to minimise the impact of cold winters, would be substantial. After all, the economic impact of last winter in the United States is put at several billion dollars.

19 January, 1978

42

Climatic impact of Soviet river diversions

JOHN GRIBBIN

A long-term plan to reorganise the flow of Soviet rivers could have significant effects on Arctic ice cover and the climate of the northern hemisphere

Serious attention is now being paid to the possibility that man's activities may be affecting, or about to affect, the Earth's climate. Most concern is expressed about the so-called "carbon dioxide greenhouse effect", which threatens a long-term global warming. But this problem is so large, and the implications so diverse, that the resulting debate can deal only in generalities – and, indeed, there is still discussion about whether burning fossil fuels or destroying tropical rain-forests plays a bigger part in increasing the carbon dioxide content of the atmosphere (*New Scientist*, 29 March, p. 1016). Present knowledge of climatic change simply cannot deal in a precise, detailed way with the broad implications of such a profound change in the climatic balance. In the past few years, however, the understanding of climatic change has improved to the point where it is realistic to assess the impact of specific human activities – on a large but not global scale – on climate. One such planned activity – almost the archetype for such climatic impact assessments – is the Soviet plan to divert the flow of major Siberian rivers south, away from the Arctic Ocean and toward new agricultural lands.

The implications of this scheme are now being studied by a team at the University of East Anglia's Climatic Research Unit, as part of a larger project, funded by the US Office of Naval Research, aimed at determining the range and, if possible, causes of past variations in the extent of the Arctic sea-ice, and the potential for

Figure 42.1

predicting Arctic sea-ice over timescales from a few months to many years. The CRU team, led by Mick Kelly and Phil Jones, is finding that the repercussions of the river diversion scheme may echo throughout the climatic system of the northern hemisphere.

This kind of study is an expansion of the work of the CRU, which in its first few years of existence made a name for its activity on climatic reconstruction – using historical and other records to tell us about the climates of the past. This expansion of the unit's research activities results from outside requests for prediction of specific climatic changes, especially those related to Man's influence. This outside pressure for predictive work simply did not exist even five years ago, and shows how much attitudes towards the study of climatic change have changed in that time.

The background to this shift of emphasis in the outsiders' (including at least some of those outsiders who hold the purse-strings) view of climatic change is the now familiar story of crop failures in the early 1970s, followed by massive purchases on the grain market by the Soviet Union, a doubling of the world wheat price and a spreading realisation that the world lives from "hand to mouth". The world's food reserves are adequate to cover a month or so, but are insufficient if we suffer one year of terrible harvests on a global scale. Increased population and agricultural/economic policies that push farming toward large-scale, one-crop production makes us increasingly vulnerable to climatic changes, whether or not the climate itself is becoming more variable.

With a large area of the world under the control of a centrally planned economy, the Soviet Union, has made the most dramatic efforts to tailor Nature to suit Man's needs and, they hope, to overcome these problems. Great efforts have been made to develop the virgin lands of Kazakhstan and Central Asia, and the rural population of Kazakhstan has increased by about $1\frac{1}{2}$ million in the past 25 years. There is now an area of 36 million hectares of arable land in the republic, much of which receives no more than 300 mm of precipitation each year. The current plan is to triple grain production with the aid of large-scale irrigation. Water from the river Irtysh is already being supplied to outlying settlements in the Kazakhstan virgin lands, and a chain of reservoirs 1000 km long is pushing into the arid desert of Bet-Pak-Dala. With artesian wells also being drilled, the area is experiencing an agricultural revolution. And, indeed, although failures of crops in the traditional grain-growing regions such as the Ukraine forced the massive Soviet purchases on the world market in 1972, it was the yields from these new lands that saved the economy from complete disaster, enabling the government to meet its commitments to export grain to East European countries, while purchasing grain for home consumption.

Five year plan

Overall, the improvement of agricultural land in the USSR has seen the irrigation or drainage of 2 million ha of land in 1978 alone, and just under half this is newly irrigated land. Over the five years 1979–83, expenditure of R40 000 million is planned for such projects, as much as in the preceding 10 years, with more than 10 million ha of land being newly drained or irrigated, and in total more than 37 million ha of desert and mountain land brought under the plough. By the mid 1980s, on this scheme, these improved lands will be producing more than one third of the total agricultural output of the USSR.

But such grand schemes bring problems of a comparable scale. Already, thanks to irrigation demands on the central Asian rivers Amu Barya and Syr Daria, the level of the Aral Sea has fallen by 1.5 m, and with the projected demand this sea may disappear altogether if no alternative water sources are found. The level of the Caspian Sea is also falling, at least partly because of the use of water from the Volga for irrigation, and fisheries are threatened both by increased salinity and changed water flow.

Figure 42.2 *The Yenisei estuary region*

Figure 42.3   *The Yenisei estuary region could become less
prone to freezing if the Soviet plan to divert southward much
of the freshwater that now flows into the Arctic from this
river goes ahead. Although this might seem beneficial locally,
the changes in sea-ice could have some unwelcome repercussions on the climate (Credit: Novosti)*

How can these difficulties be overcome? To the Soviet planners,
big problems require big solutions, and they envisage diverting the
flow of the river Pechora (now running into the White Sea) southwards into the Volga and hence the Caspian, with some water
going, via the Volga-Don canal and River Don, into the Azov Sea.
Up to 15 km^3 per year, representing about 15 per cent of the
river's annual flow, will be extracted in this way.

Meanwhile, in Central Asia the plan is to divert the flow of the
Ob' and Yenisei rivers southwards into the Aral Sea via the Turgay
steppes, providing along the way more water for Kazakhstan. This
massive engineering scheme (*New Scientist*, vol. 79, p. 834) will

result in a canal 2500 km long, 200 or 300 m wide and of navigable depth (about 12 m). The water from the river will be raised more than 100 m by pumping machinery, now under development, handling flows of up to 400 m^3 s^{-1}, with an associated network of lesser canals, tunnels, reservoirs and pumping stations.

Details of the project remain rather cloudy and uncertain, although Philip Micklin, of Western Michigan University, has been reviewing the Soviet literature and piecing together a coherent overall picture for the US National Science Foundation. It is largely on the basis of his expert interpretation of the information that does leak out that we are able to make forecasts of how much of this scheme will get moving, and when. About 100 Soviet research institutes are currently involved in a wide-ranging assessment of the implications of the diversion schemes, and there have been some shifts in emphasis as a result. For example, it is no longer proposed that nuclear devices should be used for excavation. Micklin has also noticed that there is debate about the environmental consequences of large-scale river diversion schemes within the Soviet Union itself, and says that such factors set an upper limit on what the government regards as practicable. That upper limit, however, is very high; and at the same time, Micklin believes that, within the context of the Tenth Five-Year Plan, large-scale diversions are "essential to further economic growth" and that the authorities are "single-minded about proceeding with them" (*Environmental Management*, vol. 2, p. 567).

On this basis, it seems that construction of facilities to divert 30–35 km^3/year of northern water could be underway by the mid-1980s, with the first-stage transfers, probably from the Ob' alone, running at 25–30 km^3/year, beginning by the mid-1990s. During the early decades of the next century, when the Yenisei is brought into the scheme, 75 km^3/year may be diverted from the two rivers. And, indeed, some schemes related to the Ob'/Yenisei diversions are already operational, including the 500-km-long Irtysh–Karagancha canal, which supplies water to the outlying settlements in the Kazakhstan virgin lands, and is being extended towards Dzhezkazgan to supply new state farms and an industrial complex.

Clearly, such schemes have important environmental repercussions within the area of the diversions, and these factors set the upper limits on current Soviet planning. But they may also have much wider climatic repercussions, which is why the team is interested in them. The key factor is the role of the Siberian rivers, and especially the Ob' and Yenisei, in maintaining the ice cover of the Arctic Ocean.

The presence of an ice-covered polar sea is, many climatologists believe, a key factor in maintaining the pattern of ice ages and interglacials that has dominated the climatic history of the Earth for the past few million years. One day, when the continents drift sufficiently to allow warm water to penetrate the now almost landlocked Arctic sea, the ice will disappear and the Earth will have many millions of years of a warmer climatic regime. It now seems, though, that a minor shift in the salinity balance of the Arctic waters could do the same trick.

In its top layers, the salinity of the Arctic Ocean is much less than in layers a few hundred metres deep. Although freshwater freezes more easily than brine, this is *not* the mechanism that keeps the Arctic frozen. Rather, the low density of the freshwater ensures that it sits like a lid on top of the denser waters below, preventing even warm water from reaching the surface. Between the surface and 400 m depth, the salinity increase produces an increase in density 20 times greater than the decrease in density caused by the 3 °C rise in temperature over the same depth. The old adage that warm fluid rises applies only if other things are equal, which they are not in the Arctic. So there is a salinity-forced temperature inversion, with the coldest, but least saline, water at the surface.

Five years ago, Knut Aagaard and L. K. Coachman of the University of Washington, suggested that if the freshwater flow into the Arctic were cut off completely, the salinity layering that keeps its surface cold and icy would be gone within a decade, and that if both Yenisei and Ob' (which between them supply one third of the freshwater input that maintains the salinity stratification) were diverted to run away from the Arctic, the "lid" would disappear from about a million km^2 of the Eurasian Basin (*Eos*, vol. 56, p. 484). This would have a drastic impact on the polar ice-cap. Indeed, significantly reducing the flow of the Ob' and Yenisei may also affect the ocean current system of the Arctic, as well as affecting the spring break-up of ice and the autumn formation of sea-ice and its winter spread along the Siberian coast. No one is yet planning to switch off entirely the great Siberian rivers, but the CRU team is now coming to grips with the smaller scale (in global terms) of the actual diversions envisaged.

The large scope of these schemes by human standards, and the way they edge into the big league of global events, can be seen by comparison with other great rivers. The combined flow of the Ob' and Yenisei is about 400 times that of the River Thames, and one-seventh the annual flow of the greatest terrestrial river, the Amazon. Each of the two great Siberian rivers is a member of the top five in the league table of greatest rivers in the world in its own right; and their flows are highly seasonal, with peak discharge in late May and early June, after the snows melt. The Ob' discharges 12 000 m^3 s^{-1} on average (400 km^3/year), the Yenisei 18 000 m^3 s^{-1} (550 km^3/year) and the Amazon 150 000 m^3 s^{-1} (4800 km^3/year). The extent of the envisaged tampering with this natural flow is a reduction in the fresh-water discharge into the Arctic Ocean of roughly 5 per cent by the early decades of the twenty-first century (which is likely) and, if the most grandiose schemes go ahead, a permanent reduction of the flow of up to 20 per cent by the middle of the twenty-first century (which seems rather less likely to happen). In order to assess potential effects on Arctic ice cover, these figures must be put in the context of the natural, year-to-year and decade-to-decade, variability of the fresh-water discharge into the Arctic. First, if there have been years in recent history when natural fluctuations produced a fall of 5 per cent in the flow from the long-term mean, then study of the ice patterns in those years will provide some guidance to the likely consequences of the diversion schemes (although a permanent reduction of this kind is rather different from an occasional fluctuation the same size). Secondly, if the variability of the fresh-water discharge is less than 5 per cent, then clearly the planned diversions may have a very great impact, by completely altering the salinity stratification of the Arctic Ocean.

Uncertain details

The mean fresh-water discharge into the north Arctic is, however, subject to great uncertainty, and the range of year-to-year variations about this mean has yet to be determined accurately. As well as placing the Soviet plans in the context of past changes in the fresh-water discharge into the Arctic, the CRU team is analysing a range of climatic data in order to determine the causes of variations in the climate of western Siberia and the role that the region plays in the climate system of the northern hemisphere. This investigation has produced interesting evidence of a possible feedback mechanism involving the rivers Ob' and Yenisei and the extent of sea-ice in the Kara Sea (see below). As far as can be gleaned from their publications, the Soviet authorities are not aware of this feedback; and although the ideas have yet to be fully tested, they show the difficulties of assessing the potential environmental impacts of such far-reaching schemes.

Wider implications

As well as the possibility that the planned river diversions may adversely affect precipitation in just those regions that are supposed to benefit from the irrigation, there are other far-reaching implications. Ice from the Kara Sea drifts into the open Arctic and eventually into the North Atlantic Ocean via the East Greenland current. And the extent of ice in the North Atlantic is considered to play an important part in determining climatic conditions over the Eurasian continent.

It is still far too early to be able to say how far the repercussions of such a shift would ripple through the climatic system of the northern hemisphere, but by identifying a specific "distant effect" of a change in river-flow in the long term the CRU team has certainly moved this kind of forecasting out of the famous "ballpark" in which vague predictions are usually made, and into a more precisely defined region – perhaps a tennis court? What they need now are data going back for a hundred years or more, against which the forecasts of the effects of the diversions can be set in context. Unfortunately, reasonably good figures for the annual flow of the two rivers are available only since the 1930s, and extending the data back involves a return to the techniques in which CRU has established its skills – sifting climatic information from historical and proxy evidence.

So far, it does seem that the planned five per cent reduction in flow falls at the extreme edge of what has been "normal" variability in this century, and may shift the system into a new regime (for remember that there will still be natural fluctuations both above and below the new average). River flow has been high during the 1970s, so this might be seen as returning conditions to those that were common in the period 1940–69 – but such an optimistic assessment takes no account of any natural processes that might also operate to reverse this trend. If the diversion schemes do result in a reduction of polar ice cover and a warming of the Arctic, there will be climatic changes over a wide area, and possibly on a hemispheric scale. It may be that the changes prove to be beneficial on balance, although past experience suggests that one effect would be to decrease precipitation in the regions the Soviets plan to irrigate! But, now that it seems we do have the know-how to make sensible forecasts of what the effects will be, should the schemes go ahead before the forecasts are made? Fortunately, for once a warning has been sounded sufficiently far in advance, and the project itself is operating on such a long timescale that full information should be available before the major transfers of water begin – and, just maybe, the evidence will be strong enough, and early enough, to bring about modifications to the scheme. The Soviet authorities are certainly concerned about the potential environmental impact, but there is a definite need for independent assessment outside the Soviet Union.

6 December, 1979 © *John Gribbin 1979; all rights reserved*

Sea-ice/weather feedback in Western Siberia

Statistical analysis of atmospheric circulation data for the northern hemisphere has shown that one of the major patterns of variability in the hemisphere affects Western Siberia, and is associated with major year-to-year changes in the flow of the Ob' and Yenisei and with ice conditions in the Kara Sea. When this pattern is well developed, stronger-than-usual easterly winds blow along the Siberian coast hindering the drift of ice out of the Kara Sea into the open Arctic Ocean and producing an increase in the ice cover of the Kara Sea.

At the same time, there is enhanced cyclonic activity (low-pressure systems) and increased precipitation over the catchment areas of the Ob' and Yenisei increases the flow of the two rivers. The resulting discharge of greater quantities of fresh water into the Kara Sea then reinforces the direct effect of the easterly winds, by hastening the appearance of young ice in Autumn.

Whether or not the new increase in ice extent then affects the atmospheric circulation has yet to be assessed. The complexity of the interactions between the atmospheric circulation, river-flows and ice extent does however highlight the need for greater understanding of the workings of the local climate system and its sensitivity to changes in any of its components, for example, the flow of the Ob' and Yenisei. But there is at least a hint here that decreasing the Ob'/Yenisei flow may decrease precipitation in the regions being irrigated.

6 December, 1979

43

Martian study predicts "nuclear winter"

CATHERINE CAUFIELD

Scientists have under-estimated the consequences of a nuclear war according to a study on the global atmospheric effects of nuclear bombs carried out by a group of scientists headed by Carl Sagan and published this week. There would be much more radioactive fallout than has been realised previously, and even a small-scale "limited" nuclear war can cause a "nuclear winter" – the months of darkness and freezing temperatures that will follow nuclear confrontations. One hundred megatons, less than one per cent of the world's nuclear arsenal, would be enough to plunge the Earth into nuclear winter.

The group has built on earlier work on the effects of a global dust storm on the atmosphere and climate of Mars. It obtained data on this freak event, which occurred in late 1971, because the US's Mariner 9 spacecraft was visiting Mars at the time.

The planet's surface temperature dropped as the dust absorbed the incoming sunlight. The dust warmed the upper Martian atmosphere. After some months the dust fell out of the atmosphere and temperatures there and at ground level returned to normal. The computer models developed by the team accurately predicted the slight drops in temperature resulting from injection of dust into the Earth's atmosphere after volcanic explosions.

The team ran models for several dozen war scenarios. They varied the number and size of bombs, the time of year and distribution of targets, and other factors crucial to the amount of dust generated in a nuclear war. Their standard case assumed a 5000-megaton war, a figure widely used elsewhere in such studies. The results, says Sagan, "astonished us".

Figure 43.1 *Carl Sagan, who warns of Siberian winters all year round after the bomb*

The team discovered a "new" source of radioactivity that previous studies have ignored. Up to now, researchers have taken account of both prompt fallout from exploding bombs and long-term fallout as radioactive particles that were carried into the stratosphere return to Earth about a year later, after most of the radioactivity has decayed. But, according to the new study, there will be serious fallout from radioactive particles that are intercepted by the dust before they enter the stratosphere. These particles will return to Earth with much of their radioactivity intact. For the standard case roughly 30 per cent of the land northern mid-latitudes could receive a radioactive dose greater than 250 rads. About half the northern mid-latitudes could receive a dose greater than 100 rads. The lethal dose of radiation is 400 rads.

They also determined that after a 5000-megaton war the Earth will receive only a few per cent of its normal sunlight, too little for plants to photosynthesise. Most of the northern hemisphere, where the majority of the strategic targets for bombs are, will be frozen for months. Except for narrow coastal strips, the land temperature will drop to −25 °C and stay below freezing for months, even in a summer war. Half the world will take on the climate of a deep Siberian winter. The global movement of vast quantities of heated dust would also drive temperatures below freezing in parts of the southern hemisphere, even though few bombs would fall there.

In the severe case (10 000 megatons exploded) the entire northern hemisphere will have temperatures below freezing for more than a year, and large areas of the south will have three months of freezing temperatures, followed by a longer period of severe cold (7 °C). The oceans, however, will not freeze, so nuclear war will not trigger off a new ice age. But the researchers warn that because heating the upper atmosphere and cooling the lower atmosphere stabilises the atmospheric structure, they may be "seriously underestimating" how long the cold and dark will last.

The "greatest surprise", according to Sagan, came when the group considered the possibility of a small, "contained" nuclear war. They found that exploding only 100 megatons would result in months of cold and dark almost as severe as after a full-scale 5000-megaton war.

3 November, 1983

44

Not with a bang but a winter

MICHAEL KELLY

It is rumoured that atomic scientists placed bets on whether the atmosphere would ignite during the first A-bomb test. It now appears more likely that after a nuclear war the world would freeze

No-one needs to be reminded that the explosion of even a few nuclear weapons would cause death and devastation on a massive scale. Only in recent years, however, has anyone recognised the possibility that nuclear warfare might affect the Earth's weather and climate. As nuclear strategy has turned from deterrence and mutually assured destruction towards the development of the capability to fight and survive a nuclear war, interest in the state of the world following a nuclear exchange has mounted.

It had been thought that the main atmospheric consequences would be an increase in the amount of harmful ultra-violet radiation reaching the Earth's surface as oxides of nitrogen produced in the heat of the explosions affected the ozone layer, high up in the atmosphere. The effects of the vast clouds of dust and the pall of smoke from fires ignited in urban, industrial and rural areas had, however, been neglected.

Paul Crutzen and John Birks, in 1982, were the first atmosheric scientists to assess the pollution resulting from a nuclear exchange (*Ambio*, XI(2–3), 114–126). Many researchers have since extended their study and preliminary results were reported at the conference "The World after Nuclear War" in Washington DC, late in 1983. The first quantitative model of the atmospheric effects of the nuclear cloud was published in *Science* weeks later by the TTAPS group (Turco, Toon, Ackerman, Pollack and Sagan) along with a summary, by Paul Ehrlich and collaborators, of the likely biological effects (*Science*, 222(4630), 1283–1300). The

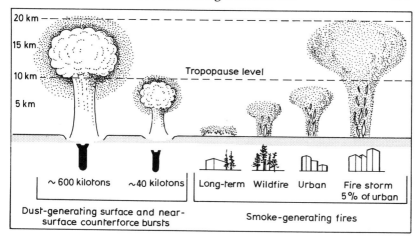

Figure 44.1   *The nuclear winter will be brought on by the cloud of dust and smoke produced by nuclear explosions. The main contaminants include: dust blasted up from the ground by the initial explosions – fine, relatively bright, particles which scatter Solar radiation; and smoke arising from the many fires in urban and rural areas ignited by the blasts – this black, oily soot very effectively absorbs the Sun's heat. Chemical products of the nuclear reactions and fires will also form part of the nuclear cloud and, if sufficient sunlight is available, may result in photochemical smog as well as affecting the ozone layer (Credit: Bill Ray)*

results of this pioneering work have recently been published in *The Cold and the Dark: the World After Nuclear War* (Sidgwick and Jackson).

It now appears possible that the dust, smoke and chemical products that would contaminate the atmosphere after a nuclear exchange could cause temperatures over much of the northern hemisphere to drop to a level that has not been experienced since the last ice age. For a period of weeks and possibly months, temperatures may remain at or below freezing over much of the northern landmasses. This is what has become known as the nuclear winter.

Predicting the effects of an event as awesome and unthinkable as nuclear war stretches to the limit our understanding of the mechanisms that underlie changes in climate. How reliable are the conclusions reached in the preliminary studies? Where do the uncertainties lie? And how do scientists see and assess their social responsibility in such a politically loaded arena?

To estimate the climatic effects of the nuclear cloud of dust and smoke is a complex process, involving a wide range of scientific disciplines and many uncertainties. The analysis begins in the realm of war games. How many and what type of weapons might be used? What kind of targets? How long could a nuclear war last? This stage of the study has to be undertaken on a "what if?" basis, second-guessing military strategists in the nuclear nations. Strategically plausible scenarios are developed covering exchanges ranging from a relatively limited attack on, say, a handful of cities to the detonation of most of the world's arsenal.

Next, researchers have to determine the characteristics of the cloud of pollution associated with each scenario (Figure 44.1). They must estimate the amount of combustible material at military bases and in cities, industrial and rural areas (particularly forests). Smoke production at targeted sites is then assessed and the quantity of dust generated by ground-bursts on, and airbursts over, these targets is calculated. The result is an estimate of the total amount of material injected into the atmosphere and some idea of its physical properties.

Inevitably, there are many areas of uncertainty in these initial stages of the analysis. Can we really know how a nuclear war might be fought? How much can we say about the physical nature of military targets? How good is our knowledge of the physics of smoke production in large fires? The size-distribution of the smoke particles is of crucial importance as this determines how much of the Sun's heat is trapped within the cloud. Aware of the many uncertainties and simplifications involved, researchers have been careful, where doubt exists, to err on the conservative side.

How will the smoke and dust be distributed within the atmosphere as they are spread by blast, by wind, by fires and by firestorms? We have to consider both the horizontal spread of the cloud and its vertical distribution. Most simulations attempted to date have assumed that the dust and smoke will spread evenly and rapidly over middle latitudes of the northern hemisphere and that the atmosphere will be in its present-day state. In fact, the cloud might spread in a patchy fashion, with areas of high and low concentration. Moreover, as the nuclear winter progresses, the state of the atmosphere will alter radically, and this will affect the further evolution of the mass of dust and smoke. Some changes may reinforce the cooling, others will counter it.

To take just one example, the cloud will be distributed between the lower atmosphere, the troposphere, and the upper atmosphere, the stratosphere. The relative proportion of the contaminants in these two distinct layers is important, because the residence time in the stratosphere is much longer (of the order of months and, possibly, years as opposed to days and weeks). The boundary, the tropopause, is at about 10 to 12 km in middle latitudes. Under normal conditions, precipitation washes pollution out of the troposphere relatively quickly. As the lower atmosphere becomes more stable, a reduction in precipitation may occur and residence times may increase. This could affect the duration of the nuclear winter.

The next stage in the analysis is to estimate the effect of the cloud on the Earth's energy balance. This is conveniently measured by the atmopshere's optical depth. An optical depth of n

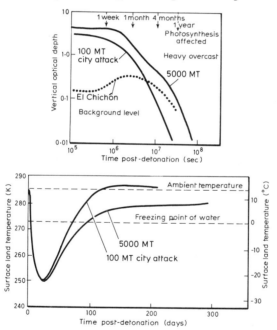

Figure 44.2 (a) *The time-independent hemispheric extinction optical depth (wavelength 550 nm) for the cloud produced by the volcano, El Chichón, and two of the series of TTAPS exchange scenarios.* (b) *The change in surface air temperature in the continental interiors of the northern hemisphere for the two exchange scenarios*

means that the incoming radiation at the top of the atmosphere will be reduced by a factor of e to the power n by the time it reaches the Earth's surface. The TTAPS group first used a particle microphysics model. This simulated the effect on the development of the nuclear cloud of processes such as gravitational settling, vertical diffusion, coagulation, agglomeration, and scavenging by precipitation. Then, considering both visible and infra-red properties, the group calculated the hemispheric optical depth for each of a range of nuclear exchange scenarios.

Turco and his colleagues tested their method on the particle cloud produced by the Mexican volcano, El Chichón, which erupted in spring 1982 (Figure 44.2(a)). Observations of this volcanic cloud confirm that the simulation is reasonable. In the case of a 5000-Mt (megaton) nuclear exchange, among the more likely of the scenarios, the model predicts optical depths in the range 2 to 4 for the first two to three months. This corresponds to a reduction over 95 per cent in the amount of Solar energy reaching the ground (averaged over the daily cycle and the hemisphere). The largest volcanoes of recent times have produced a reduction of a few per cent at most causing a cooling of about 1 °C over northern landmasses. Because attacks on cities would start a large number of fires, even a 100-Mt attack, using many small warheads targeted on cities, could have pretty much the same effect as the 5000-Mt exchange. The amount of smoke produced by a 100-Mt attack on cities would not be very different from that of the larger exchanges. Cities can burn only once!

The TTAPS group then used another computer model to predict the effects on the temperature of the atmosphere. This model took account of the processes affecting the energy balance of a single column of air, which may be over land or ocean, and modelled the vertical transfer of heat. The resulting surface air temperatures over the continental interiors are shown in Figure 44.2(b). In the case of the 5000-Mt exchange, surface temperatures drop by about 35 °C in the first month and remain below freezing for about three months. The more limited exchange of 100 Mt produces a similar cooling in the initial months.

There would be a smaller drop in temperature over the oceans, because the seas take longer to cool down. The TTAPS model predicts a fall in temperature of only a few degrees over the ocean. In the case of the 5000-Mt scenario, if we take into account the ameliorating influence of the oceans, landmasses of the northern hemisphere in the middle latitudes could expect an average surface cooling of perhaps 15 to 20 °C.

Four other studies, three in the US and one in the Soviet Union, each using different computer models, have now reproduced the TTAPS results. Contrary to claims that later work has shown the TTAPS results to be exaggerated, there is remarkable consistency between the experiments when their results are expressed in compatible form.

Mike MacCracken, at the Lawrence Livermore National Laboratory in California, using essentially the TTAPS 5000-Mt scenario, predicts a drop of 10 to 15 °C in surface temperature averaged over the land under the nuclear cloud (reported in a paper presented at the Third International Conference on Nuclear War, Erice, Sicily, 19–23 August 1983).

Vladimir Alexandrov, with a model of the atmosphere and ocean based on early American work and developed further in the Computing Centre of the Soviet Academy of Sciences, predicts a drop of 10 to 15 °C averaged over the landmasses in the months after a 10 000-Mt exchange (*The Proceeding on Applied Mathematics*, The Computing Centre of the USSR Academy of Sciences, Moscow, 1983).

Curt Covey and colleagues at the National Center for Atmospheric Research (NCAR) in Boulder, Colorado, using one of the most sophisticated climate models available, running on one of the biggest and fastest computers that dollars can buy, predict a temperature drop over land under the cloud of some 15 to 20 °C a few days after a 6500-Mt exchange (*Nature*, 308(a), 21–25, 1984).

Alan Robock, at the University of Maryland, in a range of simulations, forecasts similar drops in temperature with the effects possibly lasting for up to four or five years due to amplification by polar feedbacks (*Nature*, 310, 667–670, 1984).

Although the models used in these studies vary in their formulation and degree of sophistication, they are all based on the same understanding of the climate system and are only partly independent. Moreover, they contain many simplifications and approximations and were designed to simulate present-day conditions rather than the radically different climatic state of the nuclear winter. Nevertheless, it is encouraging that they produce results that are very close to each other and to the original TTAPS estimates. It would be unwise to rely on any one model to produce a definitive prediction of conditions in the nuclear winter, but each throws light on a different aspect of the problem.

Robock's energy-balance model handles feedback between ocean, ice and atmosphere in high latitudes explicitly. Feedback, in this case lengthens the duration of the nuclear winter as cooling alters the extent of snow and ice, producing a "knock-on" effect in following years. Covey and his colleagues produced maps showing how the cooling would affect different parts of the world (Figure 44.3). They found that the way the air circulates in the atmosphere might change as temperatures fall and that this would blow part of the nuclear cloud into the southern hemisphere. Consequently, the cooling would spread southwards across the equator. The Soviet model produced a similar result. The nuclear winter will affect combatant and non-combatant nations alike. Climate does not respect neutrality.

These models are experimental. They are not predictions in the sense that tomorrow's weather can be forecast by computer. They provide, at best, an indication of what might happen – an order-of-magnitude estimate of the impact on climate. In fact, our understanding of the processes involved in the nuclear winter may not be sufficient to make definite predictions. Steve Schneider, at

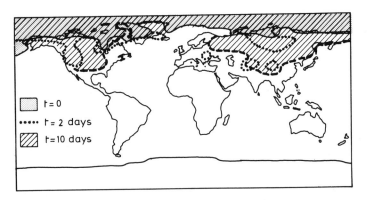

Figure 44.3 *The initial development of the nuclear winter simulated by the NCAR model for day 0, before the nuclear cloud is added, day 2 and day 10. These results are for a summer war. The shaded areas indicate temperatures below freezing. The sequence shows the advance of freezing temperatures from the poles with the oceans affording some protection to neighbouring land masses. This protection depends on the direction of the prevailing winds*

NCAR, reckons that scientists should adopt an "anticipatory" role, warning of the risk, although unable to make firm predictions. His colleague, Starley Thompson, in a guest editorial in the journal *Climatic Change* (6(2), 105–109, 1984) concludes that the problem is one of determining plausibility rather than accurate simulation.

The nature of the problem means that models cannot be verified experimentally in the real world. We can, however, better understand the physical processes involved if we study past events that are similar in some respect to a nuclear catastrophe. Such analogues include dust storms, forest fires, fires induced by conventional bombing (for example, in Dresden and Hamburg) and the atomic devastation of Hiroshima and Nagasaki, volcanic eruptions, and meteorite or asteroid impacts.

How do atmospheric scientists see the wider, political implications of these findings? On an individual level, the nuclear winter debate has, to date, been conducted in an extremely responsible fashion. Results have been reported with scrupulous honesty, and criticism has, for the most part, been informed and offered constructively. The study of climatic change has come of age in recent years and, in this context at least, is showing signs of maturity. A refreshing state of affairs.

On a more formal level, the American Meteorological Society issued the following statement in September last year: "Recognising the inevitable, widespread, devastating consequences of nuclear war by direct explosive effects, and by effects propagated through the atmosphere to the entire globe that could cause the destruction of the biological base that sustains human life, the Council of the American Meteorological Society calls on the nations of the world to take whatever measures are necessary, such as the adoption of appropriate treaties to prevent use of nuclear weapons and avoid nuclear war." (*Bulletin of the American Meteorological Society*, 64(11), 1302, 1983).

Early in 1984, the Danish Meteorological Society reprinted this statement on the front cover of its journal (*Vejret*, 6(1)) and, noting that "far too many scientists shut themselves up in their ivory towers", commented that " it is . . . gratifying that such a large and influential group of meteorologists . . . clearly supports a peaceful solution to one of the greatest problems of our time".

Yuri Izrael, a Corresponding Member of the USSR Academy of Sciences and a renowned atmospheric scientist, writing in one of the —leading Soviet journals about the ecological consequences

314 Economics, Politics and Climate

of nuclear war, concluded that: "The issue is that of life on Earth itself. Aggression, leading to the unleashing of nuclear war, is an absolute crime against humanity and the whole biosphere of the Earth." (*Meteorologiya i Gidrologiya*, 10, 5–10, 1983).

Carl Sagan, a member of the TTAPS group, has published a detailed consideration of the policy implications of the nuclear winter (*Foreign Affairs*, Winter 1983/1984, 257–292). He claims, perhaps optimistically, that a threshold, defined in terms of targeting policy and the number of warheads exploded, can be determined below which the nuclear winter effect is unlikely to be triggered. He goes on to suggest that arms limitation talks should strive for a "build-down" to this level (which, he estimates, was exceeded during the 1950s).

Sagan points out that the findings have important implications for first-strike or counterforce strategies. Even in the unlikely event of a successful first strike, there can be no winner in the nuclear winter. The victor may well suffer as much as the vanquished. Under pressure from groups such as the Natural Resources Defense Council in Washington DC, the US government has moved to consider these implications. Richard L. Wagner, assistant to Defense Secretary Caspar Weinberger, testified before a congressional committee in July 1984, that "even a small possibility of . . . catastrophic effects must be considered very seriously". Plans have been announced for a $50-million five-year research project to be administered by the National Oceanic and Atmospheric Administration. The British government has had little to say.

The research on the nuclear winter is currently being scrutinised by SCOPE (the Scientific Committee on Problems of the Environment) at the request of the International Council of Scientific Unions and by the US National Academy of Sciences. The report of the academy's study was due to be published late last year but has been delayed. While full scientific evaluation of the research awaits findings of these projects, it can be stated quite categorically that a finite risk of climatic catastrophe following a nuclear exchange has been demonstrated. The details may be in error; limited exchanges may not trigger the effect, but the danger cannot be denied.

13 September, 1984

Effects on Britain

How will Britain experience the nuclear winter? Let us consider one scenario – an average temperature drop over the world's northern middle latitudes of some 10 to 20 °C, with temperatures reduced by up to 35 °C in some continental regions but only a few degrees over the central oceans. Situated between ocean and continental landmass, Britain is likely to experience an average temperature decrease of somewhere between 10 and 20 °C. The range from day to day is likely to be great, between 5 and 35 °C below present-day values depending on whether the wind blows from the cold continental interior or the relatively warm ocean.

This temperature drop can be placed in context by considering how much climate varies naturally. From year to year, Britain can experience temperature swings between mild and severe seasons of up to 5 °C. The difference between a normal summer and winter is about 10 °C. If the nuclear exchange occurs in summer, average temperatures will drop to close to and, at times, well below freezing – more severe than a harsh winter in the present day. If the exchange occurs in winter, temperatures will drop to well below freezing. The closest parallel, in magnitude although not duration, is the drop in temperature experienced at the height of the last ice age. Alaska is, perhaps, the best analogue in the present climatic epoch.

What will we find as we emerge from under the kitchen table, pushing aside the sandbags? Twilight, day-long, with only an occasional glimpse of the Sun. Temperatures swinging between freezing and 20 ° or so below. Intense storms due to the temperature contrast between the cold land and the relatively warm ocean. Dense fogs in coastal areas, as the oceans pump moisture into the surface layers of the atmosphere. Violent thunderstorms and black rain. The seas along the coastline gradually freezing. The ground permanently covered by frost and snow. All surface water frozen.

Human survival is possible in such conditions, with adequate protection. Without Arctic survival gear, and in a physically and psychologically shattered state, survival at sub-zero temperatures is likely to prove difficult, to say the least. The casualties of a prolonged nuclear winter could equal those killed or injured in the initial days of the nuclear exchange.

Few domestic crops are likely to survive a rapid temperature drop to levels well below freezing, although the impact is, to a

certain extent, dependent on the time of year. It is extremely
unlikely that domestic livestock or wild animals would survive the
cold, the lack of food, the lack of unfrozen water, not to mention
the effects of blast and radiation poisoning. We would be reduced
to a hunter–gatherer lifestyle, with nothing to hunt and precious
little to gather.

Why will we freeze?

Under normal circumstances, the Sun's energy reaching the Earth's
surface heats the ground. This heating is balanced by infra-red
cooling of the surface and cooling throughout the lower atmosphere. The vertical temperature gradient between the warm
ground and the colder atmosphere above means that the atmosphere is unstable. Upward motion, convection, results in vertical
transfer of heat to balance the instability. The actual temperature
of the Earth's surface is the result of the fine balance between these
processes, critically determined by conditions high in the atmosphere, close to the tropopause, rather than at the Earth's surface.

The particles in the nuclear cloud affect this energy balance by
absorption in the case of the soot and scattering in the case of dust.
Absorption heats the particles up; scattering changes the direction
of the incident radiation. Solar energy is trapped at the top of the

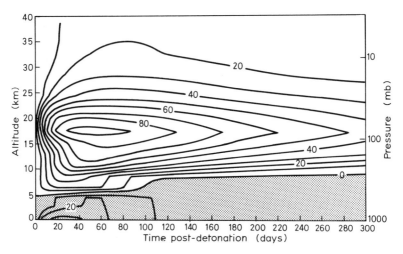

Figure 44.4   *The change in the vertical temperature profile
(°C) with time for the continental interiors. The shaded area
indicates cooling*

cloud and much of it does not reach the Earth's surface. The atmosphere at cloud-top warms, the instability in the lower atmosphere is drastically reduced (the upper levels of the troposphere become as warm as, or warmer than the surface), and the tropopause may well be brought down to the ground (Figure 44.4). The balance between the radiative and convective processes there then determines that the surface cools. Heat trapped under the cloud (for example, that stored in the oceans) will offset the cooling to a certain extent as is evidenced by the much smaller temperature changes over the oceans.

If the characteristics of the nuclear cloud are very different from those suggested by current work then the balance may not be disrupted in this way. Moreover, this account of the processes involved, although reflecting the way the TTAPS model views the world, does neglect a number of important factors such as horizontal advection of heat. It is a first approximation. Whether or not it can be improved upon significantly, given the uncertainties involved in all stages of the analysis, is a moot point. More sophisticated models may be more vulnerable to errors and approximation.

13 September, 1984

45

Volcano research backs nuclear winter theory

JOHN GRIBBIN

Strong support for the nuclear winter hypothesis has come from the latest study of how the Earth's atmosphere responds to a major volcanic eruption.

The study has been carried out by Mick Kelly and Chris Sear, at the University of East Anglia's Climatic Research Unit. It shows that several large volcanic eruptions in the northern hemisphere during the present century have produced a cooling in the continental interiors around the hemisphere of as much as 1.4 °C within a few weeks of the eruption.

Climatologists have accepted for a long time that large volcanic eruptions do affect the climate, by throwing gas and dust high into the stratosphere, where it blocks heat from the Sun. But until recently they thought that the global effects of such a dust veil took a year or more to become established. This mistaken impression was, it now seems, partly due to the lack of month-by-month temperature data to study, and partly an accident of history.

Because the experts only had figures on annual mean temperatures to work with, they were bound to find the shortest effects operating on an annual timescale. And it so happens that several of the most important eruptions, such as that of Krakatoa in 1883, occurred in the southern hemisphere, from where it did take months for the dust veil to spread to Europe and North America.

The first hint that this combination of factors was giving a misleading impression came in 1982. Then, Kelly and Sear reported the first fruits of their investigation of the monthly temperature figures following eruptions in the northern hemisphere, such as those of Pelée in the West Indies in 1902 and Bezymianni in the eastern Soviet Union in 1956.

This study was stimulated by analysis of the consequences of the eruption of Mount St Helens in the US in 1980. Since then, the eruption of El Chichón in April 1982, and now the interest in the nuclear winter scenario, have encouraged a more detailed statistical analysis of the records.

These show that when a major volcano erupts in the northern hemisphere there is an immediate, rapid decrease in surface temperatures across the hemisphere, reaching a lowest point in the second month after the eruption, and recovering only slowly over the next two years. If the eruption occurs in winter, the maximum depression of temperatures is about 1.4 °C; in summer, the effect is about one third as great (*Nature*, vol. 311, p. 741).

As yet the experts are unable to explain how a localised disturbance in the energy balance of the globe can provide such a swift response in temperatures around the hemisphere.

This is why the new study is so relevant to the nuclear winter debate. Computer models of the effects of even a limited nuclear strike suggest a massive cooling of the entire northern hemisphere within a matter of weeks (*New Scientist*, 13 September, p. 33). Some objectors have said that this is so unrealistic that the prediction casts doubt on the validity of the whole nuclear winter hypothesis.

But now that there is proof that the climate of the whole hemisphere does respond rapidly to a local injection of material into the stratosphere, the balance of that argument is tilted back in favour of the computer modellers.

As Kelly and Sear sum up: "The major significance of this work lies in the fact that it challenges commonly held beliefs concerning the response time and the sensitivity of the climate system to external forcing. Our results provide empirical support for the short response time suggested by recent attempts to simulate the climatic effects of a nuclear exchange."

1 November, 1984 © *John Gribbin, 1984; all rights reserved*

46

The subjective side of assessing risks

ERIC ASHBY

Decisions about protecting the environment inevitably involve a subjective element. To avoid rotten compromise and expediency, the decision-maker's "hunch" should be based on the principle of Mankind's responsibility to the natural world and should be open to challenge by environmental lobby groups

For many political decisions (not only decisions about the environment) there has to be an ingredient of hard data: scientific, technological, economic, statistical. But before the decision can be made, another ingredient has to be added, I called it "hunch" but a more respectable name for it is "political judgement". It can be shallow, mere vote catching; but it can also be profound, and sometimes it tips the balance even against the weight of cognitive evidence. This is a fact of life and there are two ways of looking at it. One is to regret it as a deficiency that scientists and social scientists will ultimately overcome as they are able to quantify more and more social values; computerising and putting a money tag on qualities like anxiety, suffering, joy, the beauty of the South Downs without pylons carrying power cables, the voice of a nightingale. Another way of looking at it is to commend it as an admission that some of the values that mean most to Mankind cannot be quantified, that attempts to quantify them distort them and therefore obscure the issues, and that we should expect those who have to make decisions on our behalf to have a flair for combining the cognitive with the non-cognitive, to be persons possessing what Laplace called "a happy tact given by nature" for making wise decisions.

In the simplest cases there is no argument about whether the environment should be protected (from damage, say, due to pollution). The only argument is about how much should be spent. If you have the data, you can draw a curve that shows the marginal

Figure 46.1   *Sir Eric Ashby, FRS, ex-chairman of the Royal Commission on Environmental Pollution*

cost of abating pollution, plotted against the amount of pollution abated. And on the same graph you could (if you had the data) draw another curve that shows the marginal damage done by pollution (also expressed as cost) plotted against the amount of pollution left in the air or water. The point where the two curves cross is the optimal level of pollution abatement. Beyond this optimum the damage done by pollution is less than the cost of abating it; below this optimum it is cheaper to abate pollution than to sustain the damage of not abating it.

It is not difficult to get data for the cost of abating pollution by different amounts, but despite heroic efforts, I do not think we have any really credible data for the cost of damage done by pollution. For example, it is known that high levels of sulphur dioxide and particulates in the air increase the incidence of respiratory diseases. A price tag of sorts can be attached to this: medical costs, loss of production due to illness, discounted lost earnings due to premature death; to which can be added cost of metal corrosion, more frequent laundry work, higher consumption of detergents, and an estimate of the value of the leisure time that citizens spend at weekends polishing their cars.

Suffice it to say that in my view none of these data for damage – or benefit – curves are credible enough to determine a political decision, partly because they include guesses which can so easily be challenged, but mainly for two other reasons. First, they take no account of the interests of future generations (a slow accumulation of mercury in a river, for instance, may be doing no damage at present, but the accumulated mercury could be a disaster). Secondly, they put no socially acceptable price tag on the distress of the family whose father is dying of emphysema, nor of the pleasure of looking at clean buildings. While cost-*effectiveness* studies can indicate the cheapest way to achieve an agreed level of protection, cost-*benefit* studies have very little use. Numerically cost-benefit equations cannot be solved but politically they must be. So the decision maker has to combine hard data with subjective judgement of values; he has to rank the values in some order of priority and make a decision which he will doubtless rationalise afterwards but which has in it a large component of intuition.

We have to ask how broad is the range of uncertainty within which the decision maker has to work? In policy making about the protection of the environment there are three kinds of uncertainty. There can be uncertainty about facts; there can be uncertainty about what people think about the facts; and there can be uncertainty about the future consequences of present decisions.

Consider one example of uncertainty about facts. It is agreed by all who have competence in the matter that the chlorofluorocarbons (commonly called fluorocarbons) used as propellants in aerosols persist in the lower atmosphere (the troposphere) and are accumulating there; the present concentration is about one part in 10^{10}. It is known that these substances rise into the stratosphere where they are decomposed, and one effect of the decomposition is to break down ozone some 30–40 km above the Earth's surface. There is some evidence that the amount of ozone may already have decreased by 0.6 per cent. If this continues unchecked there might be a maximum decrease of 8 per cent in the ozone layer in 100 year's time. It is known, too, that even if fluorocarbons were banned now, the material already released would go on breaking down ozone in the stratosphere for 15 years or more.

Stratospheric speculation

Beyond this we get into areas of speculation. First, since ozone is made in the stratosphere from oxygen that is there, is it being replaced automatically as quickly as it is destroyed? This is something one might expect from the common behaviour of chemical reactions. We do not know because the amount of ozone in the stratosphere varies considerably, even from day to day, sometimes by as much as 15 per cent, and this masks any long-term effects that might be due to fluorocarbons or emissions from stratospheric flight. Indeed there is still some doubt whether atomic chlorine persists in the stratosphere at all, to do the damage attributed to it. It has recently been suggested that chlorine nitrate ($ClONO_2$) might be formed there; if this were so, two potentially dangerous gases would be immobilised: chlorine and the oxide of nitrogen arising from supersonic aircraft.

Secondly, would reduction of ozone in the stratosphere (if it does occur) affect life on earth? It has been claimed by the National Academy of Sciences in the US that a one per cent reduction of ozone would allow an increased penetration of ultra-violet which would cause a two per cent increase in the incidence of skin cancer. Yet even an eight per cent decrease in ozone – the maximum predicted value – would lead to an increased penetration of ultra-violet equivalent only to that which would occur if one moved from, say, Carlisle to Torquay. A third area of speculation is the economic consequence of any ban – even if it were practicable on a world scale – on what is now a gigantic industry.

This brings me to the second uncertainty: uncertainty about what people think about the facts. In a pluralistic democracy legislators rarely lead public opinion; they have to follow it, or at best anticipate it by a very short head. But there is a subtle two-way influence. Sometimes, as over the disposal of toxic wastes, politicians are driven to act by public opinion. At other times, as over the Health and Safety at Work Act, the politicians try to educate public opinion: laws can be pedagogical as well as proscriptive. So the politician has to try to interpret social norms as well as to influence them; and this is both difficult and capricious.

In fact, the decision makers find themselves relying on the influence of pressure groups and lobbies. They watch the response of the public to the perpetual surges of synthetic publicity from the mass media. Commonly, over environmental matters, the decision makers have to wait until there is an incident of some kind which acts like a shot of adrenaline to the public conscience, and enables them to make a decision that they know will win approval. Thus both politicians and civil servants knew as far back as 1964 that toxic wastes were being tipped in unauthorised places where they might do damage. But action was taken only after the scandal broke in the press in December 1971. By January 1972 there were TV shots of cyanide drums and other nasty substances in tips all over the place. This raised public opinion to the flashpoint where government action was imperative. The Deposit of Poisonous Wastes Act 1972 was hastily drafted, squeezed into the parliamentary programme, and received the royal assent at the beginning of March.

This is not, however, the most perplexing kind of capriciousness. Much more puzzling is the apparently irrational attitude that people have toward environmental hazards. Some 7000 people are killed and some 350 000 injured each year on the roads of Britain. Yet this perpetual carnage – nearly 1000 killed or injured every day – generates no public outrage. People are as reconciled to it as they were to typhus a century and a half ago. Indeed, there is resistance to legislative measures that might reduce it, such as a lower speed limit, compulsory seat belts, and built-in safety devices in cars. But if 7 people were to be killed and 350 injured in one day in one incident at one spot – one thousandth of the annual road casualties – there would be an outcry, banner headlines, perhaps a public enquiry and possibly fresh legislation.

We have to distinguish between three measures of attitude to environmental hazards, whether they endanger human life or not: (i) the statistical assessment of a hazardous event occurring (a flood, a depletion of ozone in the stratosphere, a health risk from lead); (ii) the public perception of this hazard, which may be quite different because it is distorted on one hand by over-emphasis on propinquity and on the other hand by an under-emphasis of the probability – often very low – of the event occurring; (iii) even more subtle, the personal evaluation of the risk against the benefits. People will voluntarily accept far greater risks than they will tolerate if the risks are imposed upon them by society.

In a totalitarian state, decision makers can disregard both the public perception and the public evaluation of environmental hazards, and base policy solely on the rational assessment (if the data are available) of the probability of a hazard occurring and the severity of its occurrence. But in a pluralistic democracy it is the other two measures, the subjective perception of the hazard and the public risk–benefit impression of it, that the politician has to use for his decision making. Attempts to quantify this are in a very rudimentary state and public perception of hazards is very sensitive to propaganda from the mass media. But, as a very rough generalisation, it can be said that risks of 10^{-6} are of no great concern to the average person (though risks of nuclear power plant disasters are in the region of 10^{-9}). When the risks rise to 10^{-4} the public are willing to incur expenditure to reduce the risk (e.g. crash barriers on roads, railings at busy intersections), unless the risk is voluntary, for example cigarette smoking. At 10^{-3} a risk becomes unacceptable to the public and there is strong pressure to have it reduced. But this generalisation is greatly affected by the benefits that people get (or think they get) from the risk.

There are also irrational tendencies in the decision makers themselves. Environmental decisions are likely to benefit some people at the expense of others. To restrict the disposal of wastes, to choose a site for a reservoir or an airfield, to give – or to withhold – planning permission for mining: all these are acts that make enemies. Neither politicians nor the civil servants advising them like making enemies. It is on this account that much legislation to protect the environment is weakened by compromises. Sometimes the compromises appear as escape clauses, sometimes as secrecy clauses. The most outrageous example of these was in the Rivers (Prevention of Pollution) Act 1961. Clause 12 of this Act made it an offence, punishable by £100 fine or three months imprisonment or both, for an official of a River Authority to disclose what pollutants were being put into a river, although to pollute the river without consent made the polluter liable to a fine that might be as trivial as £25. Furthermore, decisions about the environment are likely to have very long-term effects and this predisposes the decision makers to cover themselves against unforeseen consequences.

Despite a great deal of research on the application of probability theory to decision making under the conditions of uncertainty, it is pretty evident that an unquantified – and perhaps unquantifiable – human dimension predominates in decisions about all these uncertainties. It is a subjective judgement, which I believe cannot be quantified, when you decide that you cannot wait for any more facts before making a diagnosis, or issuing a regulation. It is a subjective judgement when you allow the public perception of an environmental hazard to influence your decision in a way inconsistent with your knowledge of the statistical and rational assessment of the same hazard. It is a subjective judgement if you decide to go ahead of public opinion and require the public to forgo some benefit now for the sake of posterity.

Most difficult of all, however, is the question: what weight is to be given to the interests of posterity? There is an embarrassing contrast between the reliability of prediction in the physical sciences and its unreliability in the social sciences. There are dangers in taking the very long-term view. Arguments for making a decision about an environmental problem that will not "mature" as it were, for a century, are inevitably difficult to defend and unlikely to lead to any practical action. It is very difficult to persuade human communities to adapt themselves in anticipation of a hazard that has not yet materialised. Utopias end up in wastepaper baskets. So my rule of thumb in environmental policy making would be to make a decade rather than a century the horizon for most decision making. But let me say in the same breath that this does not mean sacrificing principle for expediency; just the opposite: it means recognition that the choices we make influence the values we come to hold.

I think there are pointers to the kind of practical machinery by which the decision makers on environmental policy can adopt a principle when legislating not only for the present but for posterity. They will, of course, have to use "hunch" in decisions; but so do their colleagues in other government departments, making decisions on foreign policy or VAT or the health service. But "hunch" based on principle is more likely to be consistent.

The principle is simply Darwin's demonstration that Mankind is an integral part of the grand symbiotic system, and that (to adapt Donne) "any tree's death diminishes me". This has to be reconciled with the necessity that Nature must be exploited for the needs of society. So we need a social device for achieving this reconciliation. One possibility would be for interest groups (bodies like the Friends of the Earth) to challenge in the courts or at public enquiries proposals that might damage the environment or to comment on draft laws and regulations for protecting the environment. Something like this already happens over applications for planning permission, so what I am suggesting would be a refinement and extension of an adversary procedure already familiar to us in Britain, with two important and essential conditions: (i) that both sides in the adversary encounter must have access to similar information and technical expertise; and (ii) that the encounter must be conducted in a formal and rational way: as in scientific discussion or in courts of law. The interest groups, in acting as guardians for the environment, would automatically be working in the interests of posterity too; and the decision makers (upon whom, of course, the final verdict has to depend) could from this evidence, assess more reliably the effects of their decision upon posterity.

19 May, 1977

Index